FAVORITE BRAND NAME BARBECUE COLLECTION

Publications International, Ltd.

Louis Weber, C.E.O.
Publications International, Ltd.
7373 N. Cicero Ave.
Lincolnwood, IL 60646

Some of the products listed in this publication may be in limited distribution.

Pictured on the front cover: *Top row, left:* Savory Grilled Tournedo (*page 10*); *Center:* Grilled Pasta Salad (*page 176*); *Right:* Micro-Grilled Pork Ribs (*page 48*). *Bottom row, left:* Spicy Microwave Grilled Chicken (*page 101*) with Fiesta Grilled Polenta (*page 164*); *Center:* Oriental Glazed Tenderloin (*page 58*); *Right:* Grilled Prawns with Salsa Vera Cruz (*page 127*).

Pictured on the back cover: *Top row, left:* Ranch-Style Fajitas (*page 13*); *Center:* Mexican and Green Onion Hamburger Toppings (*page 211*); *Right:* Marinated Grilled Chicken (*page 121*). *Bottom row, left:* Chicken Shish-Kabobs (*page 86*); *Center:* Teriyaki Trout (*page 143*); *Right:* Soy Marinated London Broil (*page 213*).

ISBN: 0-7853-1191-2

Library of Congress Catalog Card Number: 95-67188

Manufactured in U.S.A.

8 7 6 5 4 3 2 1

Microwave ovens vary in wattage. The microwave cooking times given in this publication are approximate. Use the cooking times as guidelines and check for doneness before adding more time. Consult manufacturer's instructions for suitable microwave-safe cooking dishes.

Contents

TIPS AND TECHNIQUES

Cooking over an open fire is the oldest cooking technique known to man. Developed purely in a quest for survival, this ancient art has come a long way since then—new and innovative grilling and flavoring techniques have turned standard backyard fare into cookout cuisine. This tantalizing style of cooking with its mouthwatering aromas offers endless opportunities for both the novice and experienced pro. A simple review of these barbecue basics will ensure great success with the following fabulous brand name recipes. *Favorite Brand Name Barbecue Collection* will help bring the sizzle—and fun—back to your meals.

CHOOSING A GRILL

Before you choose a grill, consider where you grill, what you'll be cooking, the seasons when you'll be grilling and the size of your budget. A small portable grill is fine if you usually barbecue smaller cuts of meat for a few people. For larger cuts of meat, bigger groups of people and year-round grilling, a large covered grill is worth the expense. Basic types of grills include gas, covered cooker and portable.

Gas Grill: Fast starts, accurate heat control, even cooking and year-round use make this the most convenient type of grill. Bottled gas heats a bed of lava rock or ceramic coals—no charcoal is required. Fat from the meat drips onto the lava rocks or coals and produces smoke for a grilled flavor. Hickory or fruitwood chips can be used to create the typical smoky flavor of charcoal.

Covered Cooker: Square, rectangular or kettle-shaped, this versatile covered grill lets you roast, steam, smoke or cook whole meals in any season of the year. Draft controls on the lid and base help control the temperature. Closing the dampers reduces the heat; opening them increases it. When the grill is covered, heat is reflected off the inside of the grill cooking the food evenly, and without the cover, the coals are hotter since added air circulation promotes their burning.

Portable Grills: These include the familiar hibachi and small picnic grills. Portability and easy storage are their main advantage.

FIRE BUILDING

For safety's sake, make sure the grill is located on a solid surface, set away from shrubbery, grass and overhangs. Also, make sure the grill vents are not clogged with ashes before starting a fire. NEVER use gasoline or kerosene as a lighter fluid starter. Either one can cause an explosion. To get a sluggish fire going, do not add lighter fluid directly to hot coals. Instead, place two to three additional coals in a small metal can and add lighter fluid. Then stack them on the previously burning coals with barbecue or long-handled tongs and light with a match. These coals will restart the fire. Flare-ups blacken food and are a fire hazard; keep a water-filled spray bottle near the grill to quench them.

Remember that coals are hot (up to 1,000°F) and that the heat transfers to the barbecue grill, grid, tools and food. Always wear heavy-duty fireproof mitts when cooking and handling grill and tools.

The number of coals required for barbecuing depends on the size and type of grill and the amount of food to be prepared. Weather conditions also have an effect; strong winds, very cold temperatures or highly humid conditions increase the number of coals needed for a good fire. As a general rule, it takes about 30 coals to grill one pound of meat under optimum weather conditions.

To light a charcoal fire, arrange the coals in a pyramid shape about 20 to 30 minutes prior to cooking. The pyramid shape provides enough ventilation for the coals to catch. To start with lighter fluid, soak the coals with about ½ cup fluid. Wait one minute to allow the fluid to soak into the coals. Light with a match.

To start with an electric starter, nestle the starter in the center of the coals. Plug the starter into a heavy-duty extension cord, then plug the cord into an outlet. After 8 to 10 minutes, when ash begins to form on the coals, unplug the starter and remove it. The electric starter will be very hot and should be cooled in a safe, heatproof place.

To start with a chimney starter, remove the grid from the grill; place the chimney starter in the base of the grill. Crumble a few sheets of newspaper; place in the bottom portion of the chimney starter. Fill the top portion with coals. Light the newspaper. Do not disturb the starter; the coals will be ready in 20 to 30 minutes. Be sure to wear fireproof mitts when pouring the hot coals from the chimney starter into the base of the grill. This method is essentially failureproof since it does not use starter fluid.

When the coals are ready, they will be about 80% ash gray during daylight and will glow at night. Spread the coals into a single layer with barbecue or long-handled tongs. To lower the cooking temperature, spread the coals farther apart or raise the grid. To raise the cooking temperature, either lower the grid or move the coals closer together and tap off the ash.

It is important to keep the grid or cooking rack clean and free of any bits of charred food. The easiest way to do this is to scrub the grid with a stiff wire brush immediately after cooking, while the grid is still warm.

COOKING METHODS

Direct Cooking: The food is placed on the grid directly over the coals. Make sure there is enough charcoal in a single layer to extend 1 to 2 inches beyond the area of the food on the grill. This method is for quick-cooking foods, such as hamburgers, steaks and fish. This is the most common method of grilling.

Indirect Cooking: The food is placed on the grid over a metal or disposable foil drip pan with the coals banked either to one side or on both sides of the pan. This method is used for slow-cooking foods, such as large roasts and whole chickens. Some fatty meats also are cooked over indirect heat to eliminate flare-ups.

When barbecuing by indirect cooking for more than 45 minutes, add 4 to 9 coals around the outer edge of the fire just before you begin grilling. When these coals are ready, add them to the center of the fire as needed to maintain a constant temperature.

Here's how to determine the number of coals needed:

Coals Needed for Indirect Cooking, Covered Grill

Coals needed on each side of drip pan for cooking 45 to 50 minutes:

Diameter of Grill (inches)	Number of Coals
26¾	30
22½	25
18½	16
14	15

Coals needed to be added on each side of drip pan every 45 minutes for longer cooking:

Diameter of Grill (inches)	Number of Coals
26¾	9
22½	8
18½	5
14	4

CHECKING CHARCOAL TEMPERATURE

A quick, easy way to estimate the temperature of the coals is to cautiously hold your hand, palm side down, about 4 inches above the coals. Count the number of seconds you can hold your hand in that position before the heat forces you to pull it away.

Seconds	Coal Temperature
2	hot, 375°F or more
3	medium-hot, 350° to 375°F
4	medium, 300° to 350°F
5	low, 200° to 300°F

FLAVORED SMOKE

Flavored smoke, a combination of heady aromas from hardwoods and fresh or dried herbs, imparts a special flavor to barbecued foods.

As a general rule, a little goes a long way. Added flavorings should complement, not overpower, food's natural taste. Always soak flavorings, such as wood chunks or chips, in water at least 20 minutes before adding to the coals so that they smolder and smoke, not burn. Small bunches of fresh or dried herbs soaked in water can also add fragrant flavor when sprinkled over hot coals. Rosemary, oregano, tarragon and bay leaves, for example, can be teamed with wood chips or simply used by themselves for an unique taste.

For a different effect, try soaking wood chips and herbs in wine, rather than water. For poultry and seafood, use white wine with either basil, rosemary, tarragon, thyme, parsley or dill sprigs. For beef and pork, use red wine with either thyme, marjoram or sage sprigs, or dried bay leaves.

Many diverse woods are available for use on the grill in supermarkets, hardware stores and specialty stores. Only hardwoods or fruitwoods, such as hickory, oak, mesquite, pear or apple should be used to produce aromatic smoke. If you chip your own wood, never use softwoods, such as cedar, pine or spruce; these emit resins that can give food an unpleasant taste.

USING A GAS GRILL

Carefully follow the instructions in your owner's manual for lighting a gas grill. Once the grill is lit, turn on all burners to "high." The grill should be ready to use in about 10 minutes.

For **direct cooking,** the burners may be left at the "high" setting to sear the food, and then reduced immediately to the "medium" setting. Continue to cook at "low" or "medium," with temperatures in the 250° to 375°F range. This is equivalent to low to medium-hot for charcoal. If flare-ups are a problem, one or more of the burners can be turned to a lower setting.

For **indirect cooking,** preheat the grill as directed. Turn the center burner to "off" and the two side burners to "medium." Place a metal or disposable foil drip pan directly on the lava rocks in the center of the grill. Place the food on the grill directly over the drip pan. If you wish to sear the food, first place it over a side burner, then move it to the center. For indirect cooking on a dual burner grill, turn one side of the grill to "off." Place the food on the unheated side of the grill over the drip pan.

Do not use water to quench flare-ups on a gas grill. Close the hood and turn the heat down until the flaring subsides. Trimming as much fat as possible from the meat before grilling or using a drip pan also helps.

Although the distinctive smoky flavor of charcoal is missing on a gas grill, wood chips and chunks are great flavor alternatives. Most manufacturers advise against putting these directly on the lava rocks, since ash can clog the gas lines. Simply soak the chips or chunks for 20 minutes, drain and place in a metal or disposable foil drip pan. Poke several small holes into the bottom of the pan and place it directly on the lava rocks. Preheat it with the grill.

DRY RUBS AND MARINADES

Dry rubs are seasoning blends rubbed onto meat before grilling and often include coarsely ground black or white pepper, paprika and garlic powder. Sometimes mustard, brown sugar and ground red pepper are used. Crushed herbs, such as sage, basil, thyme and oregano are other good choices.

Marinades add flavor and also moisten the surface of the meat to prevent it from drying out over the hot coals. Marinades include an acidic ingredient for tenderizing, such as wine, vinegar or lemon juice, combined with herbs, seasonings and oil. Fish and vegetables do not need tenderizing and should be marinated for only short periods of time. Beef, pork, lamb and chicken should be marinated for a few hours to overnight. Turn marinating foods occasionally to let the flavor infuse evenly. For safety, marinate all meats in the refrigerator. Because marinades contain an acid ingredient, marinating should be done in a glass, ceramic or stainless-steel container. The acid can cause a chemical reaction if marinating is done in an aluminum pan. Resealable plastic food storage bags are also great to hold foods as they marinate.

Reserve some of the marinade before adding the meat to use as a baste while the meat is cooking. A marinade drained from meat can also be used as a baste—just be sure to allow the meat to cook on the grill at least 5 minutes after the last application of marinade. You can also serve marinade that has been drained from the meat as a dipping sauce. However, follow food safety practices by placing the marinade in a small saucepan, bringing it to a full boil and boiling for at least 1 minute. These precautions are necessary to prevent the cooked food from becoming contaminated with bacteria from the raw meat present in the marinade.

TOOLS AND ACCESSORIES

These tools and accessories will make your barbecuing safer and more convenient.

Long-Handled Tongs, Basting Brush and Spatula: These are used to move hot coals and food around the grill, as well as for basting and turning foods. Select tools with long handles and hang them where you are working. You may want to purchase two pairs of tongs, one for coals and one for food.

Meat Thermometers: The best way to judge the doneness of meat is with a high-quality meat thermometer. Prior to grilling, insert the thermometer into the center of the largest muscle of the meat with the point away from bone, fat or rotisserie rod. An instant-read thermometer gives an accurate reading within seconds of insertion, although it is not heatproof and should not be left in the meat during grilling. Pork should be cooked to 160°F; poultry breast meat and dark meat should be cooked to 170° and 180°F respectively. Cook beef and lamb to desired doneness.

Heavy-Duty Mitts: You will prevent many burns by safeguarding your hands with heavy-duty fireproof mitts. Keep them close to the barbecue so they are always handy.

Aluminum Foil: Some vegetables and seafood are enclosed in aluminum foil packets before placing either directly on the coals or on the grid to cook. To ensure even cooking without any leakage, use the following technique. Place the food in the center of an oblong piece of heavy-duty foil, leaving at least a 2-inch border around the food. Bring the two long sides together above the food; fold down in a series of locked folds, allowing for heat circulation and expansion. Fold the short ends up and over again. Crimp to seal the foil packet.

Metal or Disposable Foil Drip Pans: A drip pan placed beneath grilling meats prevents flare-ups. The pan should be 1½ inches deep and extend about 3 inches beyond either end of the meat. The juices that collect in the drip pan may be used for a sauce or gravy. Bring drippings to a boil before using.

Water Spritzer: To quench flare-ups when grilling with charcoal, keep a water-filled spray bottle near the barbecue.

Hinged Wire Baskets: These baskets are designed to hold fish fillets and other irregularly shaped foods. They also facilitate turning for smaller pieces of meat that are too small for the cooking grid.

Rib Racks: Rib racks increase the grill's cooking capacity by standing slabs of ribs at an angle to the heat source.

Skewers: Made of either metal or bamboo, skewers are indispensable for kabobs. Bamboo skewers should be soaked in water at least 20 minutes before grilling to prevent the bamboo from burning.

BARBECUE TIPS

- Always use tongs or a spatula when handling meat. Piercing meat with a fork allows delicious juices to escape and makes meat less moist.

- If you partially cook food in the microwave or on the range, *immediately* finish cooking the food on the grill. Do not refrigerate or let stand at room temperature before cooking on the grill.

- Wash all utensils, cutting boards and containers with hot soapy water after they have been in contact with uncooked meat, poultry or seafood.

- Always serve cooked food from the grill on a *clean* plate, not one that held the raw food.

- In hot weather, food should never sit out for over 1 hour. Remember, keep hot foods hot and cold foods cold.

- The cooking rack, or grid, should be kept clean and free of any bits of charred food. The easiest way to do this is to scrub the grid with a stiff wire brush while it is still warm.

- Watch foods carefully during grilling. Total cooking time will vary with the type of food, position on the grill, weather, temperature of the coals and the degree of doneness you desire.

- Set a timer to remind you when it's time to check the food on the grill.

- Store charcoal in a dry place. Charcoal absorbs moisture readily and won't burn well if it is damp.

- Top and bottom vents should be open before starting a charcoal grill and while cooking. Close vents when cooking is finished to extinguish the coals.

- For proper air flow in a charcoal grill, remove accumulated ashes from the bottom before starting the fire. Since charcoal requires oxygen to burn, anything blocking the vents will reduce the heat generated from the coals.

- Extend the life of your charcoal grill by thoroughly cleaning it once a year. Discard accumulated ashes and remove the grid and charcoal grates. Spray the porcelain surface with oven cleaner; let stand until grease is softened. Wipe out with paper towels. Wash with a mild detergent and water; rinse. Wipe dry.

- A vinyl or plastic grill cover is an inexpensive way to protect your grill from winter's harsh elements, adding years to the life of the grill.

- Turn small cuts of meat, such as burgers, steaks and kabobs, halfway through grilling. Turn large cuts of meat, such as roasts, every 20 minutes. Whole poultry does not need to be turned.

- Firm-textured fish, such as swordfish, shark, tuna and monkfish, are excellent choices for grilling because they don't fall apart easily. If using medium-textured fish, such as salmon, halibut, orange roughy, mahi-mahi and cod, it is easier to handle steaks, fillets with the skin, or fillets that are at least ¾ inch thick.

BEEF

Savory Grilled Tournedos

⅓ cup A.1.® Steak Sauce
¼ cup ketchup
¼ cup orange marmalade
2 tablespoons lemon juice
2 tablespoons minced onion
1 clove garlic, crushed
8 slices bacon (about 5 ounces)
8 (4-ounce) beef tenderloin steaks (tournedos), about 1 inch thick
Mushroom halves, radishes and parsley sprigs for garnish

In small bowl, blend steak sauce, ketchup, marmalade, lemon juice, onion and garlic; set aside.

Wrap a bacon slice around edge of each steak; secure with string or wooden toothpick. Grill steaks over medium-high heat for 10 minutes or to desired doneness, turning occasionally and brushing often with ½ cup prepared sauce. Remove string or toothpicks; serve steaks with remaining sauce. Garnish with mushroom halves, radishes and parsley if desired.

Makes 8 servings

Texas-Style Short Ribs

5 pounds lean, meaty beef short ribs
2 tablespoons chili powder
1 tablespoon LAWRY'S® Red Pepper Seasoned Salt
2 teaspoons LAWRY'S® Garlic Powder with Parsley
2 teaspoons ground cumin
1 teaspoon ground coriander
1 bottle (12 ounces) chili sauce
1 cup finely chopped onions
1 cup dry red wine
½ cup water
½ cup beef broth
½ cup olive oil

In shallow glass dish, place ribs. In small bowl, combine chili powder, Red Pepper Seasoned Salt, Garlic Powder with Parsley, cumin and coriander. Rub ribs with spice mixture; let stand 1 hour. In medium bowl, combine remaining ingredients; pour over seasoned ribs. Cover dish and marinate in refrigerator 4 hours. Remove ribs, reserving marinade. Grill, 4 to 5 inches from heat, 45 to 60 minutes or until ribs are tender, basting and turning often with reserved marinade. In small saucepan, bring remaining marinade to a boil; boil 1 minute. Serve with heated sauce, if desired.

Makes 8 to 10 servings

Savory Grilled Tournedo

Hickory Beef Kabobs

- **2 ears fresh corn,* husked**
- **1 pound boneless beef top sirloin or tenderloin steak, cut into 1¼-inch pieces**
- **1 red or green bell pepper, cut into 1-inch squares**
- **1 small red onion, cut into ½-inch wedges**
- **½ cup beer or nonalcoholic beer**
- **½ cup chili sauce**
- **1 teaspoon dry mustard**
- **2 cloves garlic, minced**
- **1½ cups hickory chips**
- **4 metal skewers (12 inches long)**
- **3 cups hot cooked white rice**
- **¼ cup chopped fresh parsley**
- **Fresh parsley sprigs and plum tomatoes for garnish**

Place corn on cutting board. Cut crosswise into 1-inch pieces. Place beef, bell pepper, onion and corn in large resealable plastic food storage bag. Combine beer, chili sauce, mustard and garlic in small bowl; pour over beef and vegetables. Seal bag tightly; turn to coat. Marinate in refrigerator at least 1 hour or up to 8 hours, turning occasionally.

Prepare grill. Meanwhile, cover hickory chips with cold water; soak 20 minutes. Drain beef and vegetables, reserving marinade. Alternately thread beef and vegetables onto skewers. Brush with reserved marinade. Drain hickory chips; sprinkle over coals. Place kabobs on grid. Grill, on covered grill, over medium-hot coals 5 minutes. Brush with reserved marinade; turn and brush again. Discard remaining marinade. Grill, covered, 5 to 7 minutes more for medium or to desired doneness. Combine rice and chopped parsley; serve kabobs over rice mixture. Garnish, if desired. *Makes 4 servings*

*Four small ears frozen corn, thawed, can be substituted for fresh corn.

Hickory Beef Kabob

Tenderloins with Roasted Garlic Sauce

2 whole garlic bulbs, separated but not peeled (about 5 ounces)
⅔ cup A.1.® Steak Sauce, divided
¼ cup dry red wine
¼ cup finely chopped onion
4 (4- to 6-ounce) beef tenderloin steaks, about 1 inch thick

Place unpeeled garlic cloves on baking sheet. Bake at 500°F for 15 to 20 minutes or until garlic is soft; cool. Squeeze garlic pulp from skins; chop pulp slightly. In small saucepan, combine garlic pulp, ½ cup steak sauce, wine and onion. Heat to a boil; reduce heat and simmer for 5 minutes. Keep warm.

Grill steaks over medium heat for 5 minutes on each side or to desired doneness, brushing occasionally with remaining steak sauce. Serve steak with warm garlic sauce. *Makes 4 servings*

Ranch-Style Fajitas

Ranch-Style Fajitas

2 pounds flank or skirt steak
½ cup vegetable oil
⅓ cup lime juice
2 packages (1 ounce *each*) HIDDEN VALLEY RANCH® Milk Recipe Original Ranch® Salad Dressing Mix
1 teaspoon ground cumin
½ teaspoon black pepper
6 flour tortillas
Lettuce
Guacamole, prepared HIDDEN VALLEY RANCH® Salad Dressing and picante sauce for toppings

Place steak in large baking dish. In small bowl, whisk together oil, lime juice, salad dressing mix, cumin and pepper. Pour mixture over steak. Cover and refrigerate several hours or overnight.

Remove steak; place marinade in small saucepan. Bring to a boil. Grill steak over medium-hot coals 8 to 10 minutes or to desired doneness, turning once and basting with heated marinade during last 5 minutes of grilling. Remove steak and slice diagonally across grain into thin slices. Heat tortillas following package directions. Divide steak strips among tortillas; roll up to enclose. Serve with lettuce and desired toppings. *Makes 6 servings*

Marinated Oriental Beef Salad

Marinated Oriental Beef Salad

1 (1- to 1¼-pound) beef flank steak
⅓ cup REALEMON® Lemon Juice from Concentrate
¼ cup ketchup
¼ cup vegetable oil
1 tablespoon brown sugar
¼ teaspoon garlic powder
¼ teaspoon ground ginger
¼ teaspoon pepper
8 ounces fresh mushrooms, sliced (about 2 cups)
1 (8-ounce) can sliced water chestnuts, drained
1 medium sweet onion, sliced and separated into rings
4 ounces fresh pea pods *or* 1 (6-ounce) package frozen pea pods, thawed
Lettuce

Grill or broil steak 5 to 7 minutes on each side or to desired doneness; slice diagonally into thin strips. Meanwhile, in large shallow dish or plastic bag, combine ReaLemon® brand, ketchup, oil, sugar, garlic powder, ginger and pepper; mix well. Add sliced steak, mushrooms, water chestnuts and onion; mix well. Cover; marinate in refrigerator 8 hours or overnight, stirring occasionally. Before serving, add pea pods. Serve on lettuce; garnish with tomato if desired. Refrigerate leftovers. *Makes 4 servings*

Steak Ranchero

⅔ cup A.1.® Steak Sauce
⅔ cup mild, medium or hot thick and chunky salsa
2 tablespoons lime juice
1 (1-pound) beef top round steak, about ¾ inch thick
⅓ cup sliced pitted ripe olives
4 cups shredded lettuce
⅓ cup dairy sour cream

In small bowl, combine steak sauce, salsa and lime juice. Place steak in glass dish; coat both sides with ½ cup salsa mixture. Cover; chill 1 hour, turning occasionally.

In small saucepan, over medium heat, heat remaining salsa mixture. Reserve 2 tablespoons olives for garnish; stir remaining olives into sauce. Keep warm.

Remove steak from marinade; discard marinade. Grill over medium heat for 6 minutes on each side or to desired doneness, turning once.

To serve, arrange lettuce on serving platter. Thinly slice steak across grain; arrange over lettuce. Top with warm sauce and sour cream. Garnish with reserved olive slices. *Makes 4 servings*

3-Star Hot Pepper Roulades

1 (1-pound) beef top round steak, about ½ inch thick
⅓ cup A.1.® Steak Sauce, divided
½ teaspoon coarsely ground black pepper
¼ teaspoon ground red pepper
¼ teaspoon ground white pepper

Pound steak to ¼-inch thickness. Spread 2 tablespoons steak sauce over steak. Sprinkle peppers evenly over steak sauce. Roll up steak from short edge. To make roulades, cut steak crosswise into 8 rolled slices. Thread 2 roulades securely onto each of 4 (10-inch) metal skewers.

Grill roulades over medium heat for 8 to 10 minutes or to desired doneness, turning and brushing occasionally with remaining steak sauce. Serve immediately.

Makes 4 servings

Garlic-Pepper Steak

1¼ teaspoons LAWRY'S® Garlic Powder with Parsley
1¼ teaspoons LAWRY'S® Seasoned Pepper
½ teaspoon LAWRY'S® Seasoned Salt
1 pound sirloin steak

Combine Garlic Powder with Parsley, Seasoned Pepper and Seasoned Salt. Press seasoning mixture into both sides of steak with back of spoon. Let stand 30 minutes. Heat grill for medium coals or heat broiler. Grill or broil, 4 to 5 inches from heat source, 8 to 12 minutes or to desired doneness.

Makes 4 servings

Presentation: Serve with rice pilaf and a crisp green salad.

Flank Steak with Pineapple Chili Sauce

1½ to 2 pounds flank steak
1 can (8 ounces) DOLE® Crushed Pineapple, drained
¾ cup bottled chili sauce
¼ teaspoon garlic powder
1 to 2 drops hot pepper sauce

• Prepare grill or preheat broiler. Season steak with salt and black pepper, if desired. Grill over medium coals or broil on broiler pan, 4 inches from heat, 8 to 10 minutes on each side for medium or to desired doneness.

• To prepare sauce, combine remaining ingredients in small saucepan. Cook and stir until heated through.

• Slice cooked steak across grain into thin slices. Serve with sauce. Garnish with Dole® pinapple slices, if desired.

Makes 4 to 6 servings

Prep time: 10 minutes
Cooking time: 15 minutes

Flank Steak with Pineapple Chili Sauce

Korean Beef Short Ribs

1 tablespoon sesame seeds
2½ pounds flanken-style beef short ribs, cut ⅜ to ½ inch thick
¼ cup soy sauce
¼ cup water
¼ cup chopped green onions with tops
1 tablespoon sugar
2 teaspoons Oriental sesame oil
2 teaspoons grated fresh ginger
2 cloves garlic, minced
½ teaspoon black pepper

To toast sesame seeds, spread seeds in large, dry skillet. Shake skillet over medium-low heat about 3 minutes or until golden. Set aside. Place ribs in large resealable plastic food storage bag. Combine soy sauce, water, onions, sugar, oil, ginger, garlic and pepper in small bowl; pour over ribs. Seal bag tightly; turn to coat. Marinate in refrigerator at least 4 hours or up to 24 hours, turning occasionally.

Prepare grill. Drain ribs, reserving marinade. Place ribs on grid. Grill, on covered grill, over medium-hot coals 5 minutes. Brush tops lightly with reserved marinade; turn and brush again. Discard remaining marinade. Grill, covered, 5 to 6 minutes more for medium or to desired doneness. Sprinkle with sesame seeds.

Makes 4 to 6 servings

Cowboy Kabobs

⅓ cup A.1.® Steak Sauce
⅓ cup barbecue sauce
2 teaspoons prepared horseradish
1 (1½-pound) beef top round steak, cut into ½-inch strips
8 pearl onions
8 bell pepper strips

Soak 16 (10-inch) wooden skewers in water for at least 30 minutes. In small bowl, combine steak sauce, barbecue sauce and horseradish; set aside.

Thread steak strips onto skewers; place 1 onion or pepper strip on end of each skewer. Place kabobs in glass dish; coat with steak sauce mixture. Cover; chill 1 hour, turning occasionally. Grill kabobs over medium heat for 4 to 6 minutes or to desired doneness, turning occasionally. Serve immediately. *Makes 16 appetizers*

Marinated Beef on a Spit

⅔ cup tomato ketchup
½ cup KIKKOMAN® Soy Sauce
⅓ cup water
1 tablespoon brown sugar, packed
3 tablespoons vinegar
1 teaspoon garlic powder
1 bay leaf
1 (4- to 6-pound) beef roast (chuck cross rib, chuck eye, round tip or rump)

Combine ketchup, soy sauce, water, brown sugar, vinegar, garlic powder and bay leaf in small saucepan. Simmer 5 to 10 minutes, stirring occasionally. Cool. Pour sauce over roast in large plastic food storage bag. Press air out of bag; close top securely. Refrigerate 6 to 8 hours or overnight, turning bag over occasionally. Reserving marinade, remove roast. Insert rotisserie rod lengthwise through center of roast. Tighten spit forks so roast turns only with rod. Cook on rotisserie over medium coals, allowing 20 minutes per pound for medium-rare, brushing occasionally with reserved marinade. Remove roast from rotisserie. Let stand 15 minutes before carving into thin slices.

Makes 8 to 10 servings

Korean Beef Short Ribs

Succulent Grilled Tenderloin

2 teaspoons dry mustard
1¼ teaspoons water
¼ cup KIKKOMAN® Soy Sauce
¼ cup dry white wine
2 cloves garlic, pressed
¾ teaspoon ground ginger
1 (3-pound) beef tenderloin roast, trimmed

Blend mustard and water in small bowl to make a smooth paste. Cover tightly; let stand 10 minutes. Combine soy sauce, wine, garlic and ginger. Gradually add soy sauce mixture to mustard paste, stirring until blended. Place roast on grill 4 to 5 inches from medium-hot coals; brush with sauce. Cook 30 to 45 minutes, or until meat thermometer inserted into thickest part of roast registers 135°F for rare or 155°F for medium,* or to desired doneness, turning over and brushing occasionally with sauce. (Or, place roast on rack in shallow pan. Bake at 425°F about 45 minutes, or until meat thermometer inserted into thickest part of roast registers 135°F for rare or 155°F for medium, or to desired doneness, brushing with sauce every 15 minutes.)

Makes 12 servings

*Roast will rise 5°F in temperature upon standing.

Marinated Flank Steak

1 envelope LIPTON® Recipe Secrets® Onion or Onion-Mushroom Soup Mix
½ cup water
½ cup dry red wine
¼ cup olive or vegetable oil
1 tablespoon finely chopped parsley
1 flank steak (2 pounds)

In large nonaluminum baking dish or resealable plastic bag, thoroughly blend all ingredients except steak; add steak and turn to coat. Cover, or close bag, and marinate steak in refrigerator, turning occasionally, at least 4 hours. Remove steak, reserving marinade.

Grill or broil steak to desired doneness, turning once. Meanwhile, in small saucepan, bring reserved marinade to a boil over high heat. Reduce heat to low and simmer 5 minutes. If necessary, skim fat from marinade. Serve hot marinade with steak.

Makes about 8 servings

Serving Suggestion: Serve with Grilled Potatoes (page 169) and your favorite vegetable.

Grilled Steak au Poivre

½ cup A.1.® Steak Sauce, divided
1 (1½-pound) beef sirloin steak, ¾ inch thick
2 teaspoons cracked black pepper
½ cup dairy sour cream
2 tablespoons ketchup

Using 2 tablespoons steak sauce, brush both sides of steak; sprinkle 1 teaspoon pepper on each side, pressing into steak. Set aside.

In medium saucepan, over medium heat, combine remaining steak sauce, sour cream and ketchup. Cook and stir over low heat until heated through. Do not boil; keep warm.

Grill steak over medium heat for 5 minutes on each side or to desired doneness. Serve steak with warm sauce.

Makes 6 servings

Fajitas with Grilled Vegetables

Fajitas with Grilled Vegetables

1 pound boneless beef top sirloin steak, 1 inch thick
¾ cup prepared salsa
2 tablespoons olive oil
2 tablespoons lime juice
2 tablespoons tequila or additional lime juice
2 cloves garlic, minced
1 large red bell pepper, cored, cut in half and seeded
1 large yellow bell pepper, cored, cut in half and seeded
4 slices red onion, cut ¼ inch thick
8 (7-inch) flour tortillas, warmed
1 cup (4 ounces) SARGENTO® Classic Supreme Shredded Cheese For Tacos

Place beef in resealable plastic food storage bag. Add salsa, oil, lime juice, tequila and garlic. Close bag securely; turn to combine ingredients and coat beef. Add peppers and onion slices. Marinate in refrigerator at least 2 hours or up to 24 hours.

Prepare grill or preheat broiler. Remove beef and vegetables, reserving marinade. Grill over medium coals or broil 4 to 5 inches from heat source about 5 minutes per side or until beef is medium-rare (145°F) or to desired doneness. Remove to carving board; slice beef and peppers into thin strips. Separate onion slices into rings. To serve, divide beef and vegetables among tortillas. Bring remaining marinade to a rolling boil in small saucepan; drizzle over beef and vegetables. Sprinkle with Taco cheese; roll up tortillas.

Makes 4 servings

Beef with Dry Spice Rub

3 tablespoons firmly packed brown sugar
1 tablespoon black peppercorns
1 tablespoon yellow mustard seeds
1 tablespoon whole coriander seeds
4 cloves garlic
1½ to 2 pounds beef top round steak or London broil (1½ inches thick)
Vegetable or olive oil
Salt
Grilled Mushrooms (recipe follows)
Grilled New Potatoes (recipe follows)

Place brown sugar, peppercorns, mustard seeds, coriander seeds and garlic in a blender or food processor; process until seeds and garlic are crushed. Rub beef with oil, then pat on spice mixture. Season generously with salt.

Beef with Dry Spice Rub

Oil hot grid to help prevent sticking. Grill beef, on a covered grill, over medium-low KINGSFORD® Briquets, 16 to 20 minutes for medium doneness, turning once. Let stand 5 minutes before slicing. Cut across the grain into thin, diagonal slices.

Makes 6 servings

Grilled Mushrooms: Thread mushrooms, 1½ to 2 inches in diameter, onto metal or bamboo skewers. Brush lightly with oil; season with salt and pepper. Grill 7 to 12 minutes, turning occasionally.

Grilled New Potatoes: Cook or microwave small new potatoes until barely tender. Thread onto metal or bamboo skewers. Brush lightly with oil; season with salt and pepper. Grill 10 to 15 minutes, turning occasionally.

Note: Bamboo skewers should be soaked in water for at least 20 minutes to keep them from burning.

Tip: You can grill mushrooms and new potatoes on skewers over medium coals while you wait for the briquets to burn down to medium-low for cooking the beef.

Greek Grilled Pizza Wedges

⅓ cup prepared pizza sauce
¼ cup A.1.® Steak Sauce
4 (6-inch) whole wheat pita breads
2 tablespoons olive oil
4 ounces deli sliced roast beef, coarsely chopped
½ cup chopped tomato
⅓ cup sliced pitted ripe olives
½ cup crumbled feta cheese* (2 ounces)

*¾ cup shredded mozzarella cheese may be substituted.

In small bowl, combine pizza sauce and steak sauce; set aside. Brush both sides of pita bread with oil. Spread sauce mixture on one side of each pita; top evenly with roast beef, tomato, olives and feta cheese.

Grill each prepared pita, topping side up, over medium heat for 4 to 5 minutes or until topping is hot and pita is crisp. Cut each pita into 4 wedges to serve.

Makes 8 appetizer servings

Onion-Marinated Steak

2 large red onions
¾ cup *plus* 2 tablespoons WISH-BONE® Italian Dressing,* divided
1 boneless sirloin or London broil steak (2 to 3 pounds)

Cut 1 onion in half; set aside one half. Chop remaining onion to equal 1½ cups. In blender or food processor, process ¾ cup Italian dressing and chopped onion until puréed.

In large shallow nonaluminum baking dish or resealable plastic bag, place dressing-onion marinade; add steak and turn to coat. Cover, or close bag, and marinate in refrigerator, turning occasionally, 3 hours or overnight. Remove steak, reserving marinade.

Grill or broil steak to desired doneness, turning and basting frequently with reserved marinade.

Meanwhile, cut remaining onion half into thin slices. In saucepan, heat remaining 2 tablespoons Italian dressing; add onion and cook, stirring occasionally, 4 minutes or until tender. Serve over steak.

Makes 8 servings

*Also terrific with Wish-Bone® Robusto Italian or Lite Italian Dressing.

Gazpacho Steak Roll

Gazpacho Steak Roll

1 (2-pound) beef flank steak, butterflied
⅔ cup A.1.® Steak Sauce, divided
1 cup shredded Monterey Jack cheese (4 ounces)
½ cup chopped tomato
⅓ cup chopped cucumber
¼ cup chopped green bell pepper
2 tablespoons sliced green onion

Open butterflied steak like a book on smooth surface and flatten slightly. Spread ⅓ cup steak sauce over surface. Layer remaining ingredients over sauce. Roll up steak from short edge; secure with wooden toothpicks or tie with string if necessary.

Grill steak roll over medium heat for 30 to 40 minutes or to desired doneness, turning and brushing often with remaining steak sauce during last 10 minutes of cooking. Remove toothpicks; slice and serve garnished as desired.

Makes 8 servings

Fajitas with Avocado Salsa

1 beef flank steak (1¼ to 1½ pounds)
¼ cup tequila or nonalcoholic beer
3 tablespoons fresh lime juice
1 tablespoon minced jalapeño peppers*
2 large cloves garlic, minced
Avocado Salsa (recipe follows)
8 (6- to 7-inch) flour tortillas
1 large red bell pepper, halved and seeded
1 large green bell pepper, halved and seeded
4 slices red onion, cut ¼ inch thick

Place steak in large resealable plastic food storage bag. Combine tequila, lime juice, jalapeños and garlic in small bowl; pour over steak. Seal bag tightly; turn to coat. Marinate in refrigerator 1 to 4 hours, turning once.

Prepare grill. Meanwhile, prepare Avocado Salsa. Wrap tortillas in heavy-duty foil. Drain steak, discarding marinade. Place steak, bell peppers and onion slices on grid. Grill, on covered grill, over medium-hot coals 14 to 18 minutes for medium or to desired doneness, turning steak, bell peppers and onion slices halfway through grilling time. Place tortilla packet on grid during last 5 to 7 minutes of grilling; turn halfway through grilling time to heat through. Transfer steak to carving board. Carve steak across the grain into thin slices. Slice bell peppers into thin strips. Separate onion slices into rings. Divide among tortillas; roll up and top with Avocado Salsa. *Makes 4 servings*

*Jalapeño peppers can sting and irritate the skin; wear rubber gloves when handling peppers and do not touch eyes. Wash your hands after handling.

Avocado Salsa

1 ripe large avocado
1 large tomato, seeded and diced
3 tablespoons chopped fresh cilantro
1 tablespoon vegetable oil
1 tablespoon fresh lime juice
2 teaspoons minced fresh jalapeño peppers*
1 clove garlic, minced
½ teaspoon salt

Place avocado on cutting board. Insert utility knife into stem end of avocado; slice in half lengthwise to the pit, turning avocado while slicing. Twist both halves to pull apart; remove pit. Scoop avocado flesh out of shells; coarsely chop avocado flesh into ½-inch cubes. Transfer to medium bowl. Stir in all remaining ingredients until well combined. Let stand at room temperature while grilling steak. (Can be prepared up to 3 hours in advance. Cover and refrigerate. Bring to room temperature before serving.) *Makes about 1½ cups*

Fruit Glazed Beef Ribs

4 pounds beef back ribs, cut into individual ribs
⅓ cup A.1.® BOLD Steak Sauce
¼ cup ketchup
¼ cup apricot preserves
1 tablespoon lemon juice
½ teaspoon grated lemon peel

Arrange ribs on rack in large roasting pan. Bake at 400°F for 30 minutes.

In small saucepan, over medium heat, cook and stir steak sauce, ketchup, preserves, lemon juice and lemon peel until blended. Grill ribs over medium heat for 20 minutes or to desired doneness, turning and brushing often with prepared sauce. Serve immediately. *Makes 6 to 8 servings*

Fajitas with Avocado Salsa

A.1.® Dry Spice Rub

1 tablespoon peppercorn mélange (black, white, green and pink)
1 teaspoon yellow mustard seed
1 teaspoon whole coriander seed
1 tablespoon firmly packed light brown sugar
2 cloves garlic, minced
1 (1½- to 2-pound) beef T-bone or sirloin steak
3 tablespoons A.1.® BOLD Steak Sauce

In food processor or spice grinder, combine peppercorns, mustard seed and coriander seed; process until coarsely crushed. Stir in brown sugar and garlic. Brush both sides of steak with steak sauce; sprinkle each side with spice mixture, pressing firmly into steak.

Grill steak over medium heat for 20 to 25 minutes or to desired doneness, turning occasionally. Serve with additional steak sauce if desired. *Makes 6 servings*

A.1.® Dry Spice Rub

Oriental Flank Steak

½ cup WISH-BONE® Italian Dressing*
2 tablespoons soy sauce
2 tablespoons firmly packed brown sugar
½ teaspoon ground ginger (optional)
1 flank steak (1 to 1½ pounds)

In large shallow nonaluminum baking dish or resealable plastic bag, thoroughly blend all ingredients except steak; add steak and turn to coat. Cover or close bag; marinate in refrigerator, turning occasionally, 3 hours or overnight. Remove steak, reserving marinade.

Grill or broil steak to desired doneness. Meanwhile, in small saucepan, bring reserved marinade to a boil, then pour over steak. *Makes 6 servings*

*Also terrific with Wish-Bone® Robusto Italian or Lite Italian Dressing.

Easy Marinated Steak

1 beef flank steak (1½ pounds)
1 bottle (16 ounces) KRAFT® Zesty Italian Dressing, divided

• Score steak by making shallow cuts in the surface on both sides. Reserve ½ cup dressing. Pour remaining dressing over steak; cover. Refrigerate several hours or overnight to marinate. Drain; discarding dressing. Heat grill.

• Place steak on greased grill rack over medium coals. Grill 14 to 16 minutes or until desired doneness, brushing with reserved ½ cup dressing and turning occasionally. Carve steak across grain into thin slices. Serve with macaroni salad, if desired. *Makes 4 to 6 servings*

Prep time: 5 minutes plus refrigerating
Cooking time: 16 minutes

Smoke-Cooked Beef Ribs

Wood chunks or chips for smoking
4 to 6 pounds beef back ribs, cut into slabs of 3 to 4 ribs *each*
Salt and black pepper
1⅓ cups K.C. MASTERPIECE® Barbecue Sauce
Beer at room temperature *or* hot tap water
Grilled Corn-on-the-Cob (optional) (page 172)

Soak 4 wood chunks or several handfuls of wood chips in water; drain. Spread ribs on a baking sheet or tray; season with salt and pepper. Brush with half of sauce. Let stand at cool room temperature up to 30 minutes.

Arrange low KINGSFORD® Briquets on each side of a rectangular metal or foil drip pan. (Since the ribs have been brushed with sauce before cooking, low heat is needed to keep them moist.) Pour in beer to fill pan half full. Add soaked wood (all the chunks; part of the chips) to the fire.

Oil hot grid to help prevent sticking. Place ribs on grid, meaty sides up, directly above drip pan. Smoke-cook ribs, on a covered grill, about 1 hour, brushing remaining sauce over ribs 2 or 3 times during cooking. If your grill has a thermometer, maintain a cooking temperature between 250°F to 275°F. Add a few more briquets after 30 minutes, or as necessary, to maintain a constant temperature. Add more soaked wood chips every 30 minutes, if necessary. Serve with Grilled Corn-on-the-Cob, if desired.

Makes 4 to 6 servings

Smoke-Cooked Beef Ribs

Tijuana Blackened Steak

¾ teaspoon garlic powder
¾ teaspoon onion powder
¾ teaspoon ground black pepper
½ teaspoon ground white pepper
¼ teaspoon ground red pepper
4 (4- to 6-ounce) beef shell or strip steaks, about ½ inch thick
½ cup A.1.® Steak Sauce
¼ cup margarine, melted

In small bowl, combine garlic powder, onion powder and peppers; spread on waxed paper. Coat both sides of steaks with seasoning mixture.

In small bowl, combine steak sauce and margarine. Grill steaks 10 to 15 minutes or to desired doneness, turning and brushing often with ¼ cup steak sauce mixture. Serve with remaining steak sauce mixture.

Makes 4 servings

Fajitas

¼ cup lime juice
¼ cup tequila or additional lime juice
2 tablespoons vegetable oil
2 cloves garlic, minced
1 fresh or canned jalapeño pepper, stemmed, seeded and minced
1 tablespoon chopped cilantro
¼ teaspoon salt
¼ teaspoon black pepper
1½ pounds beef flank steak
2 cans (about 16 ounces *each*) refried beans
8 to 12 (8-inch) flour tortillas

Condiments

2 avocados or prepared guacamole
Lime juice
Salsa
Sour cream

To prepare marinade, combine lime juice, tequila, oil, garlic, jalapeño pepper, cilantro, salt and black pepper in small bowl. Trim any visible fat from meat; place in large resealable plastic food storage bag. Pour marinade over meat; seal bag and marinate in refrigerator 8 hours or up to 2 days, turning occasionally.

Preheat grill and grease grill rack. Place refried beans in large skillet and heat through; keep warm. Stack and wrap tortillas in foil; place tortilla packet on side of grill to heat. Remove meat, reserving marinade. Place meat on grid. Grill 4 to 6 inches over medium coals 4 minutes on each side for rare or to desired doneness, basting frequently with reserved marinade. Do not baste during last 5 minutes of grilling.) To serve, cut meat across the grain into thin slices; place on warm platter. Peel, pit and chop avocados; sprinkle with lime juice. Place tortillas, refried beans, salsa, avocados and sour cream in separate serving dishes. Place meat and condiments in tortillas; roll up to enclose.

Makes 4 to 6 servings

Shrimp or Chicken Fajitas: Follow directions for Fajitas but use 2 pounds raw medium shrimp, shelled and deveined, or 2 pounds boneless skinless chicken breasts for flank steak. Marinate 2 to 3 hours. Thread shrimp or chicken onto skewers. Place on greased grid. Grill shrimp 4 to 6 inches over low coals 3 to 4 minutes on each side or until pink and opaque, turning and basting once with reserved marinade. Grill chicken 3 to 4 minutes on each side or until no longer pink in center, turning and basting once with reserved marinade. Serve as directed.

Tournedos with Mushroom Wine Sauce

¼ cup finely chopped shallots
2 tablespoons margarine
¼ pound small mushrooms, halved
½ cup A.1.® Steak Sauce
¼ cup Burgundy or other dry red wine
¼ cup chopped parsley
4 (4-ounce) beef tenderloin steaks (tournedos), about 1 inch thick

In medium saucepan, over medium heat, sauté shallots in margarine until tender. Stir in mushrooms; sauté 1 minute. Stir in steak sauce and wine; heat to a boil. Reduce heat; simmer for 10 minutes. Stir in parsley; keep warm.

Grill steaks over medium heat for 10 to 12 minutes or to desired doneness, turning occasionally. Serve steaks topped with warm sauce.

Makes 4 servings

Greco-American Beef Kabobs

4 large pattypan squash (about 1 pound), quartered
½ cup water
1½ pounds boneless tender beef steak, 1½ inches thick
1 large red bell pepper
½ cup KIKKOMAN® Teriyaki Marinade & Sauce
2 tablespoons olive oil
4 teaspoons white wine vinegar
2 large bay leaves, each broken into 4 pieces
1 large clove garlic, pressed
¾ teaspoon dried oregano leaves, crumbled

Arrange squash in single layer in microwave-safe dish; add water. Cover. Microwave on HIGH 7 minutes, rotating dish after 4 minutes. Drain squash; cool. Meanwhile, cut beef into 1-inch square pieces; cut bell pepper into 18 square pieces. Place beef and bell peppers with squash in large plastic food storage bag. Combine teriyaki sauce, oil, vinegar, bay leaves, garlic and oregano; pour over beef and vegetables. Press air out of bag; close top securely. Turn bag over several times to coat all pieces well. Marinate 30 minutes, turning bag over frequently.

Thread each of 6 (12-inch) metal or bamboo* skewers alternately with beef and vegetables. Place kabobs 5 inches from hot coals. Cook 3 minutes on each side (for rare), or to desired doneness. (Or, place kabobs on rack of broiler pan. Broil 5 inches from heat 3 minutes on each side [for rare], or to desired doneness.)

Makes 4 to 6 servings

*Soak bamboo skewers in water 30 minutes to prevent burning.

Pesto Beef Swirls

⅓ cup A.1.® Steak Sauce
¼ cup grated Parmesan cheese
¼ cup pignoli nuts or walnuts
2 tablespoons dried basil leaves
2 cloves garlic
1 (2-pound) beef flank steak, pounded to ½-inch thickness

In blender or food processor, blend all ingredients except steak to a coarse paste; spread over top of steak. Cut steak across grain into eight 1-inch-wide strips. Roll up each strip from short edge; secure with wooden toothpick.

Grill over medium heat for 7 to 8 minutes on each side or to desired doneness, brushing often with additional steak sauce. Remove toothpicks; serve immediately.

Makes 8 servings

Greco-American Beef Kabobs

Mexican Flank Steak with Mock Tamales

1½ pounds beef flank steak
⅓ cup fresh lemon juice
⅓ cup extra virgin olive oil
6 tablespoons minced jalapeño peppers*
1 tablespoon minced fresh cilantro
1 teaspoon salt
1 teaspoon black pepper
Linda's Sassy Salsa (recipe follows)
Mock Tamales (recipe follows)
Lemon slices, whole jalapeño peppers and cilantro sprigs, for garnish

Place beef flank steak in large shallow glass dish. Combine lemon juice, oil, minced jalapeño peppers, cilantro, salt and black pepper; pour over steak, turning to coat. Cover and marinate in refrigerator 6 hours or overnight. Meanwhile, prepare Linda's Sassy Salsa and Mock Tamales.

Prepare grill. Remove steak, reserving marinade. Place steak on grid. Place Mock Tamales around outer edge of grid. Grill steak over medium-hot coals 12 to 15 minutes for rare to medium or to desired doneness, turning once and basting occasionally with marinade. (Do not baste during last 5 minutes of grilling.) Turn tamales halfway through cooking time. Place steak and tamales on serving platter. Spoon ¼ cup salsa over tamales. Carve steak across grain into thin slices and serve with remaining salsa. Garnish platter with lemon slices, whole jalapeño peppers and cilantro sprigs. *Makes 6 servings*

Linda's Sassy Salsa

2 tomatillos, hulls and tough skins removed
3 cloves garlic, peeled
2 plum tomatoes, minced
3 plum tomatoes, coarsely chopped
3 jalapeño peppers,* thinly sliced
¼ cup coarsely chopped fresh cilantro
1 tablespoon fresh lemon juice
1 teaspoon black pepper

Process tomatillos and garlic in food processor or blender until pulverized. Combine tomatillo mixture, tomatoes, jalapeño peppers, cilantro, lemon juice and black pepper. Refrigerate, covered, 1 hour or overnight to blend flavors.

Makes 2 cups

Mock Tamales

1 cup (4 ounces) shredded sharp Cheddar cheese
1 cup (4 ounces) shredded Muenster cheese
2 tablespoons minced green onion with tops
6 (7-inch) flour tortillas

Combine cheeses and onion. Place equal portion of cheese mixture in center of each tortilla. Fold bottom side of each tortilla over filling. Fold two sides over filling; fold top side over filling, envelope fashion. Wrap each tamale in 12 × 8-inch piece of foil, twisting each end. *Makes 6 servings*

*Jalapeño peppers can sting and irritate the skin; wear rubber gloves when handling peppers and do not touch eyes. Wash hands after handling.

Favorite recipe from ***National Live Stock & Meat Board***

Mexican Flank Steak with Mock Tamale

Barbecued Brandy Steak

½ cup KIKKOMAN® Teriyaki Baste & Glaze
4 teaspoons brandy
2 cloves garlic, pressed
1½ teaspoons dried marjoram leaves, crumbled
¼ teaspoon onion salt
1 (2-pound) boneless beef sirloin steak, about 1 inch thick

Combine teriyaki baste & glaze, brandy, garlic, marjoram and onion salt; set aside. Trim and score fat on edge of steak. Brush both sides of steak thoroughly with baste & glaze mixture. Place steak on grill 4 to 5 inches from hot coals. Cook about 15 minutes (for rare), or to desired doneness, turning and brushing occasionally with remaining baste & glaze mixture. (Or, place steak on rack of broiler pan. Broil steak 7 minutes on each side [for rare], or to desired doneness, brushing occasionally with baste & glaze mixture.) To serve, cut steak across grain into thin slices.

Makes 4 servings

Barbecued Brandy Steak

Grilled Sauerbraten Steak

½ cup A.1.® Steak Sauce
½ cup dry red wine
1 (1½-pound) beef sirloin steak
½ cup water
2 tablespoons margarine
2 gingersnap cookies, finely rolled into crumbs

In small bowl, combine steak sauce and wine. Place steak in glass dish; coat with ½ cup steak sauce mixture. Cover; chill 1 hour, turning occasionally.

In small saucepan, over medium heat, heat remaining steak sauce mixture, water, margarine and cookie crumbs to a boil. Reduce heat and simmer 2 to 3 minutes or until thickened; keep warm.

Remove steak from marinade; discard marinade. Grill over medium heat for 15 to 20 minutes or to desired doneness, turning once. Slice steak and serve with warm sauce. *Makes 6 servings*

Grilled Beef Salad

Grilled Beef Salad

Assorted greens such as romaine, red leaf and Bibb
Fresh basil leaves
2 thin slices red onion
½ cup mayonnaise
2 tablespoons cider vinegar or white wine vinegar
1 tablespoon spicy brown mustard
2 cloves garlic, minced
½ teaspoon sugar
1 large tomato, chopped
1 pound boneless beef top sirloin steak, cut 1 inch thick
½ teaspoon salt
½ teaspoon black pepper
½ cup purchased herb or garlic croutons
Additional black pepper (optional)

Tear enough lettuce into bite-sized pieces to measure 6 cups. Set aside. Layer basil leaves with largest leaf on bottom, then roll up jelly-roll style. Slice basil roll into very thin slices; separate into strips. Slice enough leaves to measure ⅓ cup. Separate onion slices into rings. Set aside.

Prepare grill. Meanwhile, combine mayonnaise, vinegar, mustard, garlic and sugar in small bowl; mix well. Cover and refrigerate until serving. Toss together greens, tomato, basil and onion rings in large bowl; cover and refrigerate until serving.

Sprinkle both sides of steak with salt and ½ teaspoon pepper. Grill steak, on covered grill, over medium-hot coals 10 minutes for medium-rare or to desired doneness, turning halfway through grilling time. Transfer steak to carving board. Slice in half lengthwise; carve crosswise into thin slices. Add steak and croutons to bowl with greens; toss well. Add mayonnaise mixture; toss until well coated. Serve with additional pepper.

Makes 4 servings

Peppered Beef Rib Roast

1½ tablespoons black peppercorns
1 boneless beef rib roast (2½ to 3 pounds), well trimmed
¼ cup Dijon mustard
2 cloves garlic, minced
¾ cup sour cream
2 tablespoons prepared horseradish
1 tablespoon balsamic vinegar
½ teaspoon sugar

Prepare grill with rectangular metal or foil drip pan. Bank briquets on either side of drip pan for indirect cooking. Meanwhile, place peppercorns in heavy, small resealable plastic food storage bag. Squeeze out excess air; seal bag tightly. Pound peppercorns using flat side of meat mallet or rolling pin until cracked. Pat roast dry with paper towels. Combine mustard and garlic in small bowl; spread with spatula over top and sides of roast. Sprinkle cracked pepper over mustard mixture.

Insert meat thermometer into center of thickest part of roast. Place roast, pepper side up, on grid directly over drip pan. Grill, on covered grill, over medium coals 60 to 70 minutes or until thermometer registers 150°F for medium-rare or to desired doneness, adding 4 to 9 briquets to both sides of the fire after 45 minutes to maintain medium coals. Meanwhile, combine sour cream, horseradish, vinegar and sugar in small bowl; mix well. Cover; refrigerate until serving. Transfer roast to carving board; tent with foil. Let stand 5 to 10 minutes before carving. Serve with horseradish sauce. *Makes 6 to 8 servings*

Burgundy Beef Short Ribs

½ cup KIKKOMAN® Teriyaki Marinade & Sauce
1 medium shallot, minced
1 tablespoon Burgundy wine
1 teaspoon sugar
½ teaspoon pepper
2 pounds beef short ribs, trimmed of excess fat and cut crosswise into ½-inch-thick slices

Combine teriyaki sauce, shallot, wine, sugar and pepper; pour over ribs in large plastic food storage bag. Press air out of bag; close top securely. Turn bag over several times to coat both sides of ribs. Marinate 30 minutes, turning bag over occasionally. Remove ribs from marinade; place on grill 5 inches from hot coals. Cook 4 minutes on each side. (Or, place ribs on rack of broiler pan. Broil 5 inches from heat 4 minutes on each side.)
Makes 4 to 6 servings

Steak with Horseradish Sauce

4 ounces light cream cheese, softened
½ cup A.1.® Steak Sauce, divided
2 tablespoons prepared horseradish, drained
2 tablespoons chopped green onion
4 (4-ounce) beef shell or strip steaks, about 1 inch thick

In small bowl, blend cream cheese, ¼ cup steak sauce and horseradish; stir in onion. Cover; chill until ready to serve.

Grill steaks over medium heat for 5 minutes on each side or to desired doneness, turning once and brushing occasionally with remaining steak sauce. Serve steaks topped with horseradish sauce. *Makes 4 servings*

Peppered Beef Rib Roast

Mushroom-Sauced Steak

Mushroom-Sauced Steak

½ cup sliced onion
2 tablespoons margarine
1½ cups sliced mushrooms
1 cup A.1.® BOLD Steak Sauce
½ cup dairy sour cream
2 (8-ounce) beef club or strip steaks, about 1 inch thick

In medium skillet, over medium heat, sauté onion in margarine until tender, about 5 minutes. Add mushrooms; sauté 5 minutes more. Stir in steak sauce; heat to a boil. Reduce heat and simmer 5 minutes; stir in sour cream. Cook and stir until heated through. Do not boil; keep warm.

Grill steaks over medium heat for 5 minutes on each side or to desired doneness. Serve steaks topped with mushroom sauce. *Makes 4 servings*

Peppery T-bone Steaks and Chili Corn

- **4 ears fresh sweet corn, unhusked**
  Cold water
- **1 to 2 cloves garlic, crushed**
- **½ teaspoon black pepper**
- **2 beef T-bone steaks, cut 1 to 1½ inches thick**
- **2 tablespoons butter or margarine**
- **½ teaspoon chili powder**
- **¼ teaspoon ground cumin**

Pull back corn husks from each ear of corn, leaving husks attached to base. Remove corn silk. Fold husks back around corn; tie at end of each ear with string. Soak corn in cold water 3 to 4 hours.

Prepare grill. Remove corn from water. Place on grid. Grill over medium coals 20 minutes, turning often. Meanwhile, combine garlic and pepper; rub evenly into both sides of steaks. Place steaks on grid with corn; grill steaks to desired doneness, turning steaks once and corn often. (Grill 1-inch-thick steaks 10 to 14 minutes for rare to medium. Grill 1½-inch-thick steaks 22 to 30 minutes for rare to medium.) Remove corn when tender. Meanwhile, melt butter. Stir in chili powder and cumin; keep warm. Trim excess fat before carving steaks into thick slices. Serve with corn and seasoned butter. *Makes 4 servings*

Favorite recipe from ***National Live Stock & Meat Board***

Beijing Barbecue Steak

- **½ cup KIKKOMAN® Teriyaki Baste & Glaze**
- **2 tablespoons tomato ketchup**
- **1 tablespoon dry sherry**
- **2 cloves garlic, pressed**
- **4 boneless tender beef steaks (rib eye or top loin), about ¾ inch thick**

Combine teriyaki baste & glaze, ketchup, sherry and garlic; brush steaks thoroughly with mixture. Place steaks on grill 4 to 5 inches from hot coals. Cook 4 minutes on each side (for rare), or to desired doneness, brushing frequently with remaining baste & glaze mixture. (Or, place steaks on rack of broiler pan. Broil steaks 4 minutes on each side [for rare], brushing occasionally with baste & glaze mixture.)

Makes 4 servings

Beijing Barbecue Steak

Spicy Teriyaki Glazed Beef Short Ribs

½ cup KIKKOMAN® Teriyaki Baste & Glaze
2 tablespoons minced green onion and tops
2 cloves garlic, pressed
1 teaspoon crushed red pepper
½ teaspoon vegetable oil
2 pounds beef short ribs, trimmed of excess fat and cut crosswise into ½-inch-thick slices

Spicy Teriyaki Glazed Beef Short Ribs

Combine teriyaki baste & glaze, green onion, garlic, red pepper and oil. Place ribs on grill 4 to 5 inches from hot coals; brush with baste & glaze mixture. Cook 5 minutes, turning over and brushing frequently with remaining baste & glaze mixture. (Or, place ribs on rack of broiler pan; brush with baste & glaze mixture. Broil 3 minutes; turn over. Brush with remaining baste & glaze mixture. Broil 3 minutes longer.) *Makes 4 servings*

Summertime Beef Fajitas

1 flank steak (1½ pounds)
½ cup WISH-BONE® Italian Dressing*
2 teaspoons lime juice
½ teaspoon finely shredded lime peel (optional)
½ teaspoon ground cumin (optional)
12 (8-inch) flour tortillas, warmed
Shredded lettuce, diced tomatoes, sliced onions and sour cream (optional)

With knife, score (lightly cut) both sides of steak. In large shallow nonaluminum baking dish or resealable plastic bag, combine Italian dressing, lime juice, lime peel and cumin; add steak and turn to coat. Cover, or close bag, and marinate in refrigerator, turning occasionally, 3 hours or overnight. Remove steak, reserving marinade.

Grill or broil steak to desired doneness, turning once. Meanwhile, in small saucepan, bring reserved marinade to a boil, then pour over steak. To serve, thinly slice steak. Serve in tortillas with lettuce, tomatoes, onions and sour cream.

Makes 6 servings

*Also terrific with Wish-Bone® Robusto Italian Dressing.

Tex-Mex Flank Steak

- 1 medium onion, thinly sliced
- ½ cup REALEMON® Lemon Juice from Concentrate
- ½ cup vegetable oil
- 2 tablespoons dry sherry
- 2 teaspoons WYLER'S® or STEERO® Beef-Flavor Instant Bouillon
- 2 teaspoons chili powder
- 2 teaspoons ground cumin
- 2 cloves garlic, finely chopped
- 1 (1- to 1½-pound) flank steak

In large shallow dish or plastic bag, combine all ingredients except steak. Add steak. Cover; marinate in refrigerator 6 hours or overnight. Remove steak from marinade; grill or broil 5 to 7 minutes on each side or to desired doneness, basting frequently with marinade. (Do not baste during last 5 minutes of cooking.) Refrigerate leftovers.

Makes 4 to 6 servings

Grilled Italian Steak

- ¾ cup WISH-BONE® Italian Dressing
- 2 tablespoons grated Parmesan cheese
- 2 teaspoons dried basil leaves, crushed
- ¼ teaspoon cracked black pepper
- 1 boneless sirloin or London broil steak (2 to 3 pounds)

In large shallow nonaluminum baking dish or resealable plastic bag, thoroughly blend all ingredients except steak. Add steak and turn to coat. Cover or close bag; marinate in refrigerator, turning occasionally, 3 hours or overnight. Remove steak, reserving marinade.

Grill or broil steak to desired doneness. Meanwhile, in small saucepan, bring reserved marinade to a boil, then pour over steak.

Makes 8 servings

Zesty Lemon-Glazed Steak

Zesty Lemon-Glazed Steak

- ⅓ cup A.1.® Steak Sauce
- 2 teaspoons grated lemon peel
- 1 clove garlic, minced
- ¼ teaspoon coarsely ground black pepper
- ¼ teaspoon dried oregano leaves
- 4 (4- to 6-ounce) beef shell or strip steaks, about 1 inch thick

In small bowl, combine steak sauce, lemon peel, garlic, pepper and oregano; brush on both sides of steaks.

Grill steaks over medium heat for 5 minutes on each side or to desired doneness, brushing with sauce occasionally. Serve immediately.

Makes 4 servings

Grilled Beef 'n' Vegetable-Topped Pizza

1 pound ground beef
¾ cup prepared spaghetti sauce
½ cup A.1.® BOLD Steak Sauce
1 pound frozen bread or pizza dough, thawed
2 tablespoons olive oil
2 cups shredded mozzarella cheese (8 ounces)
¼ cup chopped tomato
¼ cup sliced green onions
¼ cup sliced pitted ripe olives

In medium skillet, over medium-high heat, brown ground beef until no longer pink, stirring to break up beef; drain. Stir in spaghetti sauce and steak sauce; cook and stir until heated through. Keep warm.

Divide dough in half; shape each piece into 8-inch round. Brush one side of each dough round with oil. Grill pizza dough rounds, oil sides down, over low heat for 5 to 7 minutes or until dough is firm and brown. Brush tops of dough rounds with oil and turn over on grill surface. Top each with half the beef mixture, cheese, tomato, onions and olives. Grill, covered with lid or foil, for 5 to 7 minutes or until bottoms are golden and cheese melts. Serve hot.

Makes 2 (8-inch) pizza rounds

Grilled Beef 'n' Vegetable-Topped Pizza

Spicy Beef Back Ribs

1 cup ketchup
½ cup water
1 medium onion, grated
2 tablespoons fresh lemon juice
1 teaspoon hot pepper sauce
½ to 1 teaspoon crushed red pepper
5 pounds beef back ribs, cut into 3 to 4 rib sections

Combine ketchup, water, onion, lemon juice, pepper sauce and red pepper in small saucepan. Bring to a boil over high heat; reduce heat to low. Cook slowly, uncovered, 10 to 12 minutes, stirring occasionally; keep warm.

Prepare grill for indirect cooking.* Place beef back ribs, meaty sides up, on grid centered over drip pan. Grill, on covered grill, 45 to 60 minutes or until tender, turning occasionally. Brush reserved sauce over ribs; grill, covered, 10 minutes more.

Makes 5 to 6 servings

*To prepare grill for indirect cooking, arrange equal amount of briquets on each side of grill. Place foil drip pan in center between coals. Coals are ready when ash-covered, about 30 minutes. Make sure coals are burning equally on both sides.

Uncovered Grilling Directions: Prepare grill and sauce as directed. Place ribs, meaty sides down, in center of double-thick rectangle of heavy-duty foil. Sprinkle 2 tablespoons water over rib bones. Fold up foil, leaving space around food and crimping all ends to make packets. Place packets on grid over low to medium coals. Grill 2 hours or until tender, turning packets over every ½ hour. Remove ribs from packets and place on grid. Continue grilling 10 to 20 minutes, turning once. Brush reserved sauce over ribs; grill 10 minutes more.

Favorite recipe from ***National Live Stock & Meat Board***

Texas-Style Honey Barbecue Rub

- 4 beef top sirloin steaks, about ¾ inch thick (4 ounces *each*)
- ¼ cup honey
- 4 cloves garlic, minced
- 2 teaspoons *each* salt, black pepper, ground mustard and chili powder

Prepare grill or preheat broiler. Rub each steak with 1 tablespoon honey. Combine remaining ingredients in small bowl and rub onto steaks. Let stand 20 to 30 minutes. Place steaks on grid or broiler pan. Grill over medium coals or broil 8 to 11 minutes or to desired doneness. Serve hot.

Makes 4 servings

Serving Suggestion: Serve with grilled peppers and onions; garnish with fresh herbs.

Favorite recipe from ***National Honey Board***

Texas-Style Honey Barbecue Rub

Beef Kabobs over Lemon Rice

- ½ pound boneless beef sirloin steak, cut into 1-inch cubes
- 1 small zucchini, sliced
- 1 small yellow squash, sliced
- 1 small red bell pepper, cut into squares
- 1 small onion, cut into chunks
- ¼ cup Italian dressing
- 1 cup hot cooked rice
- 2 teaspoons fresh lemon juice
- 1 tablespoon snipped fresh parsley
- ¼ teaspoon seasoned salt

Combine beef and vegetables in large resealable plastic food storage bag; add dressing. Seal bag and marinate 4 to 6 hours in refrigerator, turning bag occasionally. Thread beef and vegetables alternately onto 4 metal skewers. Grill over medium coals, or broil 5 to 7 minutes, or to desired doneness, turning and basting with remaining marinade. Combine rice and remaining ingredients. Serve kabobs over rice mixture.

Makes 2 servings

Favorite recipe from ***USA Rice Council***

Grilled Steak and Asparagus Salad

- ½ cup bottled light olive oil vinaigrette
- ⅓ cup A.1.® Steak Sauce
- 1 (1-pound) beef top round steak
- 1 (10-ounce) package frozen asparagus spears, cooked and cooled
- ½ cup thinly sliced red bell pepper
- 8 large lettuce leaves
- 1 tablespoon toasted sesame seed

In small bowl, blend vinaigrette and steak sauce. Place steak in glass dish; coat with ¼ cup vinaigrette mixture. Cover; chill 1 hour, turning once.

In small saucepan, over medium heat, heat remaining vinaigrette mixture to a boil. Reduce heat and simmer 1 minute; keep warm.

Remove steak from marinade; discard marinade. Grill over medium heat for 12 minutes or to desired doneness, turning occasionally. Thinly slice steak. Arrange steak, asparagus and red pepper on lettuce leaves. Pour warm marinade over salad; sprinkle with sesame seed. Serve immediately. *Makes 4 servings*

Pace® Fajitas

1½ pounds beef skirt steak
1 cup PACE® Picante Sauce
¼ cup vegetable oil
1 teaspoon lemon juice
Dash black pepper
Dash garlic powder
12 (7- to 8-inch) flour tortillas, warmed
Chunky Guacamole (recipe follows)
Additional PACE® Picante Sauce

Pound meat with meat mallet to tenderize; place in resealable plastic food storage bag. Combine Pace® Picante Sauce, oil, lemon juice, pepper and garlic powder in small bowl. Pour over meat in bag; press out excess air and seal. Marinate in refrigerator at least 3 hours or up to 24 hours, turning bag several times.

Drain meat, reserving marinade. Place meat on grill over hot coals or on rack of broiler pan. Grill or broil 5 to 6 minutes on each side or to desired doneness, basting frequently with reserved marinade.

Pace® Fajitas

Remove from grill or broiler pan; slice across grain into thin strips. Place meat on tortillas; top with Chunky Guacamole and additional picante sauce. Roll up and serve. *Makes 6 servings*

Chunky Guacamole

2 ripe avocados, peeled, seeded and diced
1 medium tomato, seeded and chopped
⅓ cup green onion slices or chopped white onion
¼ cup PACE® Picante Sauce

Combine ingredients in small bowl, mixing lightly; refrigerate until ready to serve. *Makes about 2½ cups*

Citrus Grilled Steak

Citrus Grilled Steak

1 (6-ounce) can orange juice concentrate, thawed
½ cup A.1.® Steak Sauce
¼ cup dry sherry
1 clove garlic, minced
2 (8-ounce) beef club or strip steaks, about 1 inch thick

In small bowl, combine orange juice concentrate, steak sauce, sherry and garlic. Place steaks in glass dish; coat with ½ cup orange juice mixture. Cover; chill 1 hour, turning occasionally.

In small saucepan, over medium heat, heat remaining orange juice mixture; keep warm.

Remove steaks from marinade; discard marinade. Grill over medium heat for 4 minutes on each side or to desired doneness. Serve steaks with reserved warm orange sauce. *Makes 4 servings*

A to Z Kabobs

3 medium zucchini (1 pound)
Boiling water
2 pounds boneless tender beef steaks, each about 1 inch thick
½ cup KIKKOMAN® Teriyaki Marinade & Sauce
¼ cup dry white wine
1 tablespoon vegetable oil
¼ to ½ teaspoon pepper
¼ teaspoon dried oregano leaves, crumbled
1 clove garlic, pressed
2 large cooking apples

Cut each zucchini in half lengthwise, then crosswise into 1½-inch pieces. Cover with boiling water. Let stand 5 minutes; drain. Cool. Cut beef into 1½-inch pieces; place with zucchini in large plastic food storage bag. Combine teriyaki sauce, wine, oil, pepper, oregano and garlic; pour over beef and zucchini. Press air out of bag; close top securely. Marinate 30 minutes, turning bag over occasionally.

Meanwhile, core apples; cut into 1½-inch pieces. Reserving marinade, remove beef and zucchini; thread onto 6 (10-inch) metal or bamboo* skewers alternately with apples. Place kabobs on grill 5 inches from hot coals. Cook 5 minutes on each side (for rare), or to desired doneness, brushing occasionally with reserved marinade. (Or, place kabobs on rack of broiler pan. Broil 5 inches from heat 5 minutes on each side [for rare], or to desired doneness, brushing occasionally with reserved marinade.)

Makes 6 servings

*Soak bamboo skewers in water 30 minutes to prevent burning.

Beef Tenderloin with Dijon-Cream Sauce

- 2 tablespoons olive oil
- 3 tablespoons balsamic vinegar*
- 1 beef tenderloin roast (about 1½ to 2 pounds)
- Salt
- 1½ tablespoons white peppercorns
- 1½ tablespoons black peppercorns
- 3 tablespoons mustard seeds
- Dijon-Cream Sauce (recipe follows)

Combine oil and vinegar in a cup; rub onto beef. Season generously with salt. Let stand 15 minutes. Meanwhile, coarsely crush peppercorns and mustard seeds in a blender or food processor or by hand with mortar and pestle. Roll beef in crushed mixture, pressing into surface to coat.

Oil hot grid to help prevent sticking. Grill beef, on a covered grill, over medium KINGSFORD® Briquets, 16 to 24 minutes (depending on size and thickness) until a meat thermometer inserted in the center almost registers 150°F for medium-rare, turning halfway through cooking. (Cook until 160°F for medium or 170°F for well-done; add another 5 minutes for every 10°F.) Let stand 5 to 10 minutes before slicing. Slice and serve with a few spoonfuls of sauce. *Makes 6 servings*

*You may substitute 2 tablespoons red wine vinegar plus 1½ teaspoons sugar for the balsamic vinegar.

Note: When choosing a beef tenderloin roast, purchase a center-cut piece or a piece cut from the thicker end, as it will grill more evenly. Test doneness with a thermometer and remove beef from the grill just before it reaches the desired temperature. (The internal temperature can rise 5°F as the roast stands.)

Dijon-Cream Sauce

- 1 can (14½ ounces) beef broth
- 1 cup whipping cream
- 2 tablespoons butter, softened
- 1½ to 2 tablespoons Dijon mustard
- 1 to 1½ tablespoons balsamic vinegar**
- Coarsely crushed black peppercorns and mustard seeds for garnish

Bring beef broth and whipping cream to a boil in a saucepan. Boil gently until reduced to about 1 cup; sauce will be thick enough to coat a spoon. Remove from heat; stir in butter, a little at a time, until all the butter is melted. Stir in mustard and vinegar, adjusting amounts to taste. Sprinkle with peppercorns and mustard seeds. *Makes about 1 cup*

**You may substitute 2 teaspoons red wine vinegar plus 1 teaspoon sugar for the balsamic vinegar.

Beef Tenderloin with Dijon-Cream Sauce

Grilled Meat Loaf and Potatoes

1 pound ground beef
½ cup A.1.® Steak Sauce, divided
½ cup plain dry bread crumbs
1 egg
¼ cup finely chopped green bell pepper
¼ cup finely chopped onion
2 tablespoons margarine, melted
4 (6-ounce) red skin potatoes, parboiled and sliced into ¼-inch-thick rounds
Grated Parmesan cheese

In large bowl, combine ground beef, ¼ cup steak sauce, bread crumbs, egg, pepper and onion. Divide mixture and shape into 4 (4-inch) oval loaves.

In small bowl, combine remaining steak sauce and margarine; set aside.

Over medium heat, grill meat loaves for 20 to 25 minutes or until loaves are cooked through and potato slices for 10 to 12 minutes or until fork-tender, turning and brushing both occasionally with steak sauce mixture. Sprinkle potatoes with Parmesan cheese; serve immediately.

Makes 4 servings

Wine Country Steak

½ cup olive oil
Juice of 1 lime or lemon
1 cup Cabernet, Merlot or other dry red wine
¼ cup soy sauce
3 cloves garlic, minced or pressed
1½ tablespoons Dijon mustard
1 teaspoon black pepper
1 beef flank steak (about 2 pounds), pounded to about ½ inch thick

Whisk together oil, lime juice, wine, soy sauce, garlic, mustard and pepper in a medium bowl. Place beef in a shallow glass dish or large heavy plastic bag; pour marinade over beef. Cover dish or close bag. Marinate in refrigerator 12 to 24 hours, turning once or twice. Remove beef from marinade; discard marinade.

Oil grid to help prevent sticking. Grill beef, on a covered grill, over medium KINGSFORD® Briquets 6 to 8 minutes for rare doneness or 9 to 12 minutes for medium-rare doneness, turning once or twice. Cut across grain into thin, diagonal slices.

Makes 6 servings

Flank Steak Grill

¼ cup red wine vinegar
¼ cup ketchup
1 tablespoon *plus* 1 teaspoon Worcestershire sauce
1 tablespoon *plus* 1 teaspoon liquid smoke (optional)
2 teaspoons LAWRY'S® Garlic Powder with Parsley
1 teaspoon LAWRY'S® Seasoned Salt
2 pounds flank steak

In large resealable plastic bag or shallow glass dish, combine all ingredients except steak; blend well. Add flank steak to marinade; seal bag or cover dish. Marinate in refrigerator 30 minutes or overnight. Heat grill for medium coals. Remove steak, reserving marinade. Grill, 4 to 5 inches from heat, 8 to 10 minutes or to desired doneness, turning and basting often with reserved marinade.

Makes 6 servings

Presentation: Cut steak diagonally into thin slices. Garnish with fresh thyme sprigs and grilled fresh pineapple slices.

Variation: Substitute London broil or beef steak for the flank steak.

Grilled Meat Loaf and Potatoes

Guadalajara Beef

1 bottle (12 ounces) Mexican dark beer*
¼ cup soy sauce
2 cloves garlic, minced
1 teaspoon ground cumin
1 teaspoon chili powder
1 teaspoon hot pepper sauce
4 beef bottom sirloin steaks or boneless tri tip steaks (4 to 6 ounces *each*)
Salt and black pepper
Red, green and yellow bell peppers, cut lengthwise into quarters and seeded (optional)
Salsa (recipe follows)
Flour tortillas (optional)
Lime wedges

Guadalajara Beef

Combine beer, soy sauce, garlic, cumin, chili powder and hot pepper sauce in a large shallow glass dish or heavy plastic bag. Add beef; cover dish or close bag. Marinate in refrigerator up to 12 hours, turning beef several times. Remove beef from marinade; discard marinade. Season with salt and pepper.

Oil hot grid to help prevent sticking. Grill beef and peppers, if desired, on covered grill, over medium KINGSFORD® Briquets, 8 to 12 minutes, turning once. Beef should be medium doneness and peppers tender. Serve with Salsa, warmed tortillas, if desired, and lime. *Makes 4 servings*

*Substitute any beer for the Mexican dark beer.

Tip: Experiment with aromatics, such as fresh herbs and citrus peel, to vary the flavor of recipes. Our suggestion is to add 2 or 3 fresh rosemary branches and the peel of half an orange directly to coals when turning meat.

Salsa

2 cups coarsely chopped seeded tomatoes (about 1¼ pounds)
2 green onions with tops, sliced
1 clove garlic, minced
1 to 2 teaspoons minced seeded jalapeño or serrano chili pepper, fresh or canned
1 tablespoon olive or vegetable oil
2 to 3 teaspoons lime juice
8 to 10 sprigs fresh cilantro, minced (optional)
½ teaspoon salt or to taste
½ teaspoon sugar or to taste
¼ teaspoon black pepper

Combine tomatoes, green onions, garlic, chili pepper, oil and lime juice in a medium bowl. Stir in cilantro, if desired. Season with salt, sugar and black pepper. Adjust seasonings to taste, adding lime juice or chili pepper, if desired.

Makes about 2 cups

Perfectly Grilled Steak and Potatoes

- Olive oil
- 1½ teaspoons cracked black pepper
- 2 cloves garlic, pressed
- ½ teaspoon salt
- ½ teaspoon dried thyme leaves, crushed
- 4 beef fillet or strip loin steaks (1½ inches thick)
- 4 medium potatoes, sliced into ½-inch-thick rounds
- Additional salt and black pepper
- 4 lime wedges

Combine 2 tablespoons oil, 1½ teaspoons pepper, garlic, ½ teaspoon salt and thyme in cup. Brush over steaks to coat both sides. Brush potato slices with additional oil; season to taste with additional salt and pepper.

Oil hot grid to help prevent sticking. Grill beef and potatoes, on a covered grill, over medium-hot KINGSFORD® Briquets 10 to 12 minutes, turning once. Beef should be medium-rare and potatoes golden brown and tender. Serve wedges of lime to squeeze over steaks. *Makes 4 servings*

Beef and Bacon Shish Kabob

Beef and Bacon Shish Kabobs

- ½ cup A.1.® Steak Sauce
- ¼ cup sherry cooking wine
- 2 tablespoons honey
- 1 (1-pound) beef sirloin steak, cut into 1-inch cubes
- 14 slices bacon, halved crosswise (about ½ pound)
- 1 large onion, cut into wedges
- 1 large green or red bell pepper, cut into squares
- 12 small mushroom caps

In small bowl, blend steak sauce, sherry and honey. Place beef cubes in nonmetal dish; coat with ¼ cup steak sauce mixture. Cover; chill 1 hour, stirring occasionally.

Remove beef cubes from marinade; discard marinade. Wrap half bacon slice around each cube. Alternately thread beef and bacon cubes, onion, pepper and mushrooms onto 4 (10-inch) metal skewers. Grill over medium heat for 8 to 10 minutes or to desired doneness, turning and brushing occasionally with remaining steak sauce mixture. Serve immediately. *Makes 4 servings*

PORK

Micro-Grilled Pork Ribs

1 tablespoon firmly packed brown sugar
2 teaspoons ground cumin
1 teaspoon salt
½ teaspoon black pepper
Dash ground red pepper (optional)
3 pounds pork back ribs
⅓ cup water
½ cup K.C. MASTERPIECE® Barbecue Sauce
Grilled Sweet Potatoes (recipe follows)

Combine brown sugar, cumin, salt and peppers in small bowl. Rub onto ribs. Arrange ribs in single layer in 13 × 9-inch microwave-safe baking dish. Pour water over ribs; cover loosely with plastic wrap. Microwave on MEDIUM-HIGH (70% power) 15 minutes, rearranging ribs and rotating dish halfway through cooking time.

Arrange medium-hot KINGSFORD® Briquets on one side of grill. Place ribs on grid area opposite briquets. Barbecue ribs, on a covered grill, 15 to 20 minutes, turning every 5 minutes and basting with barbecue sauce the last 10 minutes. Ribs should be browned and cooked through. Serve with Grilled Sweet Potatoes. *Makes 4 servings*

Grilled Sweet Potatoes or Baking Potatoes: Slice potatoes into ¼-inch-thick rounds, allowing about ⅓ pound potatoes per serving. Brush both sides of slices lightly with oil. Place on grid around edges of medium-hot Kingsford® briquets. Cook potatoes, on a covered grill, 10 to 12 minutes until golden brown and tender, turning once.

Cranberry Glazed Pork Tenderloin

1 cup whole berry cranberry sauce
⅓ cup A.1.® Steak Sauce
¼ cup chopped green onions
2 tablespoons reduced sodium soy sauce
2 tablespoons firmly packed light brown sugar
1 teaspoon grated fresh ginger
1 (1-pound) pork tenderloin

In small saucepan, combine cranberry sauce, steak sauce, onions, soy sauce, brown sugar and ginger. Over medium heat, cook until mixture is blended and heated through. Remove ⅓ cup sauce mixture; cool slightly. Keep remaining sauce mixture warm.

Grill pork over medium heat for 20 to 30 minutes or until pork is juicy and barely pink in center, turning and brushing occasionally with ⅓ cup reserved sauce mixture. Serve hot with warm sauce.

Makes 4 servings

Micro-Grilled Pork Ribs

Grilled Chili-Marinated Pork

3 tablespoons ground seeded dried pasilla chilies
1 teaspoon coarse or kosher salt
½ teaspoon ground cumin
2 tablespoons vegetable oil
1 tablespoon fresh lime juice
3 cloves garlic, minced
2 pounds pork tenderloin or thick boneless loin pork chops, trimmed of fat
Shredded romaine lettuce (optional)
Radishes for garnish

Mix chilies, salt and cumin in small bowl. Stir in oil and lime juice to make smooth paste. Stir in garlic. Butterfly pork by cutting lengthwise about ⅔ of the way through, leaving meat in one piece; spread meat flat. Cut tenderloin crosswise into 8 equal pieces. (*Do not cut chops into pieces.*) Place pork between pieces of plastic wrap. Pound with flat side of meat mallet to ¼-inch thickness. Spread chili paste on both sides of pork pieces to coat evenly. Place in shallow glass baking dish. Cover and marinate in refrigerator 2 to 3 hours.

Prepare grill. Place pork on grid. Grill, on covered grill, over medium coals 6 inches from heat, 8 to 10 minutes or until pork is juicy and barely pink in center, turning once. Serve on lettuce-lined plate. Garnish, if desired. *Makes 6 to 8 servings*

Grilled Chili-Marinated Pork

Pork Roast with Honey-Mustard Glaze

Wood chunks or chips for smoking
⅓ cup honey
¼ cup whole-seed or coarse-grind prepared mustard
Grated peel and juice of 1 medium orange
1 teaspoon minced fresh ginger or ¼ teaspoon ground ginger
½ teaspoon salt
⅛ teaspoon ground red pepper
Apple juice at room temperature
1 boneless pork loin roast (3½ to 4 pounds)

Soak about 4 wood chunks or several handfuls of wood chips in water; drain. Mix honey, mustard, grated orange peel and juice, ginger, salt and red pepper in small bowl.

Arrange medium-low KINGSFORD® Briquets on each side of a rectangular metal or foil drip pan. Pour in apple juice to fill pan half full. Add soaked wood (all the chunks; part of the chips) to the fire.

Oil hot grid to help prevent sticking. Place pork on grid directly above drip pan. Grill pork, on a covered grill, 20 to 30 minutes per pound until a meat thermometer inserted in thickest part registers 155°F. If your grill has a thermometer, maintain a cooking temperature of about 300°F. Add a few more briquets to both sides of fire every 45 minutes to 1 hour, or as necessary, to maintain a constant temperature. Add more soaked wood chips every 30 minutes. Brush meat with honey-mustard mixture twice during the last 40 minutes of cooking. Let pork stand 10 minutes before slicing to allow the internal temperature to rise to 160°F. Slice and serve with sauce made from pan drippings (directions follow), if desired. *Makes 6 to 8 servings*

To make a sauce from pan drippings: Taste the liquid and drippings left in the drip pan. If the drippings have a mild smoky flavor they will make a nice sauce. (If a strong-flavored wood, such as hickory, or too many wood chips were used, the drippings may be overwhelmingly smoky.) Remove excess fat from drip pan with a bulb baster; discard. Measure liquid and drippings; place in a saucepan. For each cup of liquid, use 1 to 2 tablespoons cider vinegar and 2 teaspoons cornstarch mixed with a little cold water until smooth. Stir vinegar-cornstarch mixture into saucepan. Stirring constantly, bring to a boil over medium heat and boil 1 minute.
Makes 6 to 8 servings

Grilled Pork Loin with Honey and Port

1½ pounds boneless pork loin
2 tablespoons olive oil
1 tablespoon kosher salt
1½ cups tawny port
1 cup orange juice
¼ cup honey
2 tablespoons cider vinegar
¼ cup minced green onions
1 cup dried apricots
1 teaspoon dried rosemary leaves, crushed

Grilled Pork Loin with Honey and Port

Rub pork loin with olive oil and kosher salt. Place in shallow glass baking dish. Combine remaining ingredients in saucepan. Bring to a boil over medium-high heat; reduce heat to low and simmer 5 minutes. Pour hot marinade over pork; cover and marinate in refrigerator 2 to 3 hours.

Prepare grill. Remove pork, reserving marinade. Sear all sides of pork roast on grill. Place on roasting rack. Grill, on covered grill, over medium coals about 35 minutes or to an internal temperature of 150°F, basting frequently with marinade. Remove from grill. Cover and keep warm 15 minutes. Reserve all juices.

Bring reserved marinade to a boil over medium-high heat; reduce heat to low and simmer 5 minutes. Add pork juices and simmer 2 to 3 minutes more. To serve, slice pork loin; arrange on plates. Pour warm sauce over slices. *Makes 6 servings*

Prep time: 10 minutes
Cooking time: 40 minutes

Favorite recipe from **National Pork Producers Council**

Skewered Pork

Skewered Pork

½ cup unsweetened pineapple juice
3 tablespoons HEINZ® Worcestershire Sauce
1 teaspoon ground coriander
1 teaspoon minced garlic
¼ teaspoon crushed red pepper
⅛ teaspoon black pepper
1 pound boneless pork loin, cut into ⅛-inch slices

For marinade, in small bowl, combine pineapple juice, Worcestershire sauce, coriander, garlic, red pepper and black pepper. Place pork in deep glass bowl; pour marinade over pork. Cover; marinate in refrigerator about 1 hour.

Meanwhile, soak thin bamboo skewers in water. Weave skewers through pork strips so meat lies flat, discarding marinade. Place pork on grid. Grill over medium coals 2 minutes. Turn; grill an additional 2 minutes or until pork is juicy and barely pink in center. *Makes 20 to 22 appetizers*

Spicy Black Bean Tenderloin

2 pounds pork tenderloin
Black Bean Sauce (recipe follows)
8 bay leaves
1 tablespoon *each* black pepper, dried basil leaves, garlic powder, dried thyme leaves and dried oregano leaves
1 teaspoon *each* ground cloves, dry mustard and salt
½ teaspoon ground cumin
¼ teaspoon ground cinnamon
Hot cooked pasta (optional)

Prepare Black Bean Sauce. Combine all seasonings in blender or food processor; process until bay leaves are fully ground and mixture is smooth.

Prepare grill. Coat tenderloin on all sides with dry rub seasoning. Sear all sides of pork on grill. Place on roasting rack over medium coals. Grill pork about 35 minutes or to an internal temperature of 150°F. Cover and let stand 10 to 15 minutes. To serve, slice tenderloin and fan on serving plates. Drizzle with Black Bean Sauce. Serve with pasta, if desired.

Makes 8 servings

Black Bean Sauce: Heat 2 tablespoons olive oil in large stockpot; add 1 finely chopped yellow onion, 1 finely chopped carrot and 2 crushed garlic cloves. Cook and stir until onion is translucent. Add 2 cups dried black beans and stir well; add 2 quarts chicken stock and 1 pound ham hocks. Bring to a boil over high heat; reduce heat to medium-low and simmer, partially covered, 1½ hours. Remove ham hocks; discard. Process sauce in food processor or blender in batches. Season with salt and pepper to taste. Keep warm until serving.

Favorite recipe from **National Pork Producers Council**

Boneless Pork Chops with Apple-Thyme Marinade

1 can (6 ounces) frozen apple juice concentrate, thawed
¼ cup cider vinegar
2 tablespoons vegetable oil
3 tablespoons soy sauce
1 teaspoon dried thyme leaves, crushed
4 to 6 boneless center-cut pork loin chops (¾ to 1 inch thick)
Salt and black pepper

Combine juice, vinegar, oil, soy sauce and thyme in a shallow glass dish or large heavy plastic bag. Add pork; cover dish or close bag. Marinate in the refrigerator up to 8 hours, turning pork once or twice. Remove pork from marinade; discard marinade. Season pork lightly with salt and pepper.

Oil hot grid to help prevent sticking. Grill pork, on a covered grill, over medium KINGSFORD® Briquets, 8 to 14 minutes, turning once. (Pork is done at 160°F; it should be juicy and slightly pink in the center.) *Makes 4 to 6 servings*

Serving Suggestion: Delicious served with warm applesauce and grilled red onion slices.

Jerk Ribs

2 pounds pork back ribs
2 tablespoons dried minced onion
1 tablespoon onion powder
4 teaspoons ground thyme
2 teaspoons salt
2 teaspoons ground allspice
½ teaspoon ground nutmeg
½ teaspoon ground cinnamon
1 tablespoon sugar
2 teaspoons black pepper
1 teaspoon ground red pepper

Place all ingredients except ribs in small jar with tight-fitting lid; cover and shake until well blended. Rub dry mixture onto all surfaces of ribs.

Prepare grill with rectangular foil drip pan. Bank briquets on either side of drip pan for indirect cooking. Place ribs on grid over drip pan. Grill, on covered grill, over low coals 1½ hours or until ribs are tender, turning occasionally. To serve, cut into 1- or 2-rib portions. *Makes 10 servings*

Conventional Directions: Prepare rub as directed. Roast ribs on rack in shallow pan in 350°F oven for 1½ hours or until ribs are tender.

Prep time: 10 minutes
Cooking time: 90 minutes

Favorite recipe from ***National Pork Producers Council***

Jerk Ribs

Pork Tenderloin with Orange Glaze

1 cup orange juice
¼ cup cider vinegar
1 tablespoon finely grated fresh ginger
1 teaspoon finely grated orange peel
1 pork tenderloin (about 1 pound)
Orange Glaze (recipe follows)
Salt and black pepper

Combine orange juice, vinegar, ginger and orange peel in a shallow glass dish or large heavy plastic bag. Add pork tenderloin; cover dish or close bag. Marinate in refrigerator at least 4 hours, turning several times.

Meanwhile, prepare Orange Glaze. Reserve about ¼ cup for brushing on meat. Remove pork from marinade; discard marinade. Season pork with salt and pepper.

Oil hot grid to help prevent sticking. Grill pork, on a covered grill, over medium KINGSFORD® Briquets, 18 to 25 minutes until a meat thermometer inserted in the thickest part registers 155°F. Brush with reserved Orange Glaze the last 5 to 10 minutes of cooking. Let pork stand 5 to 10 minutes to allow the internal temperature to rise to 160°F before slicing. Slice and serve with remaining Orange Glaze. Garnish, if desired.

Makes 4 servings

Orange Glaze

1 cup orange marmalade
1 tablespoon finely grated ginger
2 tablespoons soy sauce
2 tablespoons cider vinegar
1 tablespoon Dijon mustard
¼ teaspoon salt
¼ teaspoon black pepper

Melt orange marmalade in a small saucepan. Stir in remaining ingredients; reduce heat to low. Cook about 10 minutes. Reserve ¼ cup of glaze for brushing pork; place remaining glaze in a small bowl to serve with pork. *Makes about 1 cup*

Pork Tenderloin with Orange Glaze

Indian Tandoori Ribs

2 slabs pork spareribs
2 cartons (8 ounces *each*) plain yogurt
2 cloves garlic, crushed
3 tablespoons grated ginger
2 jalapeño peppers, halved and seeded*
½ cup fresh cilantro leaves
1 tablespoon ground cumin
Red food coloring

Combine yogurt, garlic, ginger, jalapeños, cilantro and cumin in blender or food processor; process until smooth. Stir in a few drops red food coloring. Place ribs in large resealable plastic food storage bag; add marinade. Seal bag; toss to coat. Marinate in refrigerator overnight.

Prepare grill with rectangular foil drip pan. Bank briquets on either side of drip pan for indirect cooking. Drain ribs, discarding marinade. Place ribs on grid over drip pan. Grill, on covered grill, over low coals 1½ hours or until ribs are tender, turning occasionally. Serve immediately.

Makes 4 servings

*Jalapeño peppers can sting and irritate the skin; wear rubber gloves when handling peppers and do not touch eyes. Wash hands after handling.

Prep time: 15 minutes
Cooking time: 90 minutes

Favorite recipe from ***National Pork Producers Council***

Aztec Kabob Grill with Pineapple

Spicy Marinade

- **1 cup frozen DOLE® Pineapple Juice concentrate, thawed**
- **¼ cup water**
- **1 large onion, halved and thinly sliced**
- **1 jalapeño pepper, seeded and minced**
- **1 tablespoon dried oregano leaves**
- **1 tablespoon ground cumin**
- **2 teaspoons chili powder**

Kabobs

- **1½ pounds pork tenderloin, cut into cubes**
- **4 medium zucchini, cut crosswise into thirds**
- **2 ears corn, husked and cut crosswise into fourths**
- **2 medium red onions, cut into chunks**
- **1 DOLE® Red Bell Pepper, cut into chunks**
- **1 DOLE® Fresh Pineapple**
- **2 tablespoons DOLE® Raisins**
- **2 tablespoons chopped fresh parsley**
- **Lime wedges**

Aztec Kabob Grill with Pineapple

• Combine Spicy Marinade ingredients in medium bowl until blended.

• Arrange pork in glass casserole dish. Pour 1 cup marinade over pork. Cover and marinate in refrigerator 30 minutes or overnight. Cover and refrigerate remaining marinade for sauce.

• Prepare grill. Thread pork onto 6 metal or bamboo* skewers, placing marinade in small saucepan. Bring marinade to a boil over high heat; divide between 2 small bowls.

• Thread vegetables onto 6 separate skewers, alternating zucchini, corn, onions and bell pepper.

• Twist crown from pineapple. Cut pineapple lengthwise in half. Cut each half into 6 spears.

• Place pork and vegetable kabobs on grid. Grill 6 inches over medium-hot coals 20 to 25 minutes, brushing with heated marinade and turning occasionally. (Use separate basting brush and marinade for pork and vegetables.) Grill pineapple during last 5 minutes of grilling time, brushing with marinade for vegetables and turning occasionally.

• Stir raisins and parsley into reserved marinade for sauce in same small saucepan. Bring to a boil over high heat; cook 1 minute. Serve pork with sauce and lime.

Makes 6 servings

*Soak bamboo skewers in water 30 minutes to prevent burning.

Prep time: 30 minutes
Cooking time: 25 minutes

Lite Teriyaki Pork Chops

½ cup KIKKOMAN® Lite Teriyaki Marinade & Sauce
2 tablespoons prepared horseradish
⅛ teaspoon ground cinnamon
4 pork rib or loin chops, ¾ inch thick

Blend lite teriyaki sauce, horseradish and cinnamon; pour over chops in large plastic food storage bag. Press air out of bag; close top securely. Turn bag over several times to coat all chops well. Refrigerate 1½ hours, turning bag over occasionally. Reserving marinade, remove chops. Place chops on grill 5 to 7 inches from medium-hot coals. Cook 10 to 12 minutes, or until light pink in center, turning over and brushing occasionally with reserved marinade. (Or, place chops on rack of broiler pan. Broil 5 to 7 inches from heat 8 to 10 minutes, or until light pink in center, turning over and brushing occasionally with reserved marinade.)

Makes 4 servings

Huli-Huli Spareribs

½ cup KIKKOMAN® Soy Sauce
½ cup brown sugar, packed
½ cup chopped green onions and tops
¼ cup tomato ketchup
1 large clove garlic, pressed
1 teaspoon grated fresh ginger root
3 pounds pork spareribs, cut into 1-rib pieces

Combine soy sauce, brown sugar, green onions, ketchup, garlic and ginger in large bowl. Add spareribs; toss to thoroughly coat all pieces well. Reserving sauce, remove ribs; place, meaty sides up, in 13 × 9-inch microwave-safe baking dish. Let stand 10 minutes; cover. Microwave on MEDIUM-HIGH (70%) 16 minutes, rotating dish after 8 minutes. Place ribs on grill 4 to 5 inches from medium-hot coals; brush with reserved sauce. Cook 10 minutes, turning over and brushing occasionally with remaining sauce. (Or, place ribs on rack of broiler pan; brush with reserved sauce. Broil 4 to 5 inches from heat 6 minutes; turn over. Brush with remaining sauce. Broil 6 minutes longer.)

Makes 4 servings

Huli-Huli Spareribs

Oriental Glazed Tenderloin

Oriental Glazed Tenderloins

⅓ cup KIKKOMAN® Teriyaki Baste & Glaze
1 tablespoon dry sherry
½ teaspoon ginger juice*
¼ teaspoon grated orange peel
2 pork tenderloins (¾ pound *each*)

Combine teriyaki baste & glaze, sherry, ginger juice and orange peel; set aside. Place tenderloins on grill 4 to 5 inches from hot coals. Cook 25 minutes, turning over occasionally. Brush both sides of tenderloins with baste & glaze mixture. Cook 10 minutes longer, or until meat thermometer inserted into thickest part of meat registers 160°F, turning over and brushing frequently with remaining baste & glaze mixture. Let stand 10 minutes. To serve, cut meat across grain into thin slices.

Makes 4 to 6 servings

*Press enough fresh ginger root pieces through garlic press to measure ½ teaspoon juice.

Hickory Smoked Ham with Maple-Mustard Sauce

Hickory chunks or chips for smoking
1 fully cooked boneless ham (about 5 pounds)
¾ cup maple syrup
¾ cup spicy brown mustard or Dijon mustard

Soak about 4 wood chunks or several handfuls of wood chips in water; drain. If using a canned ham, scrape off any gelatin. If using another type of fully cooked ham, such as a bone-in shank, trim most of the fat, leaving a ⅛-inch layer. (The thinner the fat layer, the better the glaze will adhere to the ham.)

Arrange low KINGSFORD® Briquets on each side of a rectangular metal or foil drip pan. Pour in hot tap water to fill pan half full. Add soaked wood (all the chunks; part of the chips) to the fire.

Oil hot grid to help prevent sticking. Place ham on grid directly above drip pan. Grill ham, on a covered grill, 20 to 30 minutes per pound, until a meat thermometer inserted in the thickest part registers 140°F. If your grill has a thermometer, maintain a cooking temperature of about 200°F. For best flavor, cook slowly over low coals, adding a few briquets to both sides of the fire every hour, or as necessary, to maintain a constant temperature. Add more soaked hickory chips every 20 to 30 minutes.

Meanwhile, prepare Maple-Mustard Sauce by mixing maple syrup and mustard in small bowl; set aside most of the syrup mixture to serve as a sauce. Brush ham with remaining mixture several times during the last 45 minutes of cooking. Let ham stand 10 minutes before slicing. Slice and serve with Maple-Mustard Sauce.

Makes 12 to 15 servings

Note: Most of the hams available today are fully cooked and need only be heated to a temperature of 140°F. If you buy a partially cooked ham, often labeled "cook before eating," it needs to be cooked to an internal temperature of 160°F.

Tip: Smoking an ordinary canned ham over hickory chips improves its flavor tremendously. Keep the temperature low and replenish the hickory chips every 20 to 30 minutes. The 5-pound canned ham used for this recipe cooks in 2 to 2½ hours. However, you may use any bone-in or boneless ham. Just follow these directions and cook to 140°F.

Honey-Lime Pork Chops

1 envelope LIPTON® Recipe Secrets® Savory Herb with Garlic or Onion Soup Mix
3 tablespoons soy sauce
2 tablespoons honey
2 tablespoons lime juice
1 teaspoon grated fresh ginger *or* ¼ teaspoon ground ginger (optional)
4 boneless pork chops, 1½ inches thick (about 1 pound)

In large nonaluminum baking dish or resealable plastic bag, thoroughly blend all ingredients except pork chops; add chops and turn to coat. Cover and marinate in refrigerator, turning chops occasionally, at least 2 hours. Remove chops, reserving marinade.

Grill or broil chops 15 to 18 minutes or until pork is juicy and barely pink in center, turning once and basting with reserved marinade. *Makes about 4 servings*

Serving Suggestion: Serve with baked potatoes topped with plain yogurt or sour cream and your favorite vegetable.

Javanese Pork Saté

1 pound boneless pork loin
½ cup minced onion
2 tablespoons peanut butter
2 tablespoons lemon juice
2 tablespoons soy sauce
1 tablespoon brown sugar
1 tablespoon vegetable oil
1 clove garlic, minced
Dash hot pepper sauce
Hot cooked rice (optional)

Cut pork into ½-inch cubes; place in shallow dish. Combine all remaining ingredients except rice in blender or food processor; process until smooth. Pour over pork. Cover and marinate in refrigerator 10 minutes.

Prepare grill. Thread pork onto skewers.* Place skewers on grid. Grill over medium-hot coals 10 to 12 minutes or until pork is nicely browned and barely pink in center, turning occasionally. Serve with rice, if desired. *Makes 4 servings*

*If using bamboo skewers, soak in water 30 minutes to prevent burning.

Favorite recipe from **National Pork Producers Council**

Javanese Pork Saté

Dijon Baby Back Barbecued Ribs

2 to 3 teaspoons LAWRY'S® Seasoned Salt
4 pounds pork baby back ribs
1 bottle (12 ounces) LAWRY'S® Dijon & Honey Barbecue Sauce

Sprinkle Seasoned Salt onto both sides of ribs. In large resealable plastic bag or shallow glass baking dish, place ribs; seal bag or cover dish. Refrigerate at least 2 hours. Heat grill for medium coals. Grill, 4 to 5 inches from heat, 45 to 60 minutes or until ribs are tender, turning and basting with Dijon & Honey Barbecue Sauce after 30 minutes. *Makes 4 to 6 servings*

Presentation: Cut ribs into 3-bone portions to serve.

Hint: Ribs may be baked in 375°F oven 45 to 60 minutes or until ribs are tender, turning and basting with sauce every 10 minutes.

Pork Kabobs with Mustard-Bourbon Glaze

1 boneless pork loin roast (1 to 1¼ pounds)
Salt and black pepper
3 tablespoons Dijon mustard
3 tablespoons bourbon or water
¼ cup soy sauce
¼ cup firmly packed brown sugar
1 tablespoon Worcestershire sauce

Cut pork into 1-inch cubes; season with salt and pepper. Combine mustard, bourbon, soy sauce, brown sugar and Worcestershire sauce in a shallow glass dish or large heavy plastic bag. Add pork; cover dish or close bag. Marinate in refrigerator up to 4 hours. Remove pork from marinade; discard marinade. Thread pork onto metal or bamboo skewers. (Soak bamboo skewers in water for at least 20 minutes to prevent burning.)

Oil hot grid to help prevent sticking. Grill pork, on a covered grill, over medium KINGSFORD® Briquets, 8 to 12 minutes until pork is cooked through, turning once. (Pork should be juicy and slightly pink in the center.) *Makes 4 servings*

Grilled Szechuan Pork Chops

4 boneless pork chops, 1 inch thick
2 green onions with tops, finely chopped
2 tablespoons soy sauce
2 cloves garlic, minced
1 tablespoon toasted sesame oil
1 tablespoon lemon juice
2 teaspoons chile paste or Oriental chile oil
1 teaspoon sugar
1 teaspoon grated fresh ginger
½ teaspoon Oriental chile oil

For marinade, combine all ingredients except chops in small bowl. Place chops in large resealable plastic food storage bag; pour marinade over chops. Seal bag and marinate in refrigerator 4 hours or overnight.

Prepare grill. Drain chops, reserving marinade. Place chops on grid. Grill over medium-hot coals 4 to 5 minutes. Brush chops with reserved marinade; turn and brush again. Grill 4 to 5 minutes more or until pork is juicy and barely pink in center. Serve immediately. *Makes 4 servings*

Prep time: 10 minutes
Cooking time: 10 minutes

Favorite recipe from ***National Pork Producers Council***

Dijon Baby Back Barbecued Ribs

Brats 'n' Beer

- 1 can or bottle (12 ounces) beer (not dark) or nonalcoholic beer
- 4 bratwurst (about 1 pound)
- 1 large sweet or Spanish onion (about ½ pound), thinly sliced and separated into rings
- 1 tablespoon olive or vegetable oil
- ¼ teaspoon salt
- ¼ teaspoon black pepper
- 4 hot dog rolls, preferably bakery-style or onion, split
- Coarse-grain or sweet-hot mustard
- Drained sauerkraut (optional)

Prepare grill. Pour beer into heavy medium saucepan with ovenproof handle. (If not ovenproof, wrap heavy-duty foil around handle.) Set saucepan on one side of grid. Pierce each bratwurst in several places with tip of sharp knife. Carefully add bratwurst to beer; simmer, on uncovered grill, over medium coals 15 minutes, turning once.* Place onion rings on 18 × 14-inch sheet of heavy-duty foil. Drizzle with oil; sprinkle with salt and pepper. Wrap in foil, crimping all edges to make packet. Place on grid. Grill on uncovered grill, 10 to 15 minutes or until onions are tender.

Transfer bratwurst to grid; remove saucepan using heavy-duty mitt. Discard beer. Grill bratwurst, on covered grill, 9 to 10 minutes or until browned and cooked through, turning halfway through grilling time. If desired, place rolls, cut sides down, on grid to toast lightly during last 1 to 2 minutes of grilling. Place bratwurst in rolls. Open foil packet carefully. Top each bratwurst with onions. Serve with mustard and sauerkraut. *Makes 4 servings*

*If desired, bratwurst may be simmered on range top. Pour beer into medium saucepan. Bring to a boil over medium-high heat. Carefully add bratwurst to beer. Reduce heat to low and simmer, uncovered, 15 minutes, turning once.

Brat 'n' Beer

Hot and Spicy Spareribs

- 1 rack pork spareribs (3 pounds)
- 2 tablespoons butter or margarine
- 1 medium onion, finely chopped
- 2 cloves garlic, minced
- 1 can (15 ounces) tomato sauce
- ⅔ cup cider vinegar
- ⅔ cup firmly packed brown sugar
- 2 tablespoons chili powder
- 1 tablespoon prepared mustard
- ½ teaspoon black pepper

Melt butter in large skillet over low heat. Add onion and garlic; cook and stir until tender. Add all remaining ingredients except ribs. Bring to a boil over high heat; reduce heat to low and simmer 20 minutes, stirring occasionally.

Prepare grill. Place large piece of heavy-duty foil over coals to catch drippings. Baste meaty sides of ribs with sauce. Place ribs on grid, meaty sides down; baste top side. Grill, on covered grill, about 6 inches over low coals 20 minutes; turn ribs and baste. Cook 45 minutes more or until ribs are tender, basting every 10 to 15 minutes with sauce. (Do not baste during last 5 minutes of grilling.) *Makes 3 servings*

Favorite recipe from **National Pork Producers Council**

Summer Sunset Grilled Pork

2 pork tenderloins, about ¾ pound *each*
½ cup KIKKOMAN® Lite Teriyaki Marinade & Sauce
Fresh Nectarine Sauce (page 208)

Cut tenderloins lengthwise in half, being careful not to cut all the way through; press open to flatten. Pour lite teriyaki sauce over tenderloins in large plastic food storage bag. Press air out of bag; close top securely. Turn bag over several times to coat both pieces well. Refrigerate 1½ hours, turning bag over occasionally.

Meanwhile, prepare Fresh Nectarine Sauce. Reserving marinade, remove tenderloins; place on grill 5 to 7 inches from medium-hot coals. Cook 12 minutes, or until meat thermometer inserted into thickest part of meat registers 160°F, turning over and brushing occasionally with reserved marinade. (Or, place on rack of broiler pan. Broil 4 to 5 inches from heat 5 minutes; turn over. Brush with reserved marinade. Broil 5 minutes longer, or until meat thermometer inserted into thickest part of meat registers 160°F.) Let tenderloins stand 5 minutes before slicing. Serve with Fresh Nectarine Sauce. *Makes 4 servings*

Indonesian Pork Chop 'n' Zesty Relish

Indonesian Pork Chops 'n' Zesty Relish

¼ cup A.1.® Steak Sauce
¼ cup coconut milk
2 tablespoons firmly packed light brown sugar
2 cloves garlic, minced
1 teaspoon grated fresh ginger
½ cup finely diced, seeded, peeled cucumber
¼ cup finely chopped radishes
¼ cup finely chopped onion
¼ cup shredded coconut, toasted
6 (4-ounce) boneless loin pork chops

In small bowl, combine steak sauce, coconut milk, brown sugar, garlic and ginger; reserve ¼ cup for basting. Stir cucumber, radishes, onion and coconut into remaining sauce mixture; refrigerate.

Grill pork chops over medium heat for 10 minutes or until pork is juicy and barely pink in center, turning occasionally and brushing often with reserved sauce. Serve hot with cucumber relish.

Makes 6 servings

Grilled Ham Steak with Apricot Glaze

Grilled Ham Steaks with Apricot Glaze

1 pound boneless fully cooked ham, cut into 4 (½-inch-thick) slices
¼ cup apricot jam
2 teaspoons Dijon mustard
2 teaspoons cider vinegar

Prepare grill. Combine jam, mustard and vinegar in small bowl; blend well. Grill ham slices over hot coals 8 to 10 minutes or until nicely browned, brushing with apricot sauce occasionally and turning once. Serve immediately. *Makes 4 servings*

Prep time: 15 minutes
Cooking time: 8 to 10 minutes

Favorite recipe from **National Pork Producers Council**

Grilled Peppered Pork Chops with Mediterranean Relish

6 boneless pork chops, ¾ inch thick
1 jar (6 ounces) marinated artichoke hearts
1 teaspoon hot pepper sauce
1½ cups diced tomatoes
½ cup chopped bottled roasted sweet red peppers
¼ cup sliced ripe olives
1 small jalapeño pepper, seeded and finely chopped*

Drain artichoke hearts, reserving marinade. Combine reserved marinade and hot pepper sauce in shallow glass baking dish. Add chops; turn to coat. Let stand for 30 minutes, turning chops occasionally.

Prepare grill. To prepare relish, chop artichoke hearts. Combine artichoke hearts, tomatoes, red peppers, olives and jalapeño in medium bowl; set aside. Drain chops, discarding marinade. Place chops on grid. Grill over medium-hot coals 3 to 4 minutes on each side or until pork is juicy and barely pink in center. Serve with relish.
Makes 6 servings

*Jalapeño peppers can sting and irritate the skin; wear rubber gloves when handling peppers and do not touch eyes. Wash hands after handling.

Prep time: 15 minutes
Cooking time: 10 minutes

Favorite recipe from **National Pork Producers Council**

Curried Pork Kabobs

- 1 pound boneless pork loin, cut into ½-inch cubes
- 1 cup low fat plain yogurt
- 2 tablespoons orange juice
- 1 tablespoon ground coriander
- ½ teaspoon turmeric
- ½ teaspoon ground cumin
- ½ teaspoon salt
- ¼ teaspoon ground ginger

For marinade, combine all ingredients except pork cubes in medium bowl; blend well. Add pork; stir to coat with marinade. Cover and refrigerate 4 hours or overnight.

Prepare grill. Remove pork; discard marinade. Lightly pat pork dry with paper towels. Thread pork evenly onto skewers.* Grill over medium-hot coals about 10 minutes or until pork is nicely browned and barely pink in center, turning frequently. Serve immediately.

Makes 4 servings

*If using bamboo skewers, soak in cold water 30 minutes to prevent burning.

Prep time: 10 minutes
Cooking time: 10 minutes

Favorite recipe from **National Pork Producers Council**

Curried Pork Kabob

Greek-Style Loin Roast

- 1 (3-pound) boneless pork loin roast
- ¼ cup olive oil
- ¼ cup lemon juice
- 1 teaspoon dried oregano leaves, crushed
- 1 teaspoon salt
- 1 teaspoon black pepper
- 6 cloves garlic, minced
- Spicy Yogurt Sauce (recipe follows)

Place pork loin in large resealable plastic food storage bag. Combine all remaining ingredients except Spicy Yogurt Sauce in small bowl; pour over pork. Seal bag and marinate in refrigerator overnight. Meanwhile, prepare Spicy Yogurt Sauce.

Prepare grill with rectangular foil drip pan. Bank briquets on either side of drip pan for indirect cooking. Remove pork, discarding marinade. Place pork on grid over drip pan. Grill, on covered grill, over low coals 1½ hours or to an internal temperature of 155°F. Let rest 10 minutes. (Internal temperature will rise slightly upon standing.) To serve, slice roast thinly and serve with Spicy Yogurt Sauce.

Makes 8 servings

Spicy Yogurt Sauce: Combine 1 cup plain yogurt, 1 peeled and chopped cucumber, ¼ cup minced red onion, ½ teaspoon crushed garlic, ½ teaspoon crushed coriander seeds and ¼ teaspoon crushed red pepper in small bowl; blend well. Cover and refrigerate until ready to serve.

Prep time: 15 minutes
Cooking time: 60 minutes

Favorite recipe from ***National Pork Producers Council***

Baby Back Barbecued Ribs

- 2 to 3 teaspoons LAWRY'S® Seasoned Salt
- 4 pounds baby back ribs
- 1 cup vinegar
- ½ cup ketchup
- 3 tablespoons Worcestershire sauce
- 1 tablespoon sugar
- 2 large cloves garlic, crushed
- 1½ teaspoons hot pepper sauce
- 1½ teaspoons dry mustard
- 1 teaspoon LAWRY'S® Seasoned Salt

Sprinkle 2 to 3 teaspoons Seasoned Salt onto both sides of ribs. In shallow glass baking dish, place ribs; cover dish. Refrigerate 2 hours. In small saucepan, combine remaining ingredients; simmer over medium heat about 10 minutes. Heat grill for medium coals. Brush ribs with sauce. Grill, 4 to 5 inches from heat, 45 to 60 minutes or until ribs are tender, turning and basting with sauce every 10 minutes.

Makes 4 to 6 servings

Presentation: Cut ribs into 3-bone portions to serve.

Hint: Ribs may be baked in 375°F oven 45 to 60 minutes or until ribs are tender, turning and basting with sauce every 10 minutes.

Greek-Style Loin Roast

Maple-Mustard-Glazed Spareribs

Maple-Mustard-Glazed Spareribs

- **4 pounds pork spareribs**
- **½ teaspoon salt**
- **½ teaspoon pickling spices***
- **2 teaspoons vegetable oil**
- **1 small onion, coarsely chopped**
- **½ cup maple-flavored syrup**
- **¼ cup cider vinegar**
- **2 tablespoons water**
- **1 tablespoon Dijon mustard**
- **Dash salt**
- **¼ teaspoon black pepper**

Sprinkle spareribs with ½ teaspoon salt. Place pickling spices in several thicknesses of cheesecloth; tie up to make a bouquet garni. Set aside. For glaze, heat oil in small saucepan; add onion. Cook and stir until tender. Add bouquet garni. Stir in syrup, vinegar, water, mustard, dash salt and pepper. Bring to a boil over medium-high heat; reduce heat to low and simmer 20 minutes. Discard bouquet garni.

Prepare grill with rectangular foil drip pan. Bank briquets on either side of drip pan for indirect cooking. Place ribs on grid over drip pan. Grill, on covered grill, over low coals 1½ hours or until ribs are tender, turning and basting occasionally with glaze. (Do not baste during last 5 minutes of grilling.) *Makes 4 servings*

*Pickling spices is a blend of seasonings used for pickling foods. It can include allspice, bay leaves, cardamom, coriander, cinnamon, cloves, ginger, mustard seeds and/or pepper. Most supermarkets carry prepackaged pickling spices in the spice aisle.

Prep time: 20 minutes
Cooking time: 90 minutes

Favorite recipe from **National Pork Producers Council**

Calypso Pork Chops

1 ripe medium papaya
1 teaspoon paprika
½ teaspoon dried thyme leaves
¼ teaspoon salt
¼ teaspoon ground allspice
4 center-cut pork loin chops (about 1½ pounds), cut ¾ inch thick
5 tablespoons fresh lime juice, divided
2 tablespoons *plus* 1½ teaspoons seeded and chopped jalapeño peppers, divided
1 tablespoon vegetable oil
1½ teaspoons grated fresh ginger, divided
1 teaspoon sugar
¼ cup finely chopped red bell pepper
Additional chopped jalapeño pepper for garnish

To prepare papaya, remove peel with paring knife or vegetable peeler. Slice in half lengthwise. Scrape out seeds; discard. Chop papaya flesh into ¼-inch pieces. Chop enough papaya to measure 1½ cups.

Combine paprika, thyme, salt and allspice in small bowl; rub over both sides of pork chops with fingers. Place chops in large resealable plastic food storage bag. Combine 3 tablespoons lime juice, 2 tablespoons jalapeños, oil, 1 teaspoon ginger and sugar in small bowl; pour over chops. Seal bag tightly; turn to coat. Marinate in refrigerator 1 to 2 hours. Combine papaya, bell pepper, remaining 2 tablespoons lime juice, 1½ teaspoons jalapeños and ½ teaspoon ginger in another small bowl; cover and refrigerate until serving.

Prepare grill. Drain chops, discarding marinade. Place chops on grid. Grill, on covered grill, over medium coals 10 to 12 minutes or until pork is juicy and barely pink in center, turning halfway through grilling time. Serve chops topped with papaya mixture. Garnish, if desired.

Makes 4 servings

Smoked Pork Chops with Spinach, Polenta and Cranberry Chutney

6 pork chops, cured and smoked (12 ounces *each*)
Sautéed Spinach (recipe follows)
Polenta (recipe follows)
Cranberry Chutney (recipe follows)

Prepare grill. Grill chops over medium-high heat about 10 minutes or until heated through. Serve with Sautéed Spinach, Polenta and Cranberry Chutney.

Makes 6 servings

Sautéed Spinach: Melt 1 tablespoon butter in medium skillet over medium heat. Add 12 ounces cleaned fresh spinach; cook and stir 3 to 4 minutes or until softened.

Polenta: Bring 6 cups water to a boil in large saucepan; slowly pour in 1 pound coarse cornmeal and 2 teaspoons salt. Cook and stir 5 to 8 minutes. Stir in 1 cup grated Parmesan cheese and 4 tablespoons butter.

Cranberry Chutney: Heat 1 tablespoon vegetable oil in medium skillet over medium-high heat. Add 1 chopped onion; cook and stir until tender. Stir in 2 cups fresh cranberries, 1 cup water and ¾ cup sugar. Bring to a boil; boil 1 minute. Stir in 2 tablespoons dry mustard and ⅛ teaspoon *each* ground cloves, cinnamon and mace.

Prep time: 30 minutes
Cooking time: 10 minutes

Favorite recipe from ***National Pork Producers Council***

Pork Chops with Orange-Radish Relish

- 2 cups orange juice
- ⅓ cup lime juice
- ⅓ cup firmly packed brown sugar
- 3 medium oranges, peeled, seeded and cut into ¼-inch pieces
- ¼ cup chopped red onion
- ¼ cup diced radishes
- 2 tablespoons finely chopped fresh cilantro
- 6 pork chops (about ¾ inch thick)
- Salt and black pepper
- Orange curls and radishes for garnish

Combine both juices and brown sugar in a saucepan. Cook mixture at a low boil about 20 minutes until it is reduced to about ½ cup and has a syruplike consistency, stirring often. Set aside ¼ cup of sauce for basting.

Meanwhile, prepare Orange-Radish Relish by combining oranges, onion and diced radishes in a colander or strainer and drain well; transfer to a bowl. Add cilantro and gently stir in remaining orange syrup. Season pork with salt and pepper.

Oil hot grid to help prevent sticking. Grill pork, on a covered grill, over medium KINGSFORD® Briquets, 7 to 10 minutes. (Pork is done at 160°F; it should be juicy and slightly pink in the center.) Halfway through cooking, brush with reserved ¼ cup orange syrup and turn once. Serve with Orange-Radish Relish. Garnish with orange curls and radishes.

Makes 6 servings

Pork Chop with Orange-Radish Relish

Barbecued Pork Loin

2 teaspoons LAWRY'S® Seasoned Salt
1 (3- to 3½-pound) boneless pork loin
1 cup orange juice
¼ cup soy sauce
1 teaspoon LAWRY'S® Garlic Powder with Parsley
½ teaspoon LAWRY'S® Seasoned Pepper
Vegetable oil

Sprinkle Seasoned Salt onto all sides of meat. In large resealable plastic bag or shallow glass baking dish, place meat; let stand 10 to 15 minutes. Combine orange juice, soy sauce, Garlic Powder with Parsley and Seasoned Pepper; pour over meat. Seal bag or cover dish. Marinate in refrigerator at least 2 hours or overnight, turning occasionally. Heat grill for medium coals; brush grid with vegetable oil. Remove meat, reserving marinade. Grill, 4 to 5 inches from heat, 30 minutes or until internal meat temperature reaches 170°F, turning and brushing frequently with reserved marinade. Remove meat from grill; let stand about 10 minutes before thinly slicing. Meanwhile, in small saucepan, bring remaining marinade to a boil; boil 1 minute. *Makes 6 servings*

Presentation: Serve sliced meat with extra heated marinade poured over top. Garnish with fresh herb sprigs. Serve with steamed vegetables.

Conventional Directions: Marinate meat as directed. Remove meat, reserving marinade. Place meat in shallow roasting pan; brush with reserved marinade. Bake, uncovered, in 350°F oven 1 hour or until internal temperature reaches 170°F, brushing frequently with remaining marinade. Discard any unused marinade.

Barbecued Pork Loin

Grilled Smoked Sausage

1 cup apricot or pineapple preserves
1 tablespoon lemon juice
1½ pounds smoked sausage

Heat preserves in small saucepan until melted. Strain; reserve fruit pieces. Combine strained preserve liquid with lemon juice in a small bowl.

Oil hot grid to help prevent sticking. Grill whole sausage on an uncovered grill, over low KINGSFORD® Briquets, 10 minutes. Halfway through cooking, baste with glaze, then turn and continue grilling until heated through. Remove sausage from grill; baste with glaze. Garnish with reserved fruit pieces. *Makes 6 servings*

LAMB

Serbian Lamb Sausage Kabobs

1 pound lean ground lamb
1 pound lean ground beef
1 small onion, finely chopped
2 cloves garlic, minced
1 tablespoon hot Hungarian paprika
1 small egg, slightly beaten
Salt and black pepper
3 to 4 red, green or yellow bell peppers, cut into squares
Rice pilaf
Tomato slices and green onion brushes for garnish

Combine lamb, beef, chopped onion, garlic, paprika and egg in large bowl; season with salt and black pepper to taste. Place meat mixture on cutting board; pat evenly into 8 × 6-inch rectangle. Cut meat into 48 (1-inch) squares; shape each square into small oblong sausage.

Prepare grill. Place sausages on jelly-roll pan lined with waxed paper and freeze 30 to 45 minutes or until firm. *Do not freeze completely.* Alternately thread 3 sausages and 3 bell pepper pieces onto each of 16 metal skewers. Place kabobs on grid. Grill over medium-hot coals 5 to 7 minutes. Turn kabobs, taking care not to knock sausages off. Grill 5 to 7 minutes more or until meat is cooked through. Serve with rice pilaf. Garnish, if desired.

Makes 8 servings or 16 kabobs

Note: The seasonings may be adjusted, but the key to authenticity is the equal parts of beef and lamb and the garlic and paprika. You may use sweet paprika if you prefer a milder taste.

Grilled Teriyaki Lamb Chops

2 pounds lamb chops (rib, shoulder or loin), ½ to ¾ inch thick
½ cup KIKKOMAN® Teriyaki Marinade & Sauce
3 tablespoons minced fresh parsley
2 tablespoons dry white wine
2 cloves garlic, pressed
½ teaspoon pepper

Place lamb chops in single layer in large shallow pan. Combine teriyaki sauce, parsley, wine, garlic and pepper; pour over chops. Turn chops over to coat both sides well. Marinate 45 minutes, turning chops over occasionally. Reserving marinade, remove chops; place on grill 4 to 5 inches from hot coals. Cook 4 minutes on each side (for rare), or to desired doneness, turning over and brushing occasionally with reserved marinade. (Or, place lamb chops on rack of broiler pan. Broil 4 to 5 inches from heat 5 minutes; turn over. Brush with reserved marinade. Broil 5 minutes longer [for rare], or to desired doneness.)

Makes 4 servings

Serbian Lamb Sausage Kabobs

Lamb Steak Calypso

Teriyaki Lamb Riblet Appetizers

3 pounds lamb breast riblets, cut into serving-size pieces
Water
⅓ cup KIKKOMAN® Teriyaki Marinade & Sauce

Place riblets in large saucepan. Add enough water to cover. Bring to boil over high heat. Reduce heat to low; cover. Simmer 20 minutes. Remove riblets from saucepan; discard water. Pat riblets dry with paper towels. Place riblets on grill 4 to 5 inches from hot coals; brush thoroughly with teriyaki sauce. Cook 8 minutes, or until well browned on both sides, turning over and brushing frequently with remaining teriyaki sauce. (Or, place on rack of broiler pan; brush with teriyaki sauce. Broil 4 inches from heat 4 minutes on each side, or until well browned on both sides, brushing frequently with remaining teriyaki sauce.)
Makes 8 appetizer servings

Lamb Steaks Calypso

2 American lamb center leg steaks (about 2 pounds)

Marinade

1 cup chicken broth or bouillon
½ cup packed brown sugar
2 tablespoons fresh lime juice
2 tablespoons rum or additional lime juice
1 clove garlic, minced
1 teaspoon grated fresh ginger
½ teaspoon ground cloves

Combine marinade ingredients in shallow glass dish or large resealable plastic food storage bag. Add steaks. Cover and marinate in refrigerator 2 hours or overnight.

Prepare grill. Drain steaks, reserving marinade. Grill over medium coals 5 to 7 minutes on each side or to desired doneness, brushing occasionally with marinade. (Do not baste during last 5 minutes of grilling.) *Makes 4 servings*

Serving suggestion: Serve with grilled sweet potatoes and peppers.

Prep time: 5 minutes
Marinating time: 2 to 24 hours
Cooking time: 10 to 15 minutes

Favorite recipe from ***American Lamb Council***

Rosemary-Crusted Leg of Lamb

¼ cup Dijon mustard
2 cloves garlic, minced
1 boneless butterflied leg of lamb (sirloin half, about 2½ pounds), well trimmed
3 tablespoons chopped fresh rosemary leaves *or* 1 tablespoon dried rosemary leaves, crushed
Fresh rosemary sprigs (optional)
Mint jelly (optional)

Prepare grill. Combine mustard and garlic in small bowl; spread half the mixture with fingers or spatula over one side of lamb. Sprinkle with half the chopped rosemary; pat into mustard mixture. Turn lamb over; repeat with remaining mustard mixture and rosemary. Insert meat thermometer into center of thickest part of lamb. Place lamb on grid. Grill, on covered grill, over medium coals 35 to 40 minutes or until thermometer registers 160°F for medium or to desired doneness, turning every 10 minutes.

Meanwhile, soak rosemary sprigs in water. Place rosemary sprigs directly on coals during last 10 minutes of grilling. Transfer lamb to carving board; tent with foil. Let stand 10 minutes before carving into thin slices. Serve with mint jelly.

Makes 8 servings

Rosemary-Crusted Leg of Lamb

Teriyaki Butterflied Lamb

¾ cup KIKKOMAN® Teriyaki Baste & Glaze
1 teaspoon grated orange peel
1 tablespoon orange juice
1 teaspoon TABASCO® pepper sauce
4 cloves garlic, pressed
1 (4-pound) lamb leg, sirloin or shank half, boned and butterflied

Combine teriyaki baste & glaze, orange peel, orange juice, pepper sauce and garlic; set aside. Trim and discard "fell" and excess fat from lamb. Place lamb on grill 5 inches from hot coals; brush lightly with baste & glaze mixture. Cook 40 minutes, or until meat thermometer inserted into thickest part registers 140°F (for rare), or to desired doneness, turning lamb over occasionally and brushing frequently with remaining baste & glaze mixture. (Or, place lamb on rack of broiler pan. Broil 5 inches from heat 20 minutes, brushing occasionally with baste & glaze mixture. Turn lamb over. Broil 20 minutes longer, or until meat thermometer inserted into thickest part registers 140°F [for rare], or to desired doneness, brushing occasionally with remaining baste & glaze mixture.)

Makes 6 to 8 servings

Teriyaki Butterflied Lamb

Barbecued Leg of Lamb

⅓ cup A.1.® Steak Sauce
2 tablespoons red wine vinegar
2 tablespoons vegetable oil
1 teaspoon chili powder
1 teaspoon dried oregano leaves
½ teaspoon coarsely ground black pepper
½ teaspoon ground cinnamon
2 cloves garlic, crushed
1 (5- to 6-pound) leg of lamb, boned, butterflied and trimmed of fat (about 3 pounds after boning)

In small bowl, combine steak sauce, vinegar, oil, chili powder, oregano, pepper, cinnamon and garlic. Place lamb in nonmetal dish; coat with steak sauce mixture. Cover; chill 1 hour, turning occasionally.

Remove lamb from marinade. Grill over medium heat for 25 to 35 minutes or to desired doneness, turning often. Cut lamb into thin slices; serve hot.

Makes 12 servings

Southwestern Lamb Chops with Charred Corn Relish

4 lamb shoulder or blade chops (about 2 pounds), cut ¾ inch thick, well trimmed
¼ cup vegetable oil
¼ cup lime juice
1 tablespoon chili powder
2 cloves garlic, minced
1 teaspoon ground cumin
¼ teaspoon ground red pepper
Charred Corn Relish (recipe follows)
2 tablespoons chopped fresh cilantro
Hot pepper jelly (optional)

Place chops in large resealable plastic food storage bag. Combine oil, lime juice, chili powder, garlic, cumin and red pepper in small bowl; mix well. Reserve 3 tablespoons mixture for Charred Corn Relish; cover and refrigerate. Pour remaining mixture over chops. Seal bag tightly; turn to coat. Marinate in refrigerator at least 8 hours or overnight, turning occasionally.

Prepare grill and Charred Corn Relish. Drain chops, discarding marinade. Place chops on grid. Grill, on covered grill, over medium coals 13 to 15 minutes for medium or to desired doneness, turning halfway through grilling time. Sprinkle with cilantro. Serve with Charred Corn Relish and pepper jelly. *Makes 4 servings*

Charred Corn Relish

2 large or 3 small ears fresh corn, husked
½ cup finely chopped red bell pepper
¼ cup chopped fresh cilantro
3 tablespoons reserved lime mixture

Southwestern Lamb Chop with Charred Corn Relish

Place corn on grid. Grill corn, on covered grill, over medium coals 10 to 12 minutes or until charred, turning occasionally. Cool to room temperature.

Holding tip of 1 ear, stand upright on its stem end in medium bowl. Cut down the sides of cob, releasing kernels without cutting into cob. Press down along each cob with dull edge of knife to release any remaining corn and liquid. Add bell pepper, cilantro and reserved lime mixture to corn; mix well. Let stand at room temperature while grilling chops. Cover; refrigerate if preparing in advance. Bring to room temperature before serving.

Makes about 1½ cups

Mint Marinated Racks of Lamb

2 whole racks (6 ribs *each*) loin lamb chops (about 3 pounds), well trimmed
1 cup dry red wine
½ cup chopped fresh mint leaves (optional)
3 cloves garlic, minced
¼ cup Dijon mustard
2 tablespoons chopped fresh mint leaves *or* 2 teaspoons dried mint leaves, crushed
⅔ cup dry bread crumbs

Place lamb in large resealable plastic food storage bag. Combine wine, ½ cup mint and garlic in small bowl. Pour over chops. Seal bag tightly; turn to coat. Marinate in refrigerator at least 2 hours or up to 4 hours, turning occasionally.

Prepare grill. Drain lamb, discarding marinade. Pat lamb dry with paper towels. Place lamb in shallow glass dish or on cutting board. Combine mustard and 2 tablespoons mint in small bowl; spread over meaty side of lamb. Pat bread crumbs evenly over mustard mixture. Place lamb, crumb side down, on grid. Grill, on covered grill, over medium coals 10 minutes. Carefully turn; continue to grill, covered, 20 to 22 minutes more for medium or to desired doneness. Place lamb on carving board. Slice between ribs into individual chops. *Makes 4 servings*

Honey Lamb Spareribs

4 pounds lamb spareribs
Boiling water
½ cup tomato ketchup
¼ cup honey
¼ cup KIKKOMAN® Soy Sauce
¼ cup lemon juice

Cook spareribs, covered, in boiling water 1 hour; drain. Combine ketchup, honey, soy sauce and lemon juice; set aside. Place ribs on grill 5 to 6 inches from hot coals. Cook 15 minutes, or until well browned on both sides, turning over and brushing frequently with soy sauce mixture. (Or, place ribs on rack of broiler pan; brush with soy sauce mixture. Broil 4 inches from heat 5 minutes; turn over. Brush with soy sauce mixture. Broil 5 minutes longer or until well browned on both sides.) Place remaining soy sauce mixture in saucepan; bring to a boil. Serve with ribs. *Makes 4 servings*

Mint Marinated Rack of Lamb

Lamb with Fresh Mint Vinaigrette

1½ cups firmly packed mint leaves
½ cup firmly packed parsley leaves
1 clove garlic, chopped
⅓ cup olive oil
¼ cup white or red wine vinegar
2 to 4 teaspoons sugar
Salt and freshly ground black pepper
8 lamb loin chops (about 4 ounces *each*)

To make Fresh Mint Vinaigrette, place mint, parsley, garlic, oil, vinegar, 2 teaspoons sugar, ½ teaspoon salt and ¼ teaspoon pepper into a blender or food processor; process until mixture is smooth and thickened. Adjust sugar and salt to taste. Season lamb with salt and pepper.

Oil hot grid to help prevent sticking. Grill lamb, on a covered grill, over medium KINGSFORD® Briquets, 6 to 9 minutes for medium doneness, turning once. Serve with sauce. *Makes 4 servings*

Southwestern Lamb Grill

Southwestern Lamb Grill

1 rack of American lamb, 8 ribs
3 tablespoons stone ground mustard
1 tablespoon Worcestershire sauce
½ teaspoon crushed red pepper
2 cloves garlic, minced

Trim all visible fat from rack. Stir together remaining ingredients in small bowl. Spread on outside of lamb. (If desired, for maximum flavor, cover and marinate in refrigerator up to 2 days.)

Prepare grill. Place lamb on grid. Grill 6 to 8 inches over hot coals until thermometer registers 140°F for rare or 150°F for medium-rare, turning frequently.

Makes 2 servings

Conventional Directions: Prepare lamb as directed. Place lamb on rack over broiler pan. Roast in preheated 325°F oven until meat thermometer registers 140°F for rare or 150°F for medium-rare.

Serving suggestion: Slice red or green bell peppers, zucchini, chili peppers and corn to desired size; brush with mixture of oil and chopped fresh cilantro. Grill 6 to 8 inches over hot coals until tender.

Favorite recipe from ***American Lamb Council***

Savory Shish Kabobs

⅓ cup KIKKOMAN® Teriyaki Marinade & Sauce
¼ cup dry white wine
2 tablespoons olive oil
½ teaspoon pepper
¼ teaspoon dried oregano leaves, crumbled
¼ teaspoon garlic powder
2 pounds lamb cubes

Combine teriyaki sauce, wine, olive oil, pepper, oregano and garlic powder; pour over lamb in large plastic food storage bag. Press air out of bag; close top securely. Refrigerate 4 hours, turning bag over occasionally. Reserving marinade, remove lamb. Thread each of 4 (12-inch) metal or bamboo* skewers with lamb, leaving space between pieces. Place kabobs on grill 4 to 5 inches from hot coals. Cook 4 to 5 minutes on each side (for rare), or to desired doneness, brushing occasionally with reserved marinade. (Or, place kabobs on rack of broiler pan. Broil 4 to 5 inches from heat 4 minutes; turn over. Brush with reserved marinade. Broil 4 minutes longer [for rare], or to desired doneness.)

Makes 4 servings

*Soak bamboo skewers in water 30 minutes to prevent burning.

Butterflied Southern Citrus Barbecue

6 to 9 pounds butterflied leg of lamb
1½ cups grapefruit juice
3 tablespoons brown sugar
1 tablespoon grated grapefruit or lemon peel
2 cloves garlic, minced
1 teaspoon ground cloves
1 teaspoon ground allspice
½ teaspoon salt
¼ teaspoon ground pepper
Few drops hot pepper sauce

Place lamb in large glass bowl. Combine remaining ingredients in small bowl. Pour over lamb. Cover and refrigerate several hours or overnight.

Prepare grill. Drain lamb, reserving marinade. Place lamb on grid. Grill 4 to 6 inches over medium coals 1 hour and 15 minutes or until meat thermometer inserted in thickest part registers 140°F for rare or 150° to 155°F for medium, basting with marinade. (Do not baste during last 5 minutes of grilling.) *Makes 8 servings*

Favorite recipe from ***American Lamb Council***

Glazed Lamb and Nectarines en Brochette

½ cup KIKKOMAN® Teriyaki Baste & Glaze
2 cloves garlic, pressed
½ teaspoon dried oregano leaves, crumbled
⅛ teaspoon pepper
1½ pounds boneless tender lamb or beef, 1 inch thick
4 to 6 medium-size ripe nectarines

Combine teriyaki baste & glaze, garlic, oregano and pepper; set aside. Cut lamb into 1½-inch pieces. Cut nectarines in half lengthwise; carefully remove pits. Cut enough halves to make 24 wedges. Thread each of 6 (12-inch) metal or bamboo* skewers alternately with lamb and nectarines; brush thoroughly with baste & glaze mixture. Place kabobs on grill 5 to 7 inches from hot coals. Cook 5 minutes on each side (for rare), or to desired doneness, brushing occasionally with remaining baste & glaze mixture. (Or, place kabobs on rack of broiler pan. Broil 4 to 5 inches from heat 3 to 5 minutes on each side [for rare], or to desired doneness, turning over and brushing occasionally with remaining baste & glaze mixture.)

Makes 4 to 6 servings

*Soak bamboo skewers in water 30 minutes to prevent burning.

Butterflied Southern Citrus Barbecue

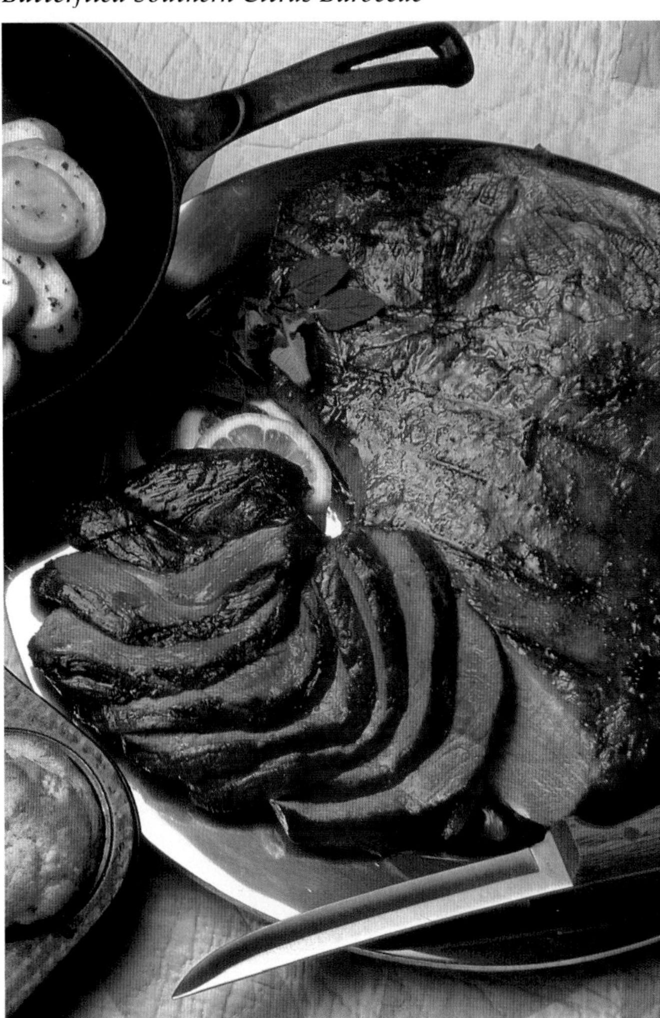

POULTRY

Chicken with Mediterranean Salsa

- ¼ cup olive oil
- 3 tablespoons lemon juice
- 4 to 6 boneless skinless chicken breast halves
- Salt and black pepper
- Rosemary sprigs (optional)
- Mediterranean Salsa (recipe follows)
- Additional rosemary sprigs for garnish

Combine olive oil and lemon juice in a shallow glass dish; add chicken. Turn chicken breasts to lightly coat with mixture; let stand 10 to 15 minutes. Remove chicken from dish and wipe off excess oil; season with salt and pepper.

Oil hot grid to help prevent sticking. Place chicken on grid and place a sprig of rosemary on each chicken breast. Grill chicken, on a covered grill, over medium KINGSFORD® Briquets, 10 to 15 minutes until chicken is no longer pink in center, turning once or twice. Serve with Mediterranean Salsa. Garnish, if desired.

Makes 4 to 6 servings

Mediterranean Salsa

- 2 tablespoons olive oil
- 2 tablespoons white wine vinegar
- 1 clove garlic, minced
- 2 tablespoons finely chopped fresh basil *or* 1 teaspoon dried basil leaves, crushed
- 1 tablespoon finely chopped fresh rosemary *or* 1 teaspoon dried rosemary, crushed
- 1 teaspoon sugar
- ¼ teaspoon black pepper
- 10 to 15 kalamata olives,* seeded and coarsely chopped *or* ⅓ cup coarsely chopped whole pitted ripe olives
- ½ cup chopped seeded cucumber
- ¼ cup finely chopped red onion
- 1 cup chopped seeded tomatoes (about ½ pound)
- ⅓ cup crumbled feta cheese

Combine oil, vinegar, garlic, basil, rosemary, sugar and pepper in a medium bowl. Add olives, cucumber and onion; toss to coat. Cover and refrigerate until ready to serve. Just before serving, gently stir in tomatoes and feta cheese.

Makes about 2 cups

*Kalamata olives are brine-cured Greek-style olives. They are available in large supermarkets.

Chicken with Mediterranean Salsa

Barbecued Chicken with Chili-Orange Glaze

1 or 2 dried de arbol chilies*
½ cup fresh orange juice
2 tablespoons tequila or additional orange juice
2 cloves garlic, minced
1½ teaspoons grated orange peel
¼ teaspoon salt
¼ cup vegetable oil
1 broiler-fryer chicken (about 3 pounds), cut into quarters
Orange slices and cilantro sprigs for garnish

Crush chilies into coarse flakes in mortar with pestle. Combine chilies, orange juice, tequila, garlic, orange peel and salt in small bowl. Gradually add oil, whisking continuously, until marinade is thoroughly blended. Arrange chicken in single layer in large shallow glass dish. Pour marinade over chicken; turn pieces to coat. Cover and marinate in refrigerator 2 to 3 hours, turning chicken over and basting with marinade several times.

Prepare grill. Drain chicken, reserving marinade in small saucepan; bring to a boil over high heat. Grill chicken 6 to 8 inches over medium coals 15 minutes, brushing frequently with marinade. Turn chicken over. Grill 15 minutes more or until chicken is no longer pink near bone, brushing frequently with marinade. Garnish, if desired. *Makes 4 servings*

*For milder flavor, seed some or all of the chilies.

Barbecued Chicken with Chili-Orange Glaze

Cold Grilled Cornish Hens with Vegetable Stuffing

3 to 4 Cornish hens (¾ to 1 pound *each*)
Salt and black pepper
⅓ cup white wine
4 teaspoons Dijon mustard
2½ teaspoons prepared liquid spice tarragon
½ cup vegetable or olive oil
4 zucchini (about 1½ pounds), halved lengthwise
1 large red bell pepper, cored, seeded and quartered
12 mushrooms, skewered
2 tablespoons chopped fresh parsley
6 slices KAVLI® Crispy Thin or Hearty Thick crispbread, crumbled
4 ounces Jarlsberg Lite cheese, cut into thin strips

Prepare grill. To butterfly hens, cut through back of each bird. Open and crack breast bones so hens lie flat. Sprinkle with salt and pepper to taste. For basting sauce, whisk together wine, mustard and liquid tarragon in small bowl until smooth. Gradually whisk in oil until well blended.

Place hens and vegetables on grid about 6 to 8 inches over medium coals. Brush vegetables with basting sauce, then brush hens. Grill vegetables about 15 minutes or until tender, turning often; grill hens 25 to 30 minutes or until no longer pink near bone, turning and basting often with sauce. (Do not baste during last 5 minutes of grilling.) Remove vegetables and hens. When cool enough to handle, cut vegetables into ¼- to ½-inch cubes. Place in large glass bowl and stir in parsley. Season with salt and pepper. Cool to room temperature; cover and refrigerate. Cut hens in half or quarters; cover and refrigerate.

Just before serving, fold crispbread crumbs and cheese into vegetable mixture. Arrange stuffing and hens on serving platter. If desired, garnish with celery leaves or additional parsley. *Makes 6 to 8 servings*

Note: Recipe may also be served warm or hot.

Favorite recipe from **Norseland, Inc.**

Grilled Teriyaki Turkey with Peppers

Grilled Teriyaki Turkey with Peppers

2 turkey breast tenderloins (about 1¼ pounds)
2 green bell peppers, seeded and quartered lengthwise
½ cup KIKKOMAN® Teriyaki Marinade & Sauce
1 tablespoon minced serrano chilies
2 teaspoons brown sugar, packed
½ teaspoon dried oregano leaves, crumbled
1 large clove garlic, pressed

Carefully cut each tenderloin equally in half lengthwise, cutting tenderloin parallel to cutting board; place with bell peppers in large plastic food storage bag. Combine teriyaki sauce, chilies, brown sugar, oregano and garlic; pour over tenderloins and peppers. Press air out of bag; close top securely. Refrigerate 4 hours, turning bag over occasionally.

Reserving marinade, remove tenderloins and peppers. Place tenderloins on grill 5 inches from medium-hot coals. Cook 2 to 3 minutes. Add peppers. Cook 6 to 8 minutes longer or until turkey is no longer pink in center and peppers are soft and browned, turning turkey and peppers over occasionally and brushing with reserved marinade. (Or, place tenderloins and peppers on rack of broiler pan. Broil 4 to 5 inches from heat about 5 minutes; turn over. Brush with reserved marinade. Broil 5 minutes longer or until turkey is no longer pink in center.) *Makes 4 servings*

Chicken Shish-Kabob

Chicken Shish-Kabobs

¼ cup CRISCO® Oil
¼ cup wine vinegar
¼ cup lemon juice
1 teaspoon dried oregano leaves
1 clove garlic, minced
¼ teaspoon black pepper
1½ pounds boneless, skinless chicken breasts, cut into 1- to 1½-inch cubes
12 bamboo or metal skewers (10 to 12 inches long)
2 medium tomatoes, cut into wedges
2 medium onions, cut into wedges
1 medium green bell pepper, cut into 1-inch squares
1 medium red bell pepper, cut into 1-inch squares
4 cups hot cooked brown rice (cooked without salt or fat)
Salt (optional)

1. Combine Crisco Oil, vinegar, lemon juice, oregano, garlic and black pepper in shallow baking dish or glass bowl. Stir well. Add chicken. Stir to coat. Cover. Marinate in refrigerator 3 hours, turning chicken several times.

2. Soak bamboo skewers in water.

3. Prepare grill or heat broiler.

4. Thread chicken, tomatoes, onions and bell peppers alternately on skewers.

5. Place skewers on grill or broiler pan. Grill or broil 5 minutes. Turn. Grill or broil 5 to 7 minutes or until chicken is no longer pink in center. Serve over hot rice. Season with salt and garnish, if desired.

Makes 6 servings

Jalapeño Chicken Fajitas

¼ cup REALIME® Lime Juice from Concentrate
2 tablespoons water
1 clove garlic, chopped
8 ounces skinned boneless chicken breasts
8 slices BORDEN® Lite-line® Jalapeño Flavor Process Cheese Product, cut in half diagonally*
8 (6-inch) flour tortillas, warmed
Garnishes: Salsa, shredded lettuce, green onions, chopped tomatoes, sliced ripe olives

In medium bowl, combine ReaLime® lime juice, water and garlic; add chicken. Marinate in refrigerator 3 to 4 hours. Remove chicken from marinade; grill or broil as desired until chicken is no longer pink in center. Place 2 Lite-line® halves on each tortilla. Slice chicken diagonally into thin strips; place on tortillas. Top with garnishes; fold tortillas. Serve immediately. Refrigerate leftovers. *Makes 8 fajitas*

*"½ the calories" 8% milkfat version

Hot, Spicy, Tangy, Sticky Chicken

- **1 chicken (3½ to 4 pounds), cut up**
- **1 cup cider vinegar**
- **1 tablespoon Worcestershire sauce**
- **1 tablespoon chili powder**
- **1 teaspoon salt**
- **1 teaspoon black pepper**
- **1 teaspoon hot pepper sauce**
- **¾ cup K.C. MASTERPIECE® Barbecue Sauce**

Place chicken in a shallow glass dish or large heavy plastic bag. Combine vinegar, Worcestershire sauce, chili powder, salt, pepper and hot pepper sauce in small bowl; pour over chicken pieces. Cover dish or seal bag. Marinate in refrigerator at least 4 hours, turning several times.

Oil hot grid to help prevent sticking. Place dark meat pieces on grill 10 minutes before white meat pieces (dark meat takes longer to cook). Grill chicken, on a covered grill, over medium KINGSFORD® Briquets, 30 to 45 minutes, turning once or twice. Turn and baste with K.C. Masterpiece® Barbecue Sauce the last 10 minutes of cooking. Remove chicken from grill; baste with barbecue sauce. Chicken is done when meat is no longer pink by bone.

Makes 4 servings

Grilled Summer Chicken & Vegetables

- **1 cup WISH-BONE® Italian Dressing,* divided**
- **4 chicken breast halves (about 2 pounds)**
- **4 ears fresh or frozen corn (about 2 pounds)**
- **2 large tomatoes, halved crosswise**

*Also terrific with Wish-Bone® Robusto Italian or Lite Italian Dressing.

In large nonaluminum baking dish or resealable plastic bag, pour ½ cup Italian dressing over chicken. In another large shallow baking dish or plastic bag, pour remaining ½ cup Italian dressing over corn and tomatoes. Cover, or close bags, and marinate chicken and vegetables in refrigerator, turning occasionally, 3 hours or overnight. Remove chicken and vegetables from marinades, reserving marinades separately.

Grill or broil chicken and corn 20 minutes, turning and basting frequently with reserved marinades. Arrange tomato halves, cut-sides-up, on grill or broiler pan and continue cooking chicken and vegetables, turning and basting frequently with reserved marinades, 10 minutes or until chicken is no longer pink near bone and corn is tender. Do not brush with marinade during last 5 minutes of cooking.

Makes 4 servings

Hot, Spicy, Tangy, Sticky Chicken

Grilled Chicken Pasta Toss

6 boneless, skinless chicken breast halves (about 1½ pounds)
1 bottle (12 ounces) LAWRY'S® Herb & Garlic Marinade with Lemon Juice, divided
3 tablespoons vegetable oil, divided
1½ cups broccoli florets and sliced stems
1 cup Chinese pea pods
1 cup diagonally sliced carrots
1 can (2¼ ounces) sliced pitted ripe olives, drained
8 ounces fettuccine or linguine noodles, cooked, drained and kept hot

Heat grill for medium coals. Pierce chicken pieces several times with fork. In large resealable plastic bag or shallow glass dish, place chicken. Add 1 cup LAWRY'S® Herb & Garlic Marinade with Lemon Juice; seal bag or cover dish. Marinate in refrigerator at least 30 minutes. Remove chicken, reserving marinade. Grill chicken, 5 inches from heat source, 5 to 7 minutes on each side or until no longer pink in center, brushing halfway through cooking time with reserved marinade. Remove chicken from grill; slice chicken. Cover and set aside. In medium skillet, heat 2 tablespoons oil. Add broccoli, pea pods and carrots; sauté until crisp-tender. In large bowl, combine sautéed vegetables, olives, hot noodles and chicken. In small bowl, combine remaining Herb & Garlic Marinade with Lemon Juice and remaining 1 tablespoon oil. Add just enough dressing to noodle mixture to coat; toss well. Serve with any remaining dressing, if desired.

Makes 4 to 6 servings

Presentation: Sprinkle with chopped fresh parsley, if desired.

Grilled Chicken Pasta Toss

Mesquite Grilled Turkey Tenderloins

1 cup mesquite chips
Caribbean Salsa (recipe follows)
2 pounds TURKEY BREAST TENDERLOINS
Black pepper to taste

Cover mesquite chips with water in small bowl. Let stand 2 hours. Meanwhile, prepare Caribbean Salsa. Prepare charcoal grill; drain water from mesquite chips and add chips to hot coals.

Sprinkle tenderloins with pepper. Place on grid, about 5 inches over coals. Grill 15 to 20 minutes or until tenderloins are no longer pink in center and register 170°F on meat thermometer, turning tenderloins over halfway through grilling time. Allow tenderloins to stand 10 minutes. To serve, slice tenderloins into ½-inch medallions and arrange on serving plate. Top with salsa.

Makes 8 servings

Caribbean Salsa

2 cups peeled ¼-inch mango cubes
½ cup peeled and seeded ¼-inch cucumber cubes
¼ cup chopped fresh cilantro
2 tablespoons finely chopped green onion
½ jalapeño pepper, seeded and finely chopped
3 tablespoons fresh lime juice
1½ teaspoons brown sugar
1 teaspoon grated fresh ginger
Dash black pepper

Combine ingredients in medium bowl. Cover and refrigerate at least 1 hour to allow flavors to blend.

Favorite recipe from ***National Turkey Federation***

Barbecued "Bistro" Chicken

Barbecued "Bistro" Chicken

6 boneless chicken breast halves
½ cup KIKKOMAN® Teriyaki Baste & Glaze
2 tablespoons Burgundy wine
2 cloves garlic, pressed
⅛ teaspoon pepper

Rinse chicken under cold water; pat dry with paper towels. Combine teriyaki baste & glaze, wine, garlic and pepper; set aside. Place chicken on grill 4 to 5 inches from hot coals. Cook 10 to 12 minutes, or until no longer pink in center, turning over and brushing frequently with baste & glaze mixture during last 5 minutes of cooking time. (Or, place chicken on rack of broiler pan; brush with baste & glaze mixture. Broil 4 to 5 inches from heat 7 minutes on each side, or until no longer pink in center, brushing occasionally with remaining baste & glaze mixture.) *Makes 6 servings*

Piquant Grape Sauce for Barbecued Turkey

½ turkey breast
1 tablespoon butter or margarine
2 tablespoons minced shallots
1 teaspoon cornstarch
½ cup chicken broth or water
1 to 2 teaspoons white wine vinegar
½ teaspoon salt
¼ teaspoon dried thyme leaves
¼ teaspoon grated lemon peel
2 cups California seedless grapes, halved
1 tablespoon minced fresh parsley

Prepare grill. Meanwhile, rinse turkey breast and pat dry. Place in microwave-safe baking dish, skin side down; cover with waxed paper and microwave at MEDIUM-HIGH (70% power) 12 minutes. Turn breast over; cover with waxed paper and microwave at MEDIUM-HIGH 12 minutes. Place turkey on grid, skin side down. Grill over medium-hot coals until internal temperature reaches 170°F, turning turkey as necessary to prevent burning.

Melt butter in medium skillet over medium heat; add shallots. Cook and stir until tender. Stir cornstarch into broth in cup until cornstarch is dissolved. Stir in vinegar, salt, thyme and lemon peel. Add to shallots; bring to boil. Stir in grapes and parsley; cook just until thoroughly heated. Slice grilled turkey and serve with grape sauce. *Makes 4 to 6 servings (about 2 cups sauce)*

Favorite recipe from ***California Table Grape Commission***

"Smacking" Wings

16 chicken wings
½ cup olive or vegetable oil
¼ cup balsamic vinegar
¼ cup honey
2 tablespoons brown sugar
2 tablespoons cane syrup or dark corn syrup
1 tablespoon TABASCO® pepper sauce
½ teaspoon red pepper flakes
½ teaspoon dried thyme leaves
1 teaspoon soy sauce
¼ teaspoon Worcestershire sauce
¼ teaspoon ground red pepper
¼ teaspoon ground nutmeg

Cut off and discard bony wing tips. Cut remaining wings in half. Combine remaining ingredients in large bowl until well blended; add wings. Cover and marinate in refrigerator 1 hour.

Prepare grill. Place wings on grid. Grill 15 to 20 minutes over medium coals, turning frequently. *Makes 32 appetizers*

Southwest Chicken Fingers

⅔ cup HELLMANN'S® or BEST FOODS® Real or Light Mayonnaise or Low Fat Cholesterol Free Mayonnaise Dressing
⅓ cup prepared salsa
1½ pounds boneless skinless chicken breasts, cut into 3 × 1-inch strips

In large bowl combine mayonnaise and salsa; set aside 6 tablespoons. Add chicken strips to mayonnaise mixture in large bowl; toss well. Let stand 30 minutes. Grill chicken 5 inches from heat, turning once, 4 minutes or until chicken is no longer pink in center. (Or, broil, without turning, 5 inches from heat.) Serve with reserved sauce. *Makes 6 to 8 appetizer servings*

Grilled Chicken Skewers

½ pound boneless, skinless chicken breasts, cut into thin strips
½ pound bacon slices
⅓ cup lemon juice
⅓ cup honey
1½ teaspoons LAWRY'S® Lemon Pepper Seasoning
½ teaspoon LAWRY'S® Seasoned Salt

Thread chicken strips and bacon slices onto wooden skewers. In shallow glass dish, combine remaining ingredients. Add prepared skewers; cover dish and marinate in refrigerator 1 hour or overnight. Heat grill for medium coals or heat broiler. Remove skewers, reserving marinade. Grill or broil skewers, 4 to 5 inches from heat source, 10 to 15 minutes or until no longer pink in center and bacon is crisp, basting with reserved marinade.

Makes 2 servings

Hint: Soak wooden skewers in water before adding chicken and bacon to prevent skewers from burning.

Grilled Chicken Skewers

Grilled Curry Chicken with Coconut Rice

4 large chicken legs (thigh-drumstick combination)
Salt and ground black pepper
2 tablespoons curry powder
2 tablespoons chili powder
2 tablespoons vegetable oil
Coconut Rice (recipe follows)

Season chicken generously with salt and pepper. Combine curry powder, chili powder and oil in small bowl until mixture forms a paste. Rub paste onto chicken.

Arrange medium KINGSFORD® Briquets on each side of a rectangular metal or foil drip pan. Pour in hot tap water to fill pan half full. Oil hot grid to help prevent sticking. Place chicken on grid directly above drip pan. Grill chicken, on a covered grill, 50 to 60 minutes, until a meat thermometer inserted into the thickest part registers 180°F. Chicken is done when meat is no longer pink by bone. Serve with Coconut Rice. *Makes 4 servings*

Chicken Caesar Salad

Coconut Rice

1 cup Basmati* or other long-grain white rice
Chicken broth
Canned coconut milk

Prepare rice according to package directions *except* omit salt and butter or oil and substitute chicken broth for half of water and coconut milk for the other half of water.

*Basmati is a long-grain rice with a fine texture and a nutty aroma and flavor. It is available in large supermarkets and Indian markets.

Chicken Caesar Salad

1 tablespoon *plus* 1½ teaspoons olive oil
4 boneless, skinless chicken breast halves (¾ to 1 pound), cut into strips
4 to 5 cups torn romaine lettuce (1 large head)
1 large Roma or 1 medium tomato, finely chopped
½ cup grated fresh Parmesan cheese
1 bottle (8 ounces) LAWRY'S® Creamy Caesar with Cracked Pepper Dressing or LAWRY'S® Classic Caesar with Imported Anchovies Dressing
Seasoned croutons

In large skillet, heat oil. Add chicken. Sauté 7 to 10 minutes or until no longer pink in center, stirring frequently. In large salad bowl, combine lettuce, tomato, Parmesan cheese and chicken; mix lightly. Refrigerate. Before serving, add enough dressing to coat all ingredients; toss lightly. Sprinkle with croutons. *Makes 4 servings*

Hint: For extra flavor, grill chicken breast halves until no longer pink in center; slice thinly. Serve on salad.

Three-Citrus Turkey Tenderloins

⅔ cup fresh orange juice, divided
½ teaspoon grated lemon peel
2 tablespoons lemon juice
½ teaspoon grated lime peel
2 tablespoons lime juice
3 tablespoons minced shallots or onion
2 whole turkey tenderloins (about ¾ pound *each*)
1 tablespoon olive oil
½ teaspoon salt
2½ tablespoons honey
1 teaspoon cornstarch

Combine ⅓ cup orange juice, lemon peel, lemon juice, lime peel, lime juice and shallots in small bowl; mix well. Reserve ⅓ cup juice mixture; cover and refrigerate. Place turkey in large resealable plastic food storage bag; add remaining juice mixture to bag. Seal bag tightly; turn to coat. Marinate in refrigerator 1 to 2 hours, turning once.

Prepare grill. Drain turkey, discarding marinade from bag. Brush turkey with oil; sprinkle with salt. Place turkey on grid. Grill, on covered grill, over medium-hot coals 15 to 20 minutes or until no longer pink in center, turning halfway through grilling time. (If desired, insert instant-read thermometer into center of thickest part of tenderloin. Thermometer should register 170°F. Do not leave in turkey while grilling.)

Meanwhile, combine reserved juice mixture and honey in small saucepan. Stir remaining ⅓ cup orange juice into cornstarch in small bowl until cornstarch is dissolved. Add to juice mixture in saucepan. Bring to a boil over high heat; reduce heat to medium and simmer, uncovered, about 5 minutes or until thickened and reduced to ½ cup. Transfer turkey to carving board. Carve turkey crosswise into thin slices; drizzle with sauce.

Makes 4 to 6 servings

Three-Citrus Turkey Tenderloin

East Indies Barbecued Chicken

4 whole broiler-fryer chicken legs (thigh and drumstick attached)
¼ cup lemon juice
2 tablespoons olive oil
1½ teaspoons turmeric
1 teaspoon salt
1 teaspoon sugar
1 teaspoon grated fresh ginger
½ teaspoon cardamom

Prepare grill. Meanwhile, place juice, oil, turmeric, salt, sugar, ginger and cardamon in food processor or blender; process until smooth. Set aside. Place chicken, skin side up, on grid. Grill 8 inches over medium coals about 40 minutes, turning every 10 minutes. Baste with sauce. Grill about 30 minutes more or until chicken is no longer pink near bone, turning and basting frequently with sauce. (Do not baste during last 5 minutes of grilling.)

Makes 4 servings

Favorite recipe from **Delmarva Poultry Industry, Inc.**

Turkey Burritos

1 tablespoon ground cumin
1 tablespoon chili powder
1½ teaspoons salt
1½ to 2 pounds turkey tenderloin, cut into ½-inch cubes
Avocado-Corn Salsa (recipe follows)
Lime wedges
Flour tortillas
Sour cream (optional)
Tomato slices for garnish

Combine cumin, chili powder and salt in cup. Place turkey cubes in a shallow glass dish or large heavy plastic bag; pour dry rub over turkey and thoroughly coat. Let turkey stand while preparing Avocado-Corn Salsa. Thread turkey onto metal or bamboo skewers. (Soak bamboo skewers in water at least 20 minutes to prevent them from burning).

Oil hot grid to help prevent sticking. Grill turkey, on a covered grill, over medium KINGSFORD® Briquets, about 6 minutes or until turkey is no longer pink in center, turning once. Remove skewers from grill; squeeze lime wedges over skewers. Warm flour tortillas in the microwave oven, or brush each tortilla very lightly with water and grill 10 to 15 seconds per side. Top with Avocado-Corn Salsa and sour cream, if desired. Garnish with tomato slices.

Makes 6 servings

Tip: This recipe is great for casual get-togethers. Just prepare the fixings and let the guests make their own burritos.

Avocado-Corn Salsa

2 small to medium, ripe avocados, finely chopped
1 cup cooked fresh corn or thawed frozen corn
2 medium tomatoes, seeded and finely chopped
2 to 3 tablespoons lime juice
2 to 3 tablespoons chopped fresh cilantro
½ to 1 teaspoon minced hot green chili pepper
½ teaspoon salt

Gently stir together all ingredients in a medium bowl; adjust flavors to taste. Cover and refrigerate until ready to serve.

Makes about 1½ cups

Summer Chicken & Squash

¾ cup WISH-BONE® Italian Dressing*
¼ cup grated Parmesan cheese
4 boneless skinless chicken breast halves (about 1¼ pounds)
2 medium zucchini or yellow squash, quartered

In large nonaluminum baking dish or resealable plastic bag, combine Italian dressing with cheese. Add chicken and zucchini; turn to coat. Cover, or close bag, and marinate in refrigerator, turning occasionally, up to 3 hours.

Grill or broil chicken and zucchini, turning and basting frequently with reserved marinade, until chicken is no longer pink in center. Do not brush with marinade during last 5 minutes of cooking.

Makes 4 servings

*Also terrific with Wish-Bone® Robusto Italian or Lite Italian Dressing.

Turkey Burritos

Black Bean Garnacha

Black Bean Garnachas

1 can (14½ ounces) DEL MONTE® Mexican Style Stewed Tomatoes
1 can (15 ounces) black or pinto beans, drained
2 cloves garlic, minced
1 to 2 teaspoons minced jalapeño chiles (optional)
½ teaspoon ground cumin
Salt and ground black pepper (optional)
1 cup cubed grilled chicken
4 flour tortillas
½ cup shredded sharp Cheddar cheese

Drain tomatoes, reserving liquid; chop tomatoes. In large skillet, combine tomatoes, reserved liquid, beans, garlic, jalapeño and cumin. Cook over medium-high heat 5 to 7 minutes or until thickened, stirring occasionally. Season with salt and pepper, if desired. Add chicken. Arrange tortillas in single layer on grill over medium-hot coals. Spread about ¾ cup chicken mixture over each tortilla. Top with cheese. Cook about 3 minutes or until bottoms of tortillas brown and cheese melts. Garnish with shredded lettuce and diced avocado, if desired.

Makes 4 servings

Teriyaki Kabobs

2 whole chicken breasts, split, boned and skinned (about 1 pound)
16 (2-inch) broccoli florets, cooked crisp-tender *or* 1 large green bell pepper, cut into 1-inch squares
16 large mushrooms, stems trimmed
½ cup PACE® Picante Sauce
¼ cup reduced-calorie Italian dressing
2 tablespoons light soy sauce
1½ teaspoons grated fresh ginger
½ teaspoon sugar
8 cherry tomatoes

Pound chicken to ½-inch thickness; cut lengthwise into 1-inch-wide strips. Place chicken, broccoli and mushrooms in large resealable plastic food storage bag. Combine Pace® Picante Sauce, Italian dressing, soy sauce, ginger and sugar in small bowl; mix well. Pour Pace® Picante Sauce mixture over chicken mixture in bag; press out air and seal. Marinate in refrigerator 1 hour, turning bag frequently. Drain chicken and vegetables, reserving marinade. Alternately thread chicken accordion-style with broccoli and mushrooms onto skewers. Place kabobs on grill over hot coals or on rack of broiler pan. Brush with marinade. Grill or broil 9 to 12 minutes or until chicken is no longer pink in center, turning and basting once with marinade. Add tomatoes to skewers during last minute of cooking.

Makes 4 servings

Healthy Grilled Chicken Salad

½ cup A.1.® Steak Sauce
½ cup prepared Italian salad dressing
1 teaspoon dried basil leaves
1 pound boneless chicken breast halves
6 cups mixed salad greens
¼ pound snow peas, blanched and halved
1 cup sliced mushrooms
1 medium red bell pepper, thinly sliced
Grated Parmesan cheese (optional)

In small bowl, combine steak sauce, dressing and basil. Place chicken in glass dish; coat with ¼ cup steak sauce mixture. Cover; chill 1 hour, turning occasionally.

Arrange salad greens, peas, mushrooms and pepper slices on 6 individual salad plates; set aside.

In small saucepan, over medium heat, heat remaining steak sauce mixture; keep dressing warm.

Remove chicken from marinade; discard marinade. Grill over medium heat for 8 to 10 minutes or until no longer pink in center, turning occasionally. Thinly slice chicken; arrange over salad greens and drizzle warm dressing over prepared salad. Serve immediately, sprinkled with Parmesan cheese if desired.

Makes 6 servings

Fresco Marinated Chicken

1 envelope LIPTON® Recipe Secrets® Savory Herb with Garlic Soup Mix
½ cup water
2 tablespoons olive or vegetable oil
1 teaspoon lemon juice or vinegar
1 pound boneless skinless chicken breast halves

In large nonaluminum baking dish or resealable plastic bag, thoroughly blend savory herb with garlic soup mix, water, oil and lemon juice; add chicken and turn to coat. Cover, or close bag, and marinate in refrigerator at least 1 hour or overnight.

On grill or broiler pan lined with heavy-duty aluminum foil, lightly sprayed with no stick cooking spray, arrange chicken; pour ½ of the marinade over chicken. Grill or broil, turning once and pouring remaining marinade over chicken, until chicken is no longer pink in center.

Makes about 4 servings

Note: Also terrific with Lipton® Recipe Secrets® Golden Onion or Golden Herb with Lemon Soup Mix.

Serving Suggestion: Serve with a tomato salad and cooked rice tossed with mushrooms and sliced green onions.

Healthy Grilled Chicken Salad

Buffalo Turkey Kabobs

⅔ cup HELLMANN'S® or BEST FOODS® Real or Light Mayonnaise or Low Fat Cholesterol Free Mayonnaise Dressing, divided
1 teaspoon hot pepper sauce
1½ pounds boneless turkey breast, cut into 1-inch cubes
2 red bell peppers or 1 red and 1 yellow bell pepper, cut into 1-inch squares
2 medium onions, cut into wedges
¼ cup (1 ounce) crumbled blue cheese
2 tablespoons milk
1 medium stalk celery, minced
1 medium carrot, minced

In medium bowl combine ⅓ cup of the mayonnaise and the hot pepper sauce. Stir in turkey. Let stand at room temperature 20 minutes. On 6 skewers, alternately thread turkey, peppers and onions. Grill or broil 5 inches from heat, brushing with remaining mayonnaise mixture and turning frequently, 12 to 15 minutes. Meanwhile, in small bowl blend remaining ⅓ cup mayonnaise with the blue cheese and milk. Stir in celery and carrot. Serve with kabobs.

Makes 6 servings

Note: For best results, use Real Mayonnaise. If using Light Mayonnaise or Low Fat Cholesterol Free Mayonnaise Dressing, use sauce the same day.

Buffalo Turkey Kabobs

Southwestern Chicken Breasts

1 can (8 ounces) tomato sauce
½ cup WISH-BONE® Italian Dressing*
3 tablespoons firmly packed brown sugar
1 tablespoon lime juice
2 teaspoons chili powder
4 boneless skinless chicken breasts (about 1¼ pounds)
8 ounces wagon wheels pasta or your favorite pasta, cooked and drained

In large nonaluminum baking dish or resealable plastic bag, thoroughly blend tomato sauce, Italian dressing, sugar, lime juice and chili powder; add chicken and turn to coat. Cover, or close bag, and marinate in refrigerator, turning occasionally, up to 3 hours. Remove chicken, reserving marinade.

Grill or broil chicken until no longer pink in center. Meanwhile, in small saucepan, bring reserved marinade to a boil. To serve, arrange chicken over pasta and top with marinade sauce. *Makes 4 servings*

*Also terrific with Wish-Bone® Robusto Italian or Lite Italian Dressing.

Mesquite Grilled Chicken en Croûte

4 boneless, skinless chicken breast halves (¾ to 1 pound)
¾ cup LAWRY'S® Mesquite Marinade with Lime Juice
½ cup chopped red bell pepper
1 can (7 ounces) diced green chiles, drained
½ cup toasted pine nuts, finely chopped
¼ cup toasted walnuts, finely chopped (optional)
1 tablespoon lime juice
½ teaspoon LAWRY'S® Seasoned Salt
½ teaspoon LAWRY'S® Garlic Powder with Parsley
1 package (11 ounces) refrigerated cornstick dough or refrigerated breadstick dough
1 egg white, beaten

In large resealable plastic bag or shallow glass dish, place chicken. Add Mesquite Marinade with Lime Juice; seal bag or cover dish. Marinate in refrigerator at least 30 minutes or overnight. Heat grill for medium coals or heat broiler. Remove chicken, discarding marinade. Grill or broil chicken, 4 to 5 inches from heat source, 7 to 10 minutes on each side or until no longer pink in center, turning over occasionally. Remove from grill; set aside.

Heat oven to 350°F. In small bowl, combine bell pepper, chiles, nuts, lime juice, Seasoned Salt and Garlic Powder with Parsley. Roll dough out into four (8-inch) squares. On each square, place one chicken breast and equal portions of vegetable-nut mixture. Wrap dough around chicken and filling; seal edges of dough. Brush dough with egg white. Bake 3 to 5 minutes or until dough is golden brown and puffy.

Makes 4 servings

Presentation: Serve with a tossed green salad and fresh fruit.

Castillian Grilled Chicken

Castillian Grilled Chicken

3 tablespoons KIKKOMAN® Lite Soy Sauce
2 tablespoons water
1 tablespoon olive oil
1 clove garlic, pressed
½ teaspoon dried oregano leaves, crumbled
¼ teaspoon ground cumin
¼ to ½ teaspoon ground red pepper (cayenne)
6 boneless, skinless chicken breast halves

Blend lite soy sauce, water, oil, garlic, oregano, cumin and pepper; pour over chicken in large plastic food storage bag. Press air out of bag; close top securely. Refrigerate 1 hour, turning bag over occasionally. Remove chicken from marinade; place on grill 4 to 5 inches from hot coals. Cook chicken 5 minutes on each side, or until no longer pink in center. (Or, place chicken on rack of broiler pan. Broil 4 to 5 inches from heat 5 to 6 minutes on each side, or until no longer pink in center.)

Makes 6 servings

Spicy Microwave Grilled Chicken

1 cup MIRACLE WHIP® Salad Dressing
1 package (1.25 ounces) taco seasoning mix
2 broiler-fryer chickens, cut up (2½ to 3 pounds *each*)

• Mix salad dressing and taco seasoning mix until well blended.

• Arrange chicken in 13 × 9-inch microwave-safe baking dish. Brush with salad dressing mixture. Cover with plastic wrap; vent.

• Microwave on HIGH 15 minutes, turning dish after 8 minutes.

• Place chicken on grill over medium-hot coals (coals will have slight glow). Grill, covered, 5 to 10 minutes on each side or until tender and browned.

Makes 6 to 8 servings

Prep time: 5 minutes
Cooking time: 20 minutes
Microwave cooking time: 15 minutes

Zesty Barbecued Chicken

1 package (6.5 ounces) RICE-A-RONI® Broccoli Au Gratin
2 teaspoons paprika
1 teaspoon garlic powder
¼ teaspoon celery salt (optional)
¼ teaspoon freshly ground black pepper
⅛ teaspoon cayenne pepper (optional)
4 skinless, boneless chicken breast halves or well-trimmed center cut ½-inch-thick pork chops
¼ cup barbecue sauce or hickory barbecue sauce

1. Prepare Rice-A-Roni® Mix as package directs.

2. While Rice-A-Roni® is simmering, combine seasonings; sprinkle evenly over both sides of chicken.

3. Place chicken on grill over medium coals *or* on rack of broiler pan. Grill or broil 3 to 4 inches from heat, 5 minutes. Brush with half of barbecue sauce. Turn; brush with remaining barbecue sauce.

4. Continue grilling or broiling 4 to 6 minutes or until chicken is no longer pink inside. Serve with rice. *Makes 4 servings*

Turkey Kabobs

1 pound boneless turkey or chicken breast, cut into 1-inch cubes
4 fresh California nectarines, pitted and cut into large wedges
2 zucchini, cut crosswise into ¼-inch slices
1 onion, cut into 8 wedges
Ginger-Soy Sauce (recipe follows)

Prepare grill or preheat broiler. Thread turkey, nectarines, zucchini and onion alternately on metal skewers. Prepare Ginger-Soy Sauce; brush onto kabobs. Place kabobs on grid or on broiler pan. Grill over medium-hot coals or broil 3 to 4 inches from heat source about 5 minutes, brushing with sauce. Discard any remaining sauce. Turn; grill or broil 5 minutes more or just until turkey is no longer pink in center.

Makes 4 servings

Ginger-Soy Sauce: Combine ¼ cup soy sauce, 3 tablespoons vegetable oil, 2 tablespoons honey and ½ teaspoon ground ginger in small bowl; blend well.

Favorite recipe from ***California Tree Fruit Agreement***

Spicy Microwave Grilled Chicken served with Fiesta Grilled Polenta (page 164)

Grilled Chicken Tostado

Grilled Chicken Tostados

1 head romaine lettuce
1 pound boneless skinless chicken breast halves
1 teaspoon ground cumin
¼ cup fresh orange juice
¼ cup *plus* 2 tablespoons prepared salsa, divided
1 tablespoon vegetable oil
2 cloves garlic, minced
8 green onions
Additional vegetable oil
1 can (16 ounces) refried beans
4 (10-inch) *or* 8 (6- to 7-inch) flour tortillas
1½ cups (6 ounces) shredded Monterey Jack cheese with jalapeño peppers
1 ripe medium avocado, seeded and chopped (optional)
1 medium tomato, seeded and chopped
Chopped fresh cilantro (optional)
Sour cream

Stack several lettuce leaves on cutting board. Cut stack lengthwise in half. Stack one section on top of the other. Cut stack crosswise into very thin slices. Slice enough lettuce to measure 2 cups. Set aside. Place chicken in single layer in large shallow glass dish; sprinkle with cumin. Combine orange juice, ¼ cup salsa, 1 tablespoon oil and garlic in small bowl; pour over chicken. Cover and marinate in refrigerator at least 2 hours or up to 8 hours, stirring mixture occasionally.

Prepare grill. Drain chicken, reserving marinade. Brush green onions with additional oil. Place chicken and onions on grid. Grill, on covered grill, over medium-hot coals 5 minutes. Brush tops of chicken with half the reserved marinade; turn and brush with remaining marinade. Turn onions. Continue to grill, covered, 5 minutes more or until chicken is no longer pink in center and onions are tender. (If onions are browning too quickly, remove before chicken is done.)

Meanwhile, combine beans and remaining 2 tablespoons salsa in small saucepan; cook over medium heat until hot, stirring occasionally. Place tortillas in single layer on grid. Grill, on uncovered grill, 1 to 2 minutes per side or until golden brown. (If tortillas puff up, pierce with tip of knife or flatten by pressing with spatula.) Transfer chicken and onions to carving board. Slice chicken crosswise into ½-inch strips. Cut green onions crosswise into 1-inch-long pieces. Spread tortillas with bean mixture; top with lettuce, chicken, onions, cheese, avocado and tomato. Sprinkle with cilantro. Serve with sour cream. *Makes 4 servings*

Mediterranean Chicken Kabobs

- 2 pounds boneless skinless chicken breasts or chicken tenders, cut into 1-inch pieces
- 1 small eggplant, peeled and cut into 1-inch pieces
- 1 medium zucchini, cut crosswise into ½-inch slices
- 2 medium onions, *each* cut into 8 wedges
- 16 medium mushrooms, stems removed
- 16 cherry tomatoes
- 1 cup ⅓-less-salt chicken broth
- ⅔ cup balsamic vinegar
- 3 tablespoons olive or vegetable oil
- 2 tablespoons dried mint leaves
- 4 teaspoons dried basil leaves
- 1 tablespoon dried oregano leaves
- 2 teaspoons grated lemon peel
- Chopped fresh parsley (optional)
- 4 cups hot cooked couscous

Alternately thread chicken, eggplant, zucchini, onions, mushrooms and tomatoes onto 16 metal skewers; place in large shallow glass dish. Combine chicken broth, vinegar, oil, mint, basil and oregano in small bowl; pour over kabobs. Cover and marinate in refrigerator 2 hours, turning kabobs occasionally.

Prepare grill. Place kabobs on grid. Grill, on covered grill, over medium-hot coals, 10 to 15 minutes or until chicken is no longer pink in center, turning kabobs halfway through cooking time. (Or, broil kabobs, 6 inches from heat source, 10 to 15 minutes or until chicken is no longer pink in center, turning kabobs halfway through cooking time.) Stir lemon peel and parsley into couscous; serve with kabobs.

Makes 8 servings

Grilled Game Hens

- ½ cup K.C. MASTERPIECE® Barbecue Sauce
- ¼ cup dry sherry
- 3 tablespoons frozen orange juice concentrate, thawed
- 4 Cornish game hens (*each* about 1 to 1½ pounds)

Combine barbecue sauce, sherry and orange juice concentrate in a small saucepan. Bring to a boil. Simmer 10 minutes; cool. Rinse hens; pat dry with paper towels. Brush sauce onto hens. Oil hot grid to help prevent sticking. Grill hens, on a covered grill, over medium-hot KINGSFORD® Briquets, 40 to 50 minutes or until thigh moves easily and juices run clear when pierced with fork, turning once. Baste with sauce during last 10 minutes of grilling. Remove hens from grill; baste with sauce.

Makes 4 to 6 servings

Mediterranean Chicken Kabobs

Tandoori Turkey Breast with Cucumber and Tomato Raita

1 Bone-in TURKEY BREAST (about 5 to 6 pounds), skin removed
⅓ cup lime juice
½ teaspoon salt
1½ cups nonfat plain yogurt
4 cloves garlic, minced
1½ teaspoons ground cumin
1 teaspoon ground red pepper
1 teaspoon ground coriander
1 teaspoon ground ginger
1 teaspoon red food coloring
¼ teaspoon ground cinnamon
⅛ teaspoon ground cloves
Vegetable cooking spray
Cucumber and Tomato Raita (recipe follows)
1 large white onion, thinly sliced
12 cherry tomatoes, quartered
3 limes, quartered and cut in half

With knife make deep slits into turkey breast. Place turkey breast in large resealable plastic food storage bag. Combine lime juice and salt in small bowl; pour over turkey breast. Combine yogurt, garlic, cumin, red pepper, coriander, ginger, food coloring, cinnamon and cloves in medium bowl. Pour yogurt mixture over turkey breast; turn to coat thoroughly. Seal bag and marinate in refrigerator overnight.

Prepare grill with foil drip pan. Bank briquets on either side of drip pan for indirect cooking. Spray grill with vegetable cooking spray. Remove turkey breast from marinade; discard marinade. Place turkey on grid over pan. Cover and grill turkey 1½ to 2 hours or until meat thermometer inserted into thickest portion of breast reaches 170° to 175°F.

Meanwhile, prepare Cucumber and Tomato Raita. To serve, place turkey breast on large platter. Arrange onion slices around edge of platter; top onion with tomatoes and limes. Serve with Cucumber and Tomato Raita.

Makes 12 servings

Cucumber and Tomato Raita

1 medium cucumber, peeled, seeded and coarsely grated
1 cup nonfat plain yogurt
1 small tomato, seeded and cut into ¼-inch cubes
1 tablespoon minced fresh cilantro
1 teaspoon ground cumin
½ teaspoon salt

Squeeze grated cucumbers to remove as much liquid as possible. Combine cucumber and remaining ingredients in medium bowl. Cover and refrigerate 1 hour.

Favorite recipe from ***National Turkey Federation***

Grilled Lemon Chicken Dijon

⅓ cup HOLLAND HOUSE® White with Lemon Cooking Wine
⅓ cup olive oil
2 tablespoons Dijon mustard
1 teaspoon dried thyme leaves
2 whole chicken breasts, skinned, boned and halved

Combine all ingredients except chicken in shallow glass baking dish or large resealable plastic food storage bag. Add chicken and turn to coat. Cover or seal bag; marinate in refrigerator 1 to 2 hours.

Prepare grill. Drain chicken, reserving marinade. Grill chicken over medium coals 15 to 20 minutes or until no longer pink in center, turning once and basting with marinade. (Do not baste during last 5 minutes of grilling.) *Makes 4 servings*

Pesto-Stuffed Grilled Chicken

2 tablespoons pine nuts or walnuts
2 cloves garlic, peeled
½ cup packed fresh basil leaves
¼ teaspoon black pepper
5 tablespoons extra-virgin olive oil, divided
¼ cup grated Parmesan cheese
1 fresh or thawed frozen roasting chicken or capon (6 to 7 pounds)
2 tablespoons fresh lemon juice
Additional fresh basil leaves and fresh red currants for garnish

Preheat oven to 350°F. To toast pine nuts, spread in single layer on baking sheet. Bake 8 to 10 minutes or until golden brown, stirring frequently. Remove pine nuts from baking sheet; cool completely. Set aside.

Prepare grill with rectangular metal or foil drip pan. Bank briquets on either side of drip pan for indirect cooking.

Meanwhile, to prepare pesto, drop garlic through feed tube of food processor with motor running. Add basil, pine nuts and black pepper; process until basil is minced. With processor running, add 3 tablespoons oil in slow, steady stream until smooth paste forms, scraping down side of bowl once. Add cheese; process until well blended.

Remove giblets from chicken cavity; reserve for another use. Rinse chicken with cold water; pat dry with paper towels. Loosen skin over breast of chicken by pushing fingers between skin and meat, taking care not to tear skin. *Do not loosen skin over wings and drumsticks.* Using rubber spatula or small spoon, spread pesto under breast skin; massage skin to evenly spread pesto. Combine remaining 2 tablespoons oil and lemon juice in small bowl; brush over chicken skin. Insert meat thermometer into center of thickest part of thigh, not touching bone. Tuck wings under back; tie legs together with wet kitchen string. Place chicken, breast side up, on grid directly over drip pan. Grill, on covered grill, over medium-low coals 1 hour 10 minutes to 1 hour 30 minutes or until thermometer registers 185°F, adding 4 to 9 briquets to both sides of the fire after 45 minutes to maintain medium-low coals. Transfer chicken to carving board; tent with foil. Let stand 15 minutes before carving. Garnish, if desired. *Makes 6 servings*

Pesto-Stuffed Grilled Chicken

Chicken Caesar

¾ cup olive oil
¼ cup lemon juice
¼ cup finely grated Parmesan cheese
1 can (2 ounces) anchovies, drained and chopped
1 clove garlic, minced
2 teaspoons Dijon mustard
½ teaspoon black pepper
Salt
4 boneless skinless chicken breast halves
½ pound green beans, trimmed, cooked and cooled
6 to 8 small new potatoes, cooked, cooled and cut into quarters
¾ cup cooked fresh corn or thawed frozen corn
1 medium carrot, thinly sliced
10 to 12 cherry tomatoes, cut into halves
2 green onions, sliced
Finely chopped parsley or basil

To make Caesar Dressing, place first 7 ingredients in a blender or food processor; process until smooth and creamy. Add salt to taste.

Place chicken in a shallow glass dish. Pour ¼ cup dressing over chicken; turn to coat. Let stand while preparing vegetables, or cover and refrigerate up to 4 hours. Place vegetables in a large bowl; toss with remaining dressing; spoon onto serving plates. Season lightly with salt.

Oil hot grid to help prevent sticking. Grill chicken, on a covered grill, over medium KINGSFORD® Briquets, 6 to 8 minutes until chicken is no longer pink in center, turning once. Slice chicken crosswise and serve with vegetables. Sprinkle with parsley or basil. Serve immediately or at room temperature. *Makes 4 servings*

Turkey Skewers with Cranberry-Ginger Sauce

1 medium orange
⅓ cup soy sauce
2 tablespoons water
1 tablespoon minced fresh ginger
2 turkey breast tenderloins (1¼ to 1¾ pounds total), cut into ¾-inch cubes
Salt and black pepper
Cranberry-Ginger Sauce (recipe follows)

Juice orange and coarsely chop up remaining fruit, including rind. Combine juice, chopped orange, soy sauce, water and ginger in a shallow glass dish or large heavy plastic bag. Add turkey; cover dish or close bag. Marinate in refrigerator up to 4 hours, turning once or twice. Remove turkey from marinade; discard marinade. Thread turkey onto metal or bamboo skewers. (Soak bamboo skewers in water at least 20 minutes to keep them from burning.) Season lightly with salt and pepper.

Oil hot grid to help prevent sticking. Grill turkey, on a covered grill, over medium KINGSFORD® Briquets, 7 to 12 minutes until turkey is cooked through, turning once. Serve with Cranberry-Ginger Sauce.
Makes 4 to 6 servings

Cranberry-Ginger Sauce

2 cans (16 ounces *each*) whole-berry cranberry sauce
1½ tablespoons minced fresh ginger
1½ teaspoons finely grated orange peel
¼ cup orange juice

Combine all ingredients in a saucepan; simmer gently about 10 minutes. Serve warm with turkey skewers.
Makes about 4 cups

Chicken Caesar

Beijing Chicken

Beijing Chicken

- 3 pounds frying chicken pieces
- ½ cup KIKKOMAN® Teriyaki Marinade & Sauce
- 1 tablespoon dry sherry
- 2 teaspoons minced fresh ginger root
- ½ teaspoon fennel seed, crushed
- ½ teaspoon grated orange peel
- ½ teaspoon honey

Rinse chicken under cold water; pat dry with paper towels. Combine teriyaki sauce, sherry, ginger, fennel, orange peel and honey; pour over chicken in large plastic food storage bag. Press air out of bag; close top securely. Refrigerate 8 hours or overnight, turning bag over occasionally. Reserving marinade, remove chicken; place on grill 5 to 7 inches from hot coals. Cook 30 to 40 minutes, or until chicken is no longer pink in center, turning over and basting occasionally with reserved marinade. (Or, place chicken on rack of broiler pan. Broil 5 to 7 inches from heat 40 minutes, or until chicken is no longer pink in center, turning over and brushing occasionally with reserved marinade.)

Makes 4 servings

Grilled Roaster with International Basting Sauces

- 1 PERDUE® Oven Stuffer® roaster (5 to 7 pounds)
- Salt and black pepper
- 1 cup vegetable oil
- ⅓ cup red wine vinegar
- 1 teaspoon paprika

Remove and discard giblets from roaster; rinse bird and pat dry with paper towels. Sprinkle inside and out with salt and pepper; set aside. To prepare basting sauce, in small jar with tight-fitting lid, combine oil, vinegar, paprika, 1 teaspoon salt and ½ teaspoon pepper. Shake well; set aside.

If using a gas grill, follow manufacturer's directions. If using a covered charcoal grill, prepare coals at least 30 minutes before grilling. Open all vents and place a drip pan at center in bottom of grill. Arrange 25 to 30 hot coals at either end of drip pan. For added smoky flavor, soak 1 cup mesquite, hickory, oak, apple or cherry wood chips in water and scatter onto hot coals.

When coals are covered with gray ash and are medium-hot (you can hold your hand over them 3 to 4 seconds), place roaster on grill over drip pan. Cover with grill lid and cook roaster about 2 hours until Bird-Watcher® thermometer pops up and juices run clear with no hint of pink when thigh is pierced. (**Note:** Smoking may cause meat to remain slightly pink. Begin checking roaster for doneness after 1¼ hours. Brush on basting sauce and grill 30 to 45 minutes longer until juices run clear when thigh is pierced.) In small saucepan, bring remaining basting sauce to a boil; serve with carved roaster. Do not reuse sauce.

Makes 6 servings

Italian Roaster: Prepare basting sauce as directed, adding 2 cloves minced garlic, 1 cup ketchup, 1 teaspoon dried oregano and ½ teaspoon dried basil to mixture. Use only in last 10 minutes of grilling.

French Roaster: Prepare basting sauce as directed, adding ⅓ cup minced shallots, ⅓ cup Dijon-style mustard and 1 teaspoon crumbled dried tarragon to mixture.

German Roaster: Prepare basting sauce as directed, adding ½ cup beer, 2 tablespoons molasses and 2 tablespoons caraway seeds to mixture. Use only in last 10 minutes of grilling.

Chinese Roaster: Prepare basting sauce as directed adding ⅓ cup soy sauce, 2 cloves minced garlic and 1 teaspoon ground ginger or 1 tablespoon grated fresh ginger root to mixture.

Lime Salsa Chicken

4 broiler-fryer chicken breast halves, boned and skinned
¼ cup lime juice
2 tablespoons sherry
2 tablespoons light olive oil
½ teaspoon dried oregano leaves
½ teaspoon garlic salt
Salsa (recipe follows)
Avocado slices
Tortilla chips

For marinade, combine lime juice, sherry, oil, oregano and garlic salt in large glass bowl or resealable plastic food storage bag. Remove 3 tablespoons marinade; set aside for Salsa. Add chicken to remaining marinade; turn to coat. Cover and marinate in refrigerator 1 hour.

Meanwhile, prepare grill and Salsa. Remove chicken, reserving marinade in small saucepan. Bring marinade to a boil; cook 1 minute. Place chicken on grid. Brush marinade over chicken. Grill 8 inches over medium coals about 16 to 20 minutes or until chicken is no longer pink in center, turning and basting frequently with marinade. (Do not baste during last 5 minutes of grilling.) Arrange chicken on platter. Serve with Salsa. Garnish with avocado slices and tortilla chips.

Makes 4 servings

Salsa: Stir together 1 peeled, seeded and chopped tomato, 1 sliced green onion, ¼ cup sliced ripe olives, 3 tablespoons reserved marinade, 1 tablespoon seeded and chopped jalapeño pepper, 1 tablespoon chopped fresh cilantro, 1 tablespoon chopped fresh mint, 1 tablespoon slivered almonds, ¼ teaspoon salt and ¼ teaspoon black pepper; refrigerate. *Makes 1 cup*

Favorite recipe from ***Delmarva Poultry Industry, Inc.***

Lime Salsa Chicken

Grilled Greek Chicken

- 1 cup MIRACLE WHIP® Salad Dressing
- ½ cup chopped fresh parsley
- ¼ cup dry white wine or chicken broth
- 1 lemon, sliced and halved
- 2 tablespoons dried oregano leaves, crushed
- 1 tablespoon *each:* garlic powder, pepper
- 2 (2½- to 3-pound) broiler-fryers, cut up

• Mix together all ingredients except chicken until well blended. Pour over chicken. Cover; marinate in refrigerator at least 20 minutes. Drain marinade; discard.

• Place chicken on grill over medium-hot coals (coals will have slight glow). Grill, covered, 20 to 25 minutes on each side or until tender.

Makes 8 servings

Hot 'n' Spicy Chicken Barbecue

- ½ cup A.1.® Steak Sauce
- ½ cup tomato sauce
- ¼ cup finely chopped onion
- 2 tablespoons cider vinegar
- 2 tablespoons maple syrup
- 1 tablespoon vegetable oil
- 2 teaspoons chili powder
- ½ teaspoon crushed red pepper flakes
- 1 (3-pound) chicken, cut up

In medium saucepan, combine steak sauce, tomato sauce, onion, vinegar, maple syrup, oil, chili powder and red pepper flakes. Over medium heat, heat mixture to a boil; reduce heat. Simmer for 5 to 7 minutes or until thickened; cool.

Grill chicken over medium heat for 30 to 40 minutes or until no longer pink near bone, turning and basting frequently with prepared sauce. Serve hot.

Makes 4 servings

Grilled Greek Chicken served with Skewered Grilled Potatoes (page 177)

Grilled Chicken à la Orange

- 1 pound boneless, skinless chicken breasts
- 1 teaspoon shredded orange peel
- ½ cup orange juice
- 1 tablespoon vegetable oil
- 2 teaspoons Worcestershire sauce
- 1 teaspoon LAWRY'S® Lemon Pepper Seasoning
- LAWRY'S® Garlic Salt

Score chicken on both sides. In shallow glass dish, place chicken. In small bowl, combine orange peel, orange juice, oil, Worcestershire sauce and Lemon Pepper Seasoning. Pour marinade over chicken to coat; let stand 30 minutes to 1 hour. Heat grill for medium coals. Remove chicken, reserving marinade. Sprinkle both sides of chicken with Garlic Salt. Grill, 4 to 5 inches from heat, 10 to 15 minutes or until no longer pink in center, turning and basting once with marinade. *Makes 4 servings*

Presentation: Garnish servings with orange slices; sprinkle with chopped green onion.

Mexican Chicken Skewers with Spicy Yogurt Sauce

- 1 package (1.25 ounces) taco seasoning mix, divided
- 6 boneless skinless chicken breast halves (about 1½ pounds), cut into 1-inch cubes
- 1 large clove garlic
- ¼ teaspoon salt
- 2 tablespoons olive oil
- 1 cup DANNON® Plain Nonfat or Lowfat Yogurt
- 1 red bell pepper, cut into chunks
- 1 green bell pepper, cut into chunks
- 1 yellow bell pepper, cut into chunks

Mexican Chicken Skewers with Spicy Yogurt Sauce

In a large bowl combine 3 tablespoons seasoning mix and chicken; toss to coat well. Cover; chill 2 hours.

To make Spicy Yogurt Sauce, in a mortar with pestle or with a large knife press garlic and salt together until a smooth paste forms. Place in a small bowl with olive oil; mix well. Stir in yogurt and remaining taco seasoning mix. Cover; chill 30 minutes before serving.

Thread chicken onto skewers alternately with peppers; grill over hot coals 10 to 12 minutes, or until chicken is no longer pink in center, turning occasionally. Serve with Spicy Yogurt Sauce. *Makes 12 servings*

Note: If using wooden skewers, soak them in water 30 minutes before serving. This will prevent skewers from charring.

Glazed Cornish Hens

2 fresh or thawed frozen Cornish game hens (1½ pounds *each*)
3 tablespoons fresh lemon juice
1 clove garlic, minced
¼ cup orange marmalade
1 tablespoon coarse-grain or country-style mustard
2 teaspoons grated fresh ginger

Remove giblets from cavities of hens; reserve for another use. Split hens in half on cutting board with sharp knife or poultry shears, cutting through breast and back bones. Rinse hens with cold water; pat dry with paper towels. Place hen halves in large resealable plastic food storage bag. Combine lemon juice and garlic in small bowl; pour over hens in bag. Seal bag tightly; turn to coat. Marinate in refrigerator 30 minutes.

Prepare grill. Drain hens, discarding marinade. Place hens, skin sides up, on grid. Grill, on covered grill, over medium-hot coals 20 minutes. Meanwhile, combine marmalade, mustard and ginger in small bowl. Brush half the mixture evenly over hens. Grill, covered, 10 minutes more. Brush with remaining mixture. Grill, covered, 5 to 10 minutes more or until tender when pierced with fork and juices run clear. *Makes 4 servings*

Caribbean Lemon Chicken

½ cup KIKKOMAN® Teriyaki Marinade & Sauce
1 teaspoon grated lemon peel
1 tablespoon lemon juice
2 teaspoons TABASCO® pepper sauce
¼ teaspoon ground cinnamon
1 (3-pound) broiler-fryer chicken, quartered

Combine teriyaki sauce, lemon peel, lemon juice, pepper sauce and cinnamon; pour over chicken in large plastic food storage bag. Press air out of bag; close top securely. Turn bag over several times to coat all pieces well. Refrigerate 8 hours or overnight, turning bag over occasionally. Remove chicken from marinade; place on grill 5 to 7 inches from hot coals. Cook 40 to 50 minutes, or until chicken is no longer pink in center, turning over frequently. (Or, place chicken on rack of broiler pan. Broil 5 to 7 inches from heat 20 to 25 minutes on each side, or until chicken is no longer pink in center.) *Makes 4 servings*

Family Barbecued Chicken

5 pounds chicken pieces
1 cup vegetable oil
⅓ cup tarragon vinegar
¼ cup sugar
¼ cup ketchup
1 tablespoon Worcestershire sauce
1½ teaspoons dry mustard
1 teaspoon LAWRY'S® Red Pepper Seasoned Salt
1 teaspoon LAWRY'S® Garlic Powder with Parsley

Place chicken in 12 × 8 × 2-inch glass ovenproof dish. In medium bowl, combine remaining ingredients; blend well and pour over chicken. Cover dish and marinate in refrigerator 6 hours or overnight. Bake, covered, in 350°F oven 25 to 30 minutes. Remove chicken, reserving marinade. Heat grill for hot coals. Grill, 4 to 5 inches from heat, about 10 minutes or until no longer pink in center, turning and basting with reserved marinade. *Makes 6 to 8 servings*

Presentation: Serve with baked beans and a fresh vegetable salad.

Glazed Cornish Hens

Buffalo Chicken Drumsticks

Buffalo Chicken Drumsticks

8 large chicken drumsticks (about 2 pounds)
3 tablespoons hot pepper sauce
1 tablespoon vegetable oil
1 clove garlic, minced
¼ cup mayonnaise
3 tablespoons sour cream
1½ tablespoons white wine vinegar
¼ teaspoon sugar
⅓ cup (1½ ounces) crumbled Roquefort or blue cheese
2 cups hickory chips
Celery sticks

Place chicken in large resealable plastic food storage bag. Combine pepper sauce, oil and garlic in small bowl; pour over chicken. Seal bag tightly; turn to coat. Marinate in refrigerator at least 1 hour or, for hotter flavor, up to 24 hours, turning occasionally.

For blue cheese dressing, combine mayonnaise, sour cream, vinegar and sugar in another small bowl. Stir in cheese; cover and refrigerate until serving.

Prepare grill. Meanwhile, cover hickory chips with cold water; soak 20 minutes. Drain chicken, discarding marinade. Drain hickory chips; sprinkle over coals. Place chicken on grid. Grill, on covered grill, over medium-hot coals 25 to 30 minutes or until chicken is tender when pierced with fork and no longer pink near bone, turning 3 to 4 times. Serve with blue cheese dressing and celery sticks.

Makes 4 servings

Savory Lemon Chicken Breast

½ cup CRISCO® Oil
1 teaspoon grated lemon peel
¼ cup lemon juice
2 tablespoons white wine vinegar
1 tablespoon dried basil leaves
2 cloves garlic, minced
½ teaspoon salt
¼ teaspoon pepper
4 boneless, skinless chicken breast halves (about 1 pound)
2⅔ cups hot cooked rice (cooked without salt or fat)

1. Combine Crisco Oil, lemon peel, lemon juice, vinegar, basil, garlic, salt and pepper in shallow baking dish. Stir until well blended. Add chicken. Turn to coat. Refrigerate 30 to 45 minutes, turning after 15 minutes.

2. Prepare grill or heat broiler.

3. Remove chicken from lemon juice mixture; discard mixture. Grill or broil 3 to 5 minutes per side or until chicken is no longer pink in center. Serve over hot rice.

Makes 4 servings

Cajun Turkey Cutlets

⅓ cup KIKKOMAN® Teriyaki Baste & Glaze
2 tablespoons prepared spicy brown mustard
1 tablespoon prepared horseradish
1 teaspoon dried thyme leaves, crumbled
¾ teaspoon garlic powder
4 turkey breast cutlets*

*Or, use a 2½- to 3-pound turkey half breast, skinned, boned and cut lengthwise into 4 to 5 equal parts.

Blend teriyaki baste & glaze, mustard and horseradish; set aside. Combine thyme and garlic powder. Rub herb mixture thoroughly onto both sides of cutlets; brush lightly with teriyaki baste & glaze mixture. Let stand 30 minutes.

Meanwhile, prepare coals for grilling. Place cutlets on grill 5 to 7 inches from hot coals; brush thoroughly with baste & glaze mixture. Cook 5 minutes; turn over. Brush with remaining baste & glaze mixture. Cook 5 minutes longer, or until turkey is no longer pink in center. (Or, place seasoned turkey cutlets on rack of broiler pan; brush thoroughly with baste & glaze mixture. Broil 4 to 5 inches from heat 7 minutes; turn over. Brush with remaining baste & glaze mixture. Broil 7 minutes longer or until turkey is no longer pink in center.)

Makes 4 servings

Cajun Turkey Cutlets

Grilled Chicken Salad

- ¾ pound boneless skinless chicken breast
- ½ teaspoon salt
- ½ teaspoon black pepper
- 1½ cups diagonally sliced small zucchini
- 3 cups cooked rice, cooled to room temperature
- 1 can (14 ounces) artichoke hearts, drained
- ¾ cup fresh snow peas, blanched*
- ½ red bell pepper, cut into 1-inch cubes
- ⅓ cup light Italian salad dressing
- 1 teaspoon chopped fresh basil leaves
- Lettuce leaves

*Substitute frozen snow peas, thawed, for fresh snow peas, if desired.

Season chicken with salt and black pepper. Grill or broil chicken breast until no longer pink in center. Add zucchini during last 5 minutes of grilling or broiling. Cover and refrigerate chicken and zucchini until chilled; cut chicken into ¾-inch cubes.

Combine rice, chicken, zucchini, artichokes, snow peas and red pepper in large bowl. Blend dressing and basil in small bowl. Pour over salad; toss lightly. Serve on lettuce leaves. *Makes 4 servings*

Favorite recipe from ***USA Rice Council***

Grilled Chicken Salad

Lime Cilantro Marinated Chicken

- 4 boneless, skinless chicken breast halves (¾ to 1 pound)
- 1 cup finely chopped red onion
- 1 cup lime juice
- ½ cup red wine vinegar
- ½ cup chopped fresh cilantro
- ¼ cup vegetable oil
- ¼ cup frozen orange juice concentrate, thawed
- 1¾ teaspoons LAWRY'S® Garlic Salt
- 1½ teaspoons LAWRY'S® Seasoned Pepper
- 1 teaspoon chopped fresh mint

Pierce chicken several times with fork. In large resealable plastic bag or shallow glass dish, place chicken. In small bowl, combine remaining ingredients. Reserve 1 cup seasoning mixture; pour remaining mixture over chicken. Seal bag or cover dish. Marinate in refrigerator at least 45 minutes. Heat grill for medium coals or heat broiler. Remove chicken, discarding marinade. Grill or broil, 4 to 5 inches from heat source, 10 to 12 minutes or until chicken is no longer pink in center, turning and brushing occasionally with reserved 1 cup seasoning mixture. *Makes 4 servings*

Presentation: Serve with rice or warm tortillas and a green salad.

Apricot-Glazed Chicken

- ½ cup WISH-BONE® Italian Dressing*
- 2 teaspoons ground ginger (optional)
- 1 chicken, cut into serving pieces (2½ to 3 pounds)
- ¼ cup apricot or peach preserves

In large nonaluminum baking dish or resealable plastic bag, blend Italian dressing and ginger; add chicken and turn to coat. Cover, or close bag, and marinate in refrigerator, turning occasionally, 3 hours or overnight. Remove chicken, reserving ¼ cup marinade.

In small saucepan, bring reserved marinade to a boil. Remove from heat and stir in preserves until melted; set aside.

Grill or broil chicken until chicken is no longer pink near bone, brushing with preserve mixture during last 5 minutes of cooking. *Makes 4 servings*

*Also terrific with Wish-Bone® Robusto Italian Dressing.

Chicken Ribbons Satay

Chicken Ribbons Satay

- ½ cup creamy peanut butter
- ½ cup water
- ¼ cup soy sauce
- 4 cloves garlic, pressed
- 3 tablespoons lemon juice
- 2 tablespoons firmly packed brown sugar
- ¾ teaspoon ground ginger
- ½ teaspoon crushed red pepper flakes
- 4 boneless skinless chicken breast halves
- Sliced green onion tops for garnish

Combine peanut butter, water, soy sauce, garlic, lemon juice, brown sugar, ginger and red pepper flakes in a small saucepan. Cook over medium heat 1 minute or until smooth; cool. Remove garlic from sauce; discard. Reserve half of sauce for dipping. Cut chicken lengthwise into 1-inch-wide strips. Thread onto 8 metal or bamboo skewers. (Soak bamboo skewers in water at least 20 minutes to keep them from burning.)

Oil hot grid to help prevent sticking. Grill chicken, on a covered grill, over medium-hot KINGSFORD® Briquets, 6 to 8 minutes until chicken is no longer pink in center, turning once. Baste with sauce once or twice during cooking. Serve with reserved sauce garnished with sliced green onion. *Makes 4 servings*

Lemon-Garlic Roasted Chicken

- **1 chicken (3½ to 4 pounds)**
- **Salt and black pepper**
- **2 tablespoons butter or margarine, softened**
- **2 lemons, cut into halves**
- **4 to 6 cloves garlic, peeled, left whole**
- **5 to 6 sprigs fresh rosemary**
- **Garlic Sauce (recipe follows)**
- **Additional rosemary sprigs and lemon wedges for garnish**

Rinse chicken; pat dry with paper towels. Season with salt and pepper, then rub the skin with butter. Place lemons, garlic and rosemary in cavity of chicken. Tuck wings under back and tie legs together with cotton string.

Arrange medium-low KINGSFORD® Briquets on each side of a rectangular metal or foil drip pan. Pour in hot tap water to fill pan half full. Place chicken, breast side up, on grid, directly above the drip pan. Grill chicken, on a covered grill, about 1 hour or until a meat thermometer inserted in the thigh registers 175° to 180°F or until the joints move easily and juices run clear when chicken is pierced. Add a few briquets to both sides of the fire, if necessary, to maintain a constant temperature.

While the chicken is cooking, prepare Garlic Sauce. When chicken is done, carefully lift it from the grill to a wide shallow bowl so that all the juices from the cavity run into the bowl. Transfer juices to a small bowl or gravy boat. Carve chicken; serve with Garlic Sauce and cooking juices. Garnish with additional rosemary sprigs and lemon wedges. *Makes 4 servings*

Garlic Sauce

- **2 tablespoons olive oil**
- **1 large head of garlic, cloves separated and peeled**
- **2 (1-inch-wide) strips lemon peel**
- **1 can (14½ ounces) low-salt chicken broth**
- **½ cup water**
- **1 sprig *each* sage and oregano *or* 2 to 3 sprigs parsley**
- **¼ cup butter, softened**

Heat oil in a saucepan; add garlic cloves and lemon peel. Sauté over medium-low heat, stirring frequently, until garlic just starts to brown in a few spots. Add broth, water and herbs; simmer to reduce mixture by about half. Discard herb sprigs and lemon peel. Transfer broth mixture to a blender or food processor; process until smooth. Return garlic purée to the saucepan and whisk in butter over very low heat until smooth. Sauce can be rewarmed before serving.

Makes about 1 cup

Fiesta Chicken Wings

- **1 cup A.1.® Steak Sauce**
- **1 cup mild, medium or hot thick and chunky salsa**
- **10 chicken wings, split and tips removed**

In medium bowl, combine steak sauce and salsa; reserve 1 cup for dipping. In nonmetal bowl, coat wings with remaining sauce. Cover; chill 1 hour, turning occasionally.

Grill wings over medium heat for 12 to 15 minutes or until no longer pink near bone, turning occasionally. Serve hot with reserved sauce. *Makes 20 appetizers*

Lemon-Garlic Roasted Chicken

Sunshine Chicken Drumsticks

Sunshine Chicken Drumsticks

½ cup A.1® Steak Sauce
¼ cup ketchup
¼ cup apricot preserves
12 chicken drumsticks (about 2½ pounds)

In small bowl, using wire whisk, blend steak sauce, ketchup and preserves until smooth. Brush chicken with sauce.

Grill chicken over medium heat for 20 minutes or until no longer pink near bone, turning and brushing with remaining sauce. (Do not baste during last 5 minutes or grilling.) Serve hot.

Makes 12 appetizers

Grilled Chicken Caesar Salad

1 pound boneless skinless chicken breast halves
½ cup extra-virgin olive oil
3 tablespoons fresh lemon juice
2 teaspoons anchovy paste
2 cloves garlic, minced
½ teaspoon salt
½ teaspoon black pepper
6 cups torn romaine lettuce leaves
4 plum tomatoes, quartered
¼ cup grated Parmesan cheese
1 cup purchased garlic croutons
Anchovy fillets (optional)
Additional black pepper (optional)

Place chicken in large resealable plastic food storage bag. Combine oil, lemon juice, anchovy paste, garlic, salt and ½ teaspoon pepper in small bowl. Reserve ⅓ cup marinade; cover and refrigerate until serving. Pour remaining marinade over chicken. Seal bag tightly; turn to coat. Marinate in refrigerator at least 1 hour or up to 4 hours, turning occasionally. Combine lettuce, tomatoes and cheese in large serving bowl. Cover; refrigerate.

Prepare grill. Drain chicken, reserving marinade from bag. Place chicken on grid. Grill, on covered grill, over medium coals 10 to 12 minutes or until chicken is no longer pink in center, brushing with reserved marinade in bag after 5 minutes and turning halfway through grilling time. Discard remaining marinade from bag. Cool chicken slightly. Slice warm chicken crosswise into ½-inch strips; add chicken and croutons to lettuce mixture in bowl. Drizzle with ⅓ cup reserved marinade; toss to coat well. Top with anchovy fillets and serve with additional pepper.

Makes 4 servings

Note: Chicken may also be refrigerated until cold before slicing.

Marinated Grilled Chicken

1 bottle (8 ounces) KRAFT® CATALINA® French Dressing
4 boneless skinless chicken breast halves (about 1¼ pounds)

• Pour dressing over chicken; cover. Refrigerate 1 hour to marinate. Drain, discarding dressing. Heat grill.

• Place chicken on greased grill over medium coals. Grill, covered, 8 to 10 minutes on each side or until cooked through. Serve with bean salad, if desired.

Makes 4 servings

Prep time: 5 minutes plus refrigerating
Cooking time: 20 minutes

Smoked Turkey

Wood chunks or chips for smoking
1 turkey (8 to 14 pounds), thawed if frozen, neck and giblets removed
1 lemon
½ cup butter or margarine, melted
⅓ cup finely chopped mixed fresh herbs*
2 cloves garlic, minced
1 teaspoon Dijon mustard
½ teaspoon salt
½ teaspoon black pepper
Fresh herbs for garnish

*Substitute ½ teaspoon *each* dried thyme, oregano, rosemary, basil and rubbed sage *plus* 2 tablespoons finely chopped fresh parsley for the mixed fresh herbs.

Soak 4 to 6 wood chunks or several handfuls of wood chips in water; drain. Rinse turkey; pat dry with paper towels. Tuck wing tips under back and tie legs together. Squeeze 1½ tablespoons juice from lemon; mix with remaining ingredients except garnish in a small bowl. Place remaining lemon in cavity of turkey.

Arrange medium-low KINGSFORD® Briquets on each side of a rectangular metal or foil drip pan. Pour in hot tap water to fill pan half full. Add soaked wood (all the chunks; part of the chips) to the fire.

Oil hot grid to help prevent sticking. Place turkey, breast side up, on grid, directly over drip pan. Smoke-cook turkey, on a covered grill, 11 to 14 minutes per pound until a meat thermometer inserted in the thigh registers 180°F or until joints move easily and juices run clear when turkey is pierced. Baste turkey three or four times with butter mixture during grilling. If your grill has a thermometer, maintain a cooking temperature of about 300°F. Add a few more briquets to both sides of the fire every 45 minutes to 1 hour, or as necessary, to maintain a constant temperature. Add more soaked wood chips every 30 to 45 minutes. Let turkey stand 10 to 20 minutes before slicing. Garnish with fresh herbs.

Makes 8 to 14 servings

Tip: A small turkey is perfect for family meals or informal gatherings. When buying a turkey, allow ¾ to 1 pound per person—leftovers make terrific sandwiches.

Marinated Grilled Chicken

Grilled Marinated Chicken

8 chicken hind quarters (thigh and drumsticks attached)
6 ounces frozen lemonade concentrate, thawed
2 tablespoons white wine vinegar
1 tablespoon grated lemon peel
2 cloves garlic, minced

Remove skin and all visible fat from chicken. Place chicken in large shallow glass dish. Combine remaining ingredients in small bowl, blending well. Pour over chicken. Cover and marinate in refrigerator 3 hours or overnight, turning chicken occasionally.

Prepare grill and lightly coat grid with vegetable cooking spray. Place chicken on grid. Grill over medium coals 10 to 15 minutes on each side or until tender when pierced with fork and juices run clear. (Do not overcook or chicken will be dry.) Garnish as desired. *Makes 8 servings*

Grilled Marinated Chicken

Southwestern Grilled Chicken Salad

1½ cups LAWRY'S® Fajitas Barbecue Sauce, divided
¾ cup vegetable oil
¾ cup red wine vinegar
1 tablespoon chopped fresh parsley
1 teaspoon sugar
1½ teaspoons LAWRY'S® Garlic Salt, divided
8 boneless, skinless chicken breast halves (about 2 pounds)
1 teaspoon LAWRY'S® Seasoned Pepper
2 quarts torn salad greens
½ red onion, sliced thin
1 large tomato, cut into thin wedges
1 can (2¼ ounces) sliced ripe olives, drained
1 avocado, peeled, seeded and sliced

In small bowl, combine ½ cup Fajitas Barbecue Sauce, oil, vinegar, parsley, sugar and ½ teaspoon Garlic Salt; blend well and refrigerate. Heat grill for hot coals or heat broiler. Season chicken with 1 teaspoon *each* Garlic Salt and Seasoned Pepper. Grill or broil, 4 to 5 inches from heat source, about 10 minutes on each side or until no longer pink in center. Spread 1 cup Fajitas Barbecue Sauce over both sides of chicken during last 5 minutes of cooking. Slice chicken diagonally into strips.

For each salad place 2 sliced breast halves on 2 cups salad greens. Top each salad with equal portions of onion, tomato, olives and avocado. Serve with reserved Fajitas Barbecue Sauce mixture.

Makes 4 entrée salads

Presentation: No garnish necessary, just serve with tortilla chips on the side.

Jalapeño-Glazed Turkey Breast

- **1 (4- to 4½-pound) fresh bone-in turkey breast half**
- **½ cup water**
- **2 teaspoons cornstarch**
- **2 teaspoons WYLER'S® or STEERO® Chicken-Flavor Instant Bouillon**
- **¼ cup jalapeño jelly or apple jelly**
- **1 tablespoon finely chopped fresh cilantro**
- **2 cloves garlic, finely chopped**
- **½ teaspoon ground cumin**
- **¼ teaspoon red pepper flakes (optional)**

Grill or roast turkey according to manufacturer's directions, 45 minutes to 2 hours or until meat thermometer reaches 170°F. In small saucepan, combine water, cornstarch and bouillon; stir in remaining ingredients. Over medium heat, cook and stir until slightly thickened. Brush turkey with 2 tablespoons sauce during last 5 to 10 minutes of cooking. Serve turkey with remaining sauce. Refrigerate leftovers.

Makes 6 servings

Almond Chicken Kabobs

- **⅓ cup A.1.® BOLD Steak Sauce**
- **1 tablespoon Dijon mustard**
- **1 tablespoon honey**
- **1 tablespoon vegetable oil**
- **1 tablespoon lemon juice**
- **1 clove garlic, crushed**
- **4 boneless chicken breast halves (about 1 pound)**
- **¼ cup toasted slivered almonds, finely chopped**

Almond Chicken Kabobs

In small bowl, combine steak sauce, mustard, honey, oil, lemon juice and garlic; set aside.

Cut each chicken breast half into 8 cubes. In medium nonmetal bowl, combine chicken cubes and ½ cup steak sauce mixture. Cover; chill 1 hour, turning occasionally.

Soak 16 (10-inch) wooden skewers in water for at least 30 minutes. Thread 2 chicken cubes onto each skewer. Grill kabobs over medium heat for 6 to 8 minutes or until chicken is no longer pink in center, turning and brushing with remaining sauce. Remove from grill; quickly roll kabobs in almonds. Serve immediately.

Makes 16 appetizers

SEAFOOD

Grilled Salmon with Creamy Tarragon Sauce

- 1 cup DANNON® Plain Nonfat or Lowfat Yogurt
- 1 tablespoon reduced-calorie mayonnaise
- ¼ cup minced green onions
- 1 tablespoon minced fresh tarragon or dill weed
- 2 teaspoons lime juice
- 1 teaspoon hot pepper sauce
- 12- to 16-ounce salmon fillet (1 inch thick), skinned
- 1 tablespoon olive oil

In a small glass bowl combine yogurt, mayonnaise, green onions, tarragon, lime juice and hot pepper sauce. Cover; chill at least 1 hour.

Cut salmon into 4 equal portions; brush with olive oil. Grill salmon over medium-hot coals 5 minutes on each side or until fish flakes easily with fork. Serve with tarragon sauce. *Makes 4 servings*

Note: Fish may be broiled 4 to 6 inches from heat source 3 to 4 minutes on each side or until fish flakes easily with fork.

Lemony Lobster Supreme

- 4 frozen lobster tails (about 8 ounces *each*), thawed
- ½ cup butter or margarine, melted
- ½ teaspoon grated lemon peel
- 2 tablespoons lemon juice
- 2 tablespoons dry sherry
- 1 tablespoon KIKKOMAN® Soy Sauce
- ½ teaspoon parsley flakes
- ¼ teaspoon ground ginger
- ⅛ teaspoon paprika

Cut along underside of tails with scissors. Peel back soft undershell; discard. Bend tails to crack shell or insert long skewers lengthwise between shell and meat to prevent curling. Combine butter, lemon peel, lemon juice, sherry, soy sauce, parsley, ginger and paprika; brush lobster meat with sauce. Place tails, meat sides up, on grill 4 to 5 inches from hot coals. Cook 5 to 8 minutes; turn tails over. Brush shells with sauce. Cook 5 to 10 minutes longer, or until meat becomes opaque. Bring remaining sauce to a boil. (Or, place tails, meat sides up, on rack of broiler pan. Broil 4 to 5 inches from heat 5 to 8 minutes. Turn tails over; brush shells with sauce. Broil 5 to 10 minutes longer, or until meat becomes opaque.) Serve immediately with warmed sauce. *Makes 4 servings*

Grilled Salmon with Creamy Tarragon Sauce

Pacific Rim Honey Barbecued Fish

¼ cup honey
¼ cup chopped onion
2 tablespoons *each* lime juice, soy sauce and hoisin sauce
2 cloves garlic, minced
1 jalapeño pepper, seeded and minced
1 teaspoon minced fresh ginger *or* ½ teaspoon ground ginger
1 pound swordfish steaks

Combine all ingredients except fish in large shallow glass dish; mix well. Add fish; turn to coat. Cover and marinate in refrigerator 1 to 2 hours. Prepare grill or preheat broiler. Place fish on grid or broiler pan. Grill over medium-hot coals or broil 10 minutes for every inch of thickness until fish flakes when tested with fork. *Makes 4 servings*

Favorite recipe from ***National Honey Board***

Pacific Rim Honey Barbecued Fish

Grilled Herb Trout

6 whole cleaned trout* (*each* at least 10 ounces), boned, butterflied and head removed if desired
Salt and black pepper
6 bacon slices
6 sprigs dill or tarragon
1 or 2 medium onions, cut into wedges
Grilled New Potatoes (recipe follows)
Lemon wedges
Dill or tarragon sprigs for garnish

Rinse fish; pat dry with paper towels. Season lightly with salt and pepper. Place 1 slice of bacon and 1 herb sprig in the cavity of each trout; close fish. (There's no need to tie the fish; it will remain closed during cooking.) Place fish in a fish basket, if desired.

Oil hot grid to help prevent sticking. Grill fish, on a covered grill, over medium-hot KINGSFORD® Briquets, 8 to 12 minutes. Halfway through cooking time, turn fish and add onions to grill. Continue grilling until fish turns from transparent to opaque throughout. Serve with lemon. (The bacon does not become crispy; it flavors and bastes the fish during cooking. It can be removed, if desired, just before serving.) Garnish with dill. *Makes 6 servings*

*Just-caught perch, pike or any other whole freshwater fish can be substituted for the trout.

Grilled New Potatoes: Cook or microwave new potatoes until barely tender. Brush lightly with oil; season with salt and pepper. Grill over medium-hot Kingsford® briquets, 8 to 10 minutes, turning occasionally.

Grilled Prawns with Salsa Vera Cruz

- 1 can (14½ ounces) DEL MONTE® Mexican Style Stewed Tomatoes
- 1 orange, peeled and chopped
- ¼ cup sliced green onions
- ¼ cup chopped cilantro or parsley
- 1 tablespoon olive oil
- 1 to 2 teaspoons minced jalapeño chile
- 1 small clove garlic, crushed
- 1 pound medium shrimp, peeled and deveined

Drain tomatoes, reserving liquid; chop tomatoes. In medium bowl, combine tomatoes, reserved liquid, orange, green onions, cilantro, oil, jalapeño and garlic. Season to taste with salt and pepper, if desired. Thread shrimp on skewers; season with salt and pepper, if desired. Brush grill with oil. Cook shrimp over hot coals about 3 minutes per side or until shrimp just turn opaque pink. Top with salsa. Serve over rice, if desired. *Makes 4 servings*

Prep time: 27 minutes
Cooking time: 6 minutes

Helpful Hint: Thoroughly rinse shrimp in cold water before cooking.

Grilled Prawns with Salsa Vera Cruz

Walter Bridge's Grilled Swordfish Steaks

- 1 (8-ounce) bottle NEWMAN'S OWN® Ranch Dressing
- ¼ cup dry white wine
- 2 tablespoons lemon juice
- 2 tablespoons lime juice
- 1 tablespoon chopped fresh rosemary
- 1 tablespoon chopped fresh dill
- 1 tablespoon minced capers
- 2 (12-ounce) swordfish steaks, *each* 1 inch thick

Combine Newman's Own® Ranch Dressing, white wine, lemon juice, lime juice, chopped rosemary, dill and capers in 13 × 9-inch glass baking dish until blended. Cut swordfish steaks crosswise in half and add to marinade; turn to coat. Cover and marinate in refrigerator at least 1 hour, turning occasionally.

Preheat grill. Drain swordfish, reserving marinade. Place swordfish on grid. Grill over medium coals about 5 minutes on each side or until swordfish flakes easily when tested with a fork, brushing steaks once halfway through grilling with reserved marinade. Discard remaining marinade. Place swordfish on platter; garnish with lemon and lime slices and rosemary sprigs. *Makes 4 servings*

Teriyaki Salmon Steak

Teriyaki Salmon Steaks

½ cup LAWRY'S® Teriyaki Marinade with Pineapple Juice
¼ cup dry sherry
2 tablespoons orange juice
1 tablespoon Dijon-style mustard
4 salmon steaks (about 2 pounds)
1 large tomato, diced
½ cup thinly sliced green onions

In medium bowl, blend together Teriyaki Marinade with Pineapple Juice, sherry, orange juice and mustard with wire whisk. In large resealable plastic bag or shallow glass dish, place salmon; cover with marinade mixture. Seal bag or cover dish. Marinate in refrigerator at least 40 minutes, turning occasionally. Heat grill for medium-hot coals or heat broiler. In small bowl, combine tomato and green onions; set aside. Remove salmon from marinade, reserving marinade. Grill or broil, 4 inches from heat source, 3 to 5 minutes, brushing once with reserved marinade. Turn salmon over. Spoon reserved vegetables over salmon; grill or broil 3 to 5 minutes longer or until thickest part of salmon flakes easily with fork. Garnish as desired.

Makes 4 servings

Presentation: Delicious served with sautéed julienne potatoes or hot fluffy rice.

Citrus Shrimp Kabobs

3 medium oranges
¼ cup WISH-BONE® Italian Dressing*
2 tablespoons snipped fresh dill**
1 pound large shrimp, peeled and deveined

Grate 1 teaspoon peel from 1 orange, then squeeze out ¼ cup juice. Cut remaining 2 oranges into 16 wedges; set aside.

In large nonaluminum baking dish or resealable plastic bag, combine orange peel, ¼ cup orange juice, Italian dressing and dill. Add shrimp and turn to coat. Cover, or close bag, and marinate in refrigerator, turning occasionally, 30 minutes. Remove shrimp. Bring reserved marinade to a boil.

On 8 skewers, alternately thread shrimp and orange wedges. Grill or broil, turning and basting with reserved marinade, until shrimp turn pink. If desired, bring remaining reserved marinade to a boil and serve over kabobs or toss with hot cooked rice.

Makes 4 servings

*Also terrific with Wish-Bone® Robusto Italian or Lite Italian Dressing.

**Substitution: Use 1 teaspoon dried dill weed.

Snapper with Pesto Butter

- ½ cup butter or margarine, softened
- 1 cup packed fresh basil leaves, coarsely chopped *or* ½ cup chopped fresh parsley plus 2 tablespoons dried basil leaves, crushed
- 3 tablespoons finely grated fresh Parmesan cheese
- 1 clove garlic, minced
- Olive oil
- 2 to 3 teaspoons lemon juice
- 4 to 6 red snapper, rock cod, salmon or other medium-firm fish fillets (at least ½ inch thick)
- Salt and black pepper
- Lemon wedges
- Fresh basil or parsley sprigs and lemon strips for garnish

To make Pesto Butter, place butter, basil, cheese, garlic and 1 tablespoon oil in a blender or food processor; process until blended. Stir in lemon juice to taste. Rinse fish; pat dry with paper towels. Brush one side of fish lightly with oil; season with salt and pepper.

Oil hot grid to help prevent sticking. Grill fillets, oil sides down, on a covered grill, over medium KINGSFORD® Briquets, 5 to 9 minutes. Halfway through cooking time, brush tops with oil and season with salt and pepper, then turn and continue grilling until fish turns from translucent to opaque throughout. (Grilling time depends on the thickness of fish; allow 3 to 5 minutes for each ½ inch of thickness.) Serve each fillet with a spoonful of Pesto Butter and a wedge of lemon. Garnish with basil sprigs and lemon strips. *Makes 4 to 6 servings*

Lemon Tarragon Fish

- ½ cup CRISCO® Oil
- 1 teaspoon grated lemon peel (optional)
- ½ cup lemon juice
- 2 teaspoons dried parsley flakes
- 2 teaspoons dried tarragon leaves
- ¼ teaspoon salt
- ⅛ teaspoon pepper
- 4 cod, halibut or haddock steaks (about 1 pound)
- 2⅔ cups hot cooked rice (cooked without salt or fat)

1. Combine Crisco Oil, lemon peel (if used), lemon juice, parsley, tarragon, salt and pepper in shallow baking dish. Stir to mix well.

2. Place fish in lemon juice mixture. Turn to coat. Refrigerate 30 minutes, turning after 15 minutes.

3. Prepare grill or heat broiler.

4. Remove fish from marinade. Grill or broil 3 to 5 minutes per side or until fish flakes easily with fork. Serve with hot rice.

Makes 4 servings

Snapper with Pesto Butter

Seafood Kabobs

24 large sea scallops
12 medium shrimp, shelled and deveined
1 can (8½ ounces) whole small artichoke hearts, drained and cut into halves
2 red or yellow bell peppers, cut into 2-inch pieces
¼ cup olive or vegetable oil
¼ cup lime juice
Lime slices and sage sprigs for garnish

Thread scallops, shrimp, artichoke hearts and peppers alternately onto metal or bamboo skewers. (Soak bamboo skewers in water at least 20 minutes to keep them from burning.) Combine oil and lime juice in a small bowl; reserve half of lime mixture. Brush kabobs with some of remaining lime mixture.

Oil hot grid to help prevent sticking. Grill kabobs, on an uncovered grill, over low KINGSFORD® Briquets, 6 to 8 minutes. Halfway through cooking time, baste top with remaining lime mixture, then turn kabobs and continue grilling until scallops and shrimp firm up and turn opaque throughout. Remove kabobs from grill; baste with reserved lime mixture using *clean* basting brush. Garnish with lime slices and sage sprigs. *Makes 6 servings*

Cheesy Trout Surprise

1 (8-ounce) sole, pollock or salmon fillet
2 egg whites
8 pieces thin-style KAVLI® Norwegian crispbread, crushed
½ cup low fat milk
¼ teaspoon ground nutmeg
¼ teaspoon black pepper
8 ounces grated Jarlsberg cheese
⅔ cup packed chopped fresh basil
4 whole fresh trout, boned (about ½ pound *each*)

Seafood Kabobs

Prepare grill. Place fish fillet in food processor; process until it forms smooth paste. Add egg whites, crispbreads, milk, nutmeg and pepper. Process until smooth, scraping down sides of bowl. Stir in Jarlsberg and basil; mix well. Stuff trout cavities evenly with fish mixture. Prepare grill. Wrap each fish in foil, leaving space around edges and crimping all ends to make packets.* Place packets on grid. Grill over medium coals about 20 minutes or until fish flakes easily with fork.

Makes 4 servings

*Recipe may be made up to this point and frozen. Thaw before cooking.

Conventional Directions: Prepare as directed and wrap in foil. Bake foil packets in preheated 350°F oven 35 minutes or until fish flakes easily with fork.

Microwave Directions: Prepare as directed (do not wrap in foil) and arrange trout in 13 × 9-inch microwave-safe dish. Cover tightly with plastic wrap. Microwave on HIGH (100% power) 6 minutes or until fish flakes easily with fork, turning once. Let stand, covered, 2 minutes.

Favorite recipe from **Norseland, Inc.**

A.1.® Grilled Fish Steaks

1 pound salmon steaks or other fish steaks, about 1 inch thick
¼ cup A.1.® Steak Sauce
1 tablespoon margarine, melted
½ teaspoon garlic powder

Coat large sheet of aluminum foil with nonstick cooking spray; place fish steaks on foil. In small bowl, combine steak sauce, margarine and garlic powder; spoon over fish. Fold edges of foil together to seal; place seam side up on grill. Grill for about 10 minutes or until fish flakes easily with fork. Carefully remove from grill. Serve immediately. *Makes 4 servings*

Grilled Swordfish with Pineapple Salsa

Pineapple Salsa (recipe follows)
1 tablespoon lime juice
2 cloves garlic, minced
4 swordfish steaks (5 ounces *each*)
½ teaspoon chili powder or coarse ground black pepper

Spray cold grid with nonstick cooking spray. Adjust grid 4 to 6 inches above heat. Prepare grill. Prepare Pineapple Salsa; set aside. Combine juice and garlic on plate. Dip swordfish in juice; sprinkle with chili powder. Place fish on grid. Grill, on covered grill, over medium-hot coals 2 to 3 minutes. Turn over; grill 1 to 2 minutes more or until just opaque in center and still very moist. Top each serving with about 3 tablespoons Pineapple Salsa.

Makes 4 servings

Grilled Swordfish with Pineapple Salsa

Pineapple Salsa

½ cup finely chopped fresh pineapple
¼ cup finely chopped red bell pepper
1 green onion, thinly sliced
2 tablespoons lime juice
½ jalapeño pepper, seeded and minced
1 tablespoon chopped fresh cilantro or basil

Combine ingredients in small glass bowl. Serve at room temperature.

Makes 4 servings

Bacon-Wrapped Shrimp

1 pound fresh or frozen large raw shrimp, shelled and deveined
1 small onion, finely chopped
½ cup olive oil
½ teaspoon sugar
½ teaspoon garlic powder
½ teaspoon ground red pepper
¼ teaspoon salt
¼ teaspoon dried oregano leaves, crushed
½ pound bacon
Mexican Fried Rice (recipe follows)

Thaw shrimp, if frozen. For marinade, in small bowl, combine onion, oil, sugar, garlic powder, red pepper, salt and oregano. Place shrimp in a large heavy plastic food bag; set bag in a deep bowl. Pour marinade over shrimp in bag; seal bag. Marinate shrimp for 3 hours in refrigerator or 1 hour at room temperature, turning occasionally.

Halve bacon slices lengthwise and crosswise. In a large skillet, partially cook bacon. Drain on paper towels. Drain shrimp; discard marinade. Wrap bacon strips around shrimp; secure with wooden toothpicks. Place wrapped shrimp in a fish basket or on 12 × 9-inch piece of heavy-duty aluminum foil. (If using foil, puncture the foil in several places.)

Grill shrimp on uncovered grill directly over medium-hot KINGSFORD® Briquets 12 minutes or until bacon is done and shrimp are opaque, turning basket or individual shrimp once. Serve with Mexican Fried Rice. *Makes 6 servings*

Mexican Fried Rice

3 tablespoons vegetable oil
1 cup long grain rice
1 (8-ounce) package frozen raw shrimp, shelled and deveined (optional)
1 cup salsa
½ cup chopped green bell pepper
1 small onion, chopped
1 clove garlic, minced
2 cups water
Additional salsa (optional)

Heat oil in large skillet over medium heat. Add rice; cook until golden brown, stirring frequently. Stir in shrimp, salsa, bell pepper, onion, garlic and 2 cups water. Bring mixture to a boil; reduce heat to low. Cover; simmer 15 to 20 minutes or until rice is tender. Season to taste; serve with additional salsa, if desired.

Makes 6 servings

Grilled Salmon with Cilantro Butter

1 clove garlic, peeled
⅓ cup packed fresh cilantro leaves
¼ cup butter or margarine, softened
½ teaspoon grated lime or lemon peel
¼ teaspoon black pepper
4 salmon fillets (about 6 ounces *each*)
Salt (optional)
Lime or lemon wedges

Grilled Salmon with Cilantro Butter

Drop garlic through feed tube of food processor with motor running. Add cilantro; process until cilantro is coarsely chopped. Add butter, lime peel and pepper; process until well combined and cilantro is finely chopped. Place butter mixture on sheet of waxed paper. Using waxed paper as a guide, roll mixture back and forth into 1-inch-diameter log, 2 inches long. Wrap waxed paper around butter mixture to seal; refrigerate about 30 minutes or until firm.

Prepare grill. Lightly sprinkle salmon with salt. Place salmon, skin side down, on grid. Grill, on covered grill, over medium coals 8 to 10 minutes or until salmon flakes easily when tested with fork. Transfer salmon to serving plates. Cut butter log crosswise into 8 slices; top each fillet with 2 slices. Serve with lime or lemon wedges.

Makes 4 servings

Seafood Tacos with Fruit Salsa

Seafood Tacos with Fruit Salsa

2 tablespoons lemon juice
1 teaspoon chili powder
1 teaspoon ground allspice
1 teaspoon olive oil
1 teaspoon minced garlic
1 to 2 teaspoons grated lemon peel
¼ teaspoon ground cloves
1 pound halibut or snapper fillets
12 (6-inch) corn tortillas *or* 6 (7- to 8-inch) flour tortillas
3 cups shredded romaine lettuce
1 small red onion, halved and thinly sliced
Fruit Salsa (recipe follows)

Combine lemon juice, chili powder, allspice, oil, garlic, lemon peel and cloves in small bowl. Rub fish with spice mixture; cover and refrigerate 1 to 3 hours. (Fish may be cut into smaller pieces for easier handling.)

Spray cold grid with nonstick cooking spray. Adjust grid 4 to 6 inches above heat. Prepare grill. Place fish on grid. Grill, covered, over medium-hot coals 3 minutes or until fish is lightly seared on bottom. Carefully turn fish over; grill 2 minutes more or until fish is opaque in center and flakes easily when tested with fork. Remove from heat and cut into 12 pieces, removing bones if necessary. Cover to keep warm.

Place tortillas on grill in single layer and grill 5 to 10 seconds; turn over and grill 5 to 10 seconds more or until hot and pliable. Stack; cover to keep warm. Top each tortilla with ¼ cup lettuce and sprinkle evenly with red onion. Add 1 piece fish and top with Fruit Salsa.

Makes 6 servings

Fruit Salsa

1 small ripe papaya, peeled, seeded and finely chopped
1 firm small banana, finely chopped
2 green onions, minced
3 tablespoons chopped fresh cilantro or mint
3 tablespoons lime juice
2 jalapeño peppers, seeded and minced*

Combine ingredients in small bowl. Serve at room temperature.

*Jalapeño peppers can sting and irritate the skin; wear rubber gloves when handling peppers and do not touch eyes. Wash your hands after handling.

Grilled Baja Swordfish

- **¼ cup chopped onion**
- **1 tablespoon olive oil**
- **1 can (14½ ounces) whole tomatoes, cut up**
- **1 teaspoon dried basil leaves, finely crushed**
- **½ teaspoon LAWRY'S® Seasoned Salt**
- **½ teaspoon LAWRY'S® Seasoned Pepper**
- **¼ teaspoon LAWRY'S® Garlic Powder with Parsley**
- **¼ teaspoon finely chopped fresh cilantro**
- **2 swordfish steaks (about ½ pound *each*)**
- **Fresh lemon (optional)**

Heat grill for hot coals. In large skillet, sauté onion in oil. Add all remaining ingredients except swordfish and lemon. Bring to a boil; reduce heat. Cover and simmer 15 minutes, stirring occasionally. Uncover and continue simmering 10 minutes. Grill swordfish, 4 to 5 inches from heat, about 5 minutes on each side or until fish flakes easily with fork. Squeeze fresh lemon juice over fish while grilling, if desired. Serve tomato sauce mixture over fish. *Makes 2 servings*

Presentation: Garnish with fresh sprigs of cilantro.

Maui Sunset Grill

- **4 fish steaks (halibut, sea bass or salmon), *each* ¾ inch thick**
- **½ cup KIKKOMAN® Teriyaki Marinade & Sauce**
- **2 tablespoons papaya nectar**
- **1 tablespoon chopped fresh cilantro**
- **1 teaspoon vegetable oil**
- **Nonstick cooking spray**
- **Maui Sunset Sauce (recipe follows)**
- **¼ cup chopped macadamia nuts or toasted almonds**

Place fish steaks in single layer in large shallow pan. Blend teriyaki sauce, papaya nectar, cilantro and oil; pour over fish. Turn fish over to coat both sides. Cover and refrigerate 45 minutes, turning fish over occasionally. Meanwhile, coat grill rack with cooking spray; place 4 to 5 inches from hot coals. Reserving marinade, remove fish; place on rack. Cook 3 minutes on each side, or until fish flakes easily with fork. (Or, place fish on rack of broiler pan. Broil 3 minutes on each side, or until fish flakes easily with fork.) Remove fish to serving platter; keep warm while preparing Maui Sunset Sauce. To serve, spoon sauce over fish steaks; sprinkle with nuts.

Makes 4 servings

Maui Sunset Sauce: Combine ⅓ cup reserved marinade, ⅓ cup papaya nectar, ¼ cup water, 1½ teaspoons cornstarch and 1 teaspoon sugar in small saucepan. Cook and stir over medium heat until mixture boils and becomes slightly thickened.

Maui Sunset Grill

Blackened Sea Bass

Hardwood charcoal*
2 teaspoons paprika
1 teaspoon garlic salt
1 teaspoon dried thyme leaves, crushed
¼ teaspoon ground white pepper
¼ teaspoon ground red pepper
¼ teaspoon ground black pepper
3 tablespoons butter or margarine
4 skinless sea bass or catfish fillets (4 to 6 ounces *each*)
Lemon halves
Fresh dill sprigs for garnish

Prepare grill. Meanwhile, combine paprika, garlic salt, thyme, white, red and black peppers in small bowl; mix well. Set aside. Melt butter in small saucepan over medium heat. Pour melted butter into pie plate or shallow bowl. Cool slightly. Dip sea bass into melted butter, evenly coating both sides. Sprinkle both sides of sea bass evenly with paprika mixture. Place sea bass on grid. (Fire will flare up when sea bass is placed on grid, but will subside when grill is covered.) Grill, on covered grill, over hot coals 4 to 6 minutes or until sea bass is blackened and flakes easily with fork, turning halfway through grilling time. Serve with lemon halves. Garnish, if desired. *Makes 4 servings*

*Hardwood charcoal takes somewhat longer than regular charcoal to become hot, but results in a hotter fire than regular charcoal. A hot fire is necessary to seal in the juices and cook fish quickly. If hardwood charcoal is not available, scatter dry hardwood, mesquite or hickory chunks over hot coals to create a hot fire.

Grilled Fish with Garlic Salsa

½ cup fruity olive oil or extra-virgin olive oil
5 tablespoons lemon juice, divided
4 cloves fresh garlic, peeled and slivered
½ cup chopped fresh cilantro, divided
Salt and black pepper
6 (6-ounce) firm fleshed fish fillets, about ¾ inch thick*
¼ pound unsalted (sweet) butter, divided
¼ cup chopped sweet red onion
2 small hot green or jalapeño chilies, finely minced
1 tablespoon finely minced fresh garlic
1 pound ripe tomatoes, peeled, chopped
Lemon wedges for garnish
Fresh cilantro sprigs for garnish

Combine oil, 4 tablespoons lemon juice, slivered garlic, ¼ cup chopped cilantro, and salt and pepper to taste in large shallow glass dish until blended. Add fish fillets; turn to coat. Cover and marinate 1 hour or refrigerate overnight.

Prepare grill. Melt 2 tablespoons butter in medium skillet over medium heat; add onion, chilies and minced garlic. Cook and stir until soft. Add tomatoes and remaining 1 tablespoon juice. Cook 10 minutes, stirring often. Remove from heat; season with salt and pepper. Stir in remaining ¼ cup chopped cilantro. Slowly stir in remaining 6 tablespoons butter until melted. Place fish on grid. Grill over low coals about 7 minutes or until fish flakes easily with fork, turning once. Remove to warm serving platter. Top with tomato mixture. Garnish with lemon wedges and cilantro sprigs. *Makes 6 servings*

*Angler, also called monkfish, is particularly good in this recipe.

Favorite recipe from **Christopher Ranch Garlic**

Blackened Sea Bass

Oriental Shrimp & Steak Kabobs

1 envelope LIPTON® Recipe Secrets® Savory Herb with Garlic or Onion Soup Mix
¼ cup soy sauce
¼ cup lemon juice
¼ cup olive or vegetable oil
¼ cup honey
½ pound uncooked medium shrimp, peeled and deveined
½ pound boneless sirloin steak, cut into 1-inch cubes
16 cherry tomatoes
2 cups mushroom caps
1 medium green bell pepper, cut into chunks

In large nonaluminum baking dish, blend savory herb with garlic soup mix, soy sauce, lemon juice, oil and honey; set aside.

Oriental Shrimp & Steak Kabobs

On skewers, alternately thread shrimp, steak, tomatoes, mushrooms and green pepper. Add prepared skewers to baking dish; turn to coat. Cover and marinate in refrigerator, turning skewers occasionally, at least 2 hours. Remove prepared skewers, reserving marinade. Grill or broil, turning and basting frequently with reserved marinade, until shrimp turn pink and steak is done. Do not brush with marinade during last 5 minutes of cooking.

Makes about 8 servings

Serving Suggestion: Serve with corn-on-the-cob, a mixed green salad and grilled garlic bread.

Vegetable-Topped Fish Pouches

4 firm fish fillets, such as flounder, cod or halibut (about 1 pound)
1 carrot, cut into very thin strips
1 rib celery, cut into very thin strips
1 medium red onion, cut into thin wedges
1 medium zucchini or yellow squash, sliced
8 mushrooms, sliced
½ cup shredded Swiss cheese (about 2 ounces)
½ cup WISH-BONE® Italian Dressing*

On four 18 × 9-inch pieces heavy-duty aluminum foil, divide fish equally. Evenly top with vegetables, then cheese. Drizzle with Italian dressing. Wrap foil loosely around fillets and vegetables, sealing edges airtight with double fold. Let stand to marinate 15 minutes. Grill or broil pouches, seam sides up, 15 minutes or until fish flakes easily with fork. *Makes 4 servings*

*Also terrific with Wish-Bone® Robusto Italian or Lite Italian Dressing.

Grilled Fresh Fish

3 to 3½ pounds fresh tuna or catfish
¾ cup prepared HIDDEN VALLEY RANCH® Original Ranch® Salad Dressing
Chopped fresh dill
Lemon wedges (optional)

Place fish on heavy-duty foil. Cover with salad dressing. Grill over medium-hot coals until fish turns opaque and flakes easily when tested with fork, 20 to 30 minutes. (Or broil fish 15 to 20 minutes.) Sprinkle with dill; garnish with lemon wedges, if desired. *Makes 6 servings*

Polynesian-Style Barbecued Fish Steaks

4 fish steaks (halibut, salmon or swordfish), *each* about ¾ inch thick
½ cup KIKKOMAN® Teriyaki Marinade & Sauce
⅓ cup unsweetened pineapple juice
2 tablespoons sliced green onions and tops
½ teaspoon grated fresh ginger root
Summer Squash Haystacks (recipe follows)

Place fish in single layer in shallow pan. Combine teriyaki sauce, pineapple juice, green onions and ginger; pour over fish. Turn fish over to coat both sides. Marinate 30 minutes, turning fish over occasionally. Meanwhile, prepare coals for cooking. Reserving marinade, remove fish; place on grill 4 inches from medium-hot coals. Cook 5 minutes; brush with reserved marinade. Turn over; cook 5 minutes longer, or until fish flakes easily with fork. (Or, place fish on rack of broiler pan. Broil 4 to 5 inches from heat 5 minutes; brush with reserved marinade. Turn over; cook 4 to 5 minutes longer, or until fish flakes easily with fork.) Meanwhile, prepare Summer Squash Haystacks. Serve with fish.
Makes 4 servings

Polynesian-Style Barbecued Fish Steaks

Summer Squash Haystacks

1¼ pounds assorted summer squash (zucchini, pattypan and yellow crookneck)
1 tablespoon butter or margarine
1 small clove garlic, pressed
2 tablespoons KIKKOMAN® Teriyaki Marinade & Sauce
2 tablespoons freshly grated Parmesan cheese (optional)

Coarsely shred squash. Melt butter in large skillet over medium-high heat. Add garlic and squash; cook and stir 2 to 3 minutes, or until squash is tender. Add teriyaki sauce; toss to coat. Sprinkle with cheese, if desired. Serve immediately.
Makes 4 servings

Grilled Swordfish with Tomato Relish

Barbecued Salmon

4 salmon steaks (*each* at least ¾ inch thick)
3 tablespoons lemon juice
2 tablespoons soy sauce
Salt and black pepper
½ cup K.C. MASTERPIECE® Barbecue Sauce, divided

Rinse fish; pat dry with paper towels. Combine lemon juice and soy sauce in a shallow glass dish. Place steaks in dish; let stand at room temperature no more than 15 to 20 minutes, turning steaks several times. Remove fish; discard marinade. Season lightly with salt and pepper.

Oil hot grid to help prevent sticking. Grill salmon, on a covered grill, over medium KINGSFORD® Briquets, 10 to 14 minutes. Halfway through cooking time, brush top with ¼ cup barbecue sauce, then turn and continue grilling until fish turns from translucent to opaque throughout. (Grilling time depends on thickness of the fish; allow 3 to 5 minutes for each ½ inch of thickness.) Remove fish from grill; brush with remaining ¼ cup barbecue sauce using *clean* basting brush. *Makes 4 servings*

Grilled Swordfish with Tomato Relish

1½ pounds tomatoes, peeled and chopped
1½ cups chopped onions
1 medium red bell pepper, chopped
1 cup sugar
1 cup HEINZ® Apple Cider Vinegar
⅓ cup HEINZ® 57 Sauce
½ cup golden raisins
2 teaspoons minced fresh ginger
1 clove garlic, crushed
½ teaspoon ground coriander
¼ teaspoon crushed red pepper
2 tablespoons vegetable oil
1 tablespoon lemon juice
¼ teaspoon lemon pepper seasoning
⅛ teaspoon garlic powder
6 swordfish steaks, *each* cut ¾ inch thick

For Tomato Relish, combine tomatoes, onions, bell pepper, sugar, vinegar, Heinz® 57 Sauce, raisins, ginger, garlic, coriander and crushed red pepper in large saucepan. Cook, stirring occasionally, over medium-low heat 1 hour or until thick. Cover; refrigerate. (Mixture may be stored in refrigerator for up to 3 weeks.) Let relish stand at room temperature 1 hour before serving.

For swordfish, combine oil, lemon juice, lemon pepper seasoning and garlic powder in small bowl. Brush mixture over swordfish. Spray grid with nonstick cooking spray. Place swordfish on grid. Grill over medium-hot coals 5 minutes on each side or until fish flakes easily when tested with fork. Serve swordfish topped with Tomato Relish. *Makes 6 servings*

Note: Tomato Relish may also be served with chicken, pork, ham or other mild-flavored fish.

Fish in Foil

1 (8-ounce) can stewed tomatoes
⅓ cup A.1.® BOLD Steak Sauce
1 clove garlic, minced
4 (4-ounce) firm fish fillets
2 cups frozen mixed vegetables

In small bowl, combine stewed tomatoes, steak sauce and garlic; set aside.

Place each fish fillet in center of heavy-duty or double thickness foil; top each with ½ cup mixed vegetables and ¼ cup steak sauce mixture. Wrap foil securely around fish. Grill fish packets over medium heat for 8 to 10 minutes or until fish flakes easily with fork. Serve immediately.

Makes 4 servings

Barbecued Shrimp with Spicy Rice

1 pound large shrimp, peeled and deveined
4 wooden* or metal skewers
⅓ cup prepared barbecue sauce
Vegetable cooking spray
Spicy Rice (recipe follows)

Thread shrimp onto skewers. To grill, place skewered shrimp over hot coals; grill 4 minutes. Brush with barbecue sauce. Turn and brush with remaining barbecue sauce. Grill 4 to 5 minutes longer or until shrimp turn pink and opaque. (To broil, place on broiler rack coated with cooking spray. Broil 4 to 5 inches from heat 4 minutes. Brush with barbecue sauce. Turn and brush with remaining barbecue sauce. Broil 2 to 4 minutes longer or until shrimp turn pink and opaque.) Serve with Spicy Rice.

Makes 4 servings

*Soak wooden skewers 30 minutes in water before using to prevent burning.

Spicy Rice

1 tablespoon vegetable oil
½ cup sliced green onions with tops
½ cup minced carrots
½ cup minced red bell pepper
1 jalapeño or serrano pepper, minced
2 cups cooked rice (cooked in chicken broth)
2 tablespoons snipped fresh cilantro
1 tablespoon lime juice
1 teaspoon soy sauce
Hot pepper sauce to taste

Heat oil in large skillet over medium-high heat; add onions, carrots, red pepper and jalapeño pepper. Cook and stir until crisp-tender. Stir in rice, cilantro, lime juice, soy sauce and pepper sauce; cook until thoroughly heated. Serve with Barbecued Shrimp.

Microwave Directions: Combine onions, carrots, red pepper, jalapeño pepper and oil in 2-quart microproof baking dish. Cook on HIGH 2 to 3 minutes or until vegetables are crisp-tender. Add rice, cilantro, lime juice, soy sauce and pepper sauce. Cook on HIGH 3 to 4 minutes, stirring after 2 minutes, or until thoroughly heated. Serve with Barbecued Shrimp.

Favorite recipe from ***USA Rice Council***

Barbecued Shrimp with Spicy Rice

Teriyaki Trout

4 whole trout (about 2 pounds)
¾ cup LAWRY'S® Teriyaki Marinade with Pineapple Juice
½ cup sliced green onions
2 medium lemons, sliced
Chopped fresh parsley (optional)

Pierce skin of trout several times with fork. Brush the inside and outside of each trout with Teriyaki Marinade with Pineapple Juice; stuff with green onions and lemon slices. Place in shallow glass dish. Pour all but ¼ cup Teriyaki Marinade with Pineapple Juice over trout; cover dish. Marinate in refrigerator at least 30 minutes. Heat grill for medium-hot coals. Remove trout, reserving marinade. Place trout in oiled hinged wire grill basket; brush with reserved marinade. Grill, 4 to 5 inches from heat source, 10 minutes or until trout flakes easily with fork, turning and brushing occasionally with reserved ¼ cup Teriyaki Marinade with Pineapple Juice. Sprinkle with parsley, if desired.

Makes 4 servings

Presentation: For a delicious side dish, cook sliced bell pepper, onion and zucchini brushed with vegetable oil on grill with trout.

Hot Honey Grilled Florida Amberjack Steaks

2 pounds Florida Amberjack Steaks, fresh or frozen
1 cup honey
½ cup prepared mustard
1 teaspoon white pepper
1 teaspoon lemon juice
⅛ teaspoon ground red pepper

Thaw steaks if frozen. Prepare grill. Combine honey, mustard, white pepper, juice and red pepper in small bowl until well blended. Baste steaks with honey mixture. Place in well-greased hinged wire grill basket. Place basket on grid. Grill about 4 inches above medium-hot coals 10 minutes per inch of thickness on each side or until fish flakes easily with fork, basting with sauce often. (Do not baste during last 5 minutes of grilling.) *Makes 4 servings*

Favorite recipe from ***Florida Department of Agriculture and Consumer Services***

Scallop Kabobs

¼ cup REALEMON® Lemon Juice from Concentrate
2 tablespoons vegetable oil
1 teaspoon dried oregano leaves
½ teaspoon dried basil leaves
1 clove garlic, finely chopped
⅛ teaspoon salt
1 pound sea scallops
8 ounces fresh mushrooms
2 small zucchini, cut into chunks
2 small onions, cut into wedges
½ red, yellow or green bell pepper, cut into bite-size pieces
Additional REALEMON® Brand

In shallow dish, combine ¼ cup ReaLemon® brand, oil and seasonings; add scallops. Cover; marinate in refrigerator 2 hours, stirring occasionally. Remove scallops from marinade; discard marinade. Thread scallops onto 8 skewers alternately with vegetables. Grill or broil just until scallops are opaque, basting frequently with additional ReaLemon® brand. Refrigerate leftovers.

Makes 8 kabobs

Teriyaki Trout

Surf and Turf Brochettes

1 (12-ounce) beef top round steak, cut into ¾-inch cubes
24 small shrimp, peeled and deveined
1 green bell pepper, cut into 1-inch squares
¾ cup orange juice
½ cup A.1.® Steak Sauce
2 tablespoons white wine
1 clove garlic, minced
1½ teaspoons cornstarch

Soak 12 (10-inch) wooden skewers in water for at least 30 minutes. Alternately thread beef cubes, shrimp and green pepper onto skewers.

In small saucepan, combine orange juice, steak sauce, wine and garlic; reserve ½ cup mixture for basting. Blend cornstarch into remaining steak sauce mixture in saucepan. Over medium heat, cook and stir until sauce thickens and begins to boil; keep warm.

Grill brochettes over medium heat for 8 to 10 minutes or until shrimp turn pink and opaque and beef is cooked, turning and brushing often with reserved steak sauce mixture. Serve brochettes with warm sauce for dipping. *Makes 12 appetizers*

Surf and Turf Brochette

Caribbean Isle Fish Steaks

½ DOLE® Fresh Pineapple
4 white fish steaks, 1 inch thick
½ cup DOLE® Pine-Orange-Guava Juice frozen concentrate
4 teaspoons fresh lime juice
1 serrano or jalapeño pepper, seeded and minced
¾ teaspoon ground ginger
¾ teaspoon ground coriander
½ teaspoon salt
2 tablespoons water

Tropical Sauce

⅔ cup water
¼ cup DOLE® Pine-Orange-Guava Juice frozen concentrate
1 tablespoon cornstarch
1 serrano or jalapeño pepper, seeded and minced

• Cut pineapple from shell; discard shell. Cut fruit crosswise into ½-inch-thick slices.

• Prepare grill or preheat broiler. Meanwhile, place fish in shallow casserole dish. Combine ½ cup juice concentrate, lime juice, 1 pepper, ginger, coriander and salt; pour over fish and turn to coat both sides. Marinate 15 minutes. Remove fish from marinade; stir 2 tablespoons water into marinade. Transfer marinade to large skillet. Bring to a boil; remove from heat. Add pineapple to marinade; turn to coat.

• Combine Tropical Sauce ingredients in small microwave-safe bowl. Microwave 2 to 3 minutes on HIGH (100% power) or until mixture boils and thickens, stirring occasionally. Set aside.

• Grill fish over medium-hot coals or broil on broiler pan, 4 to 6 inches from heat, 5 minutes on each side or until fish flakes easily with fork, turning and brushing once with marinade. Grill or broil pineapple during last 2 minutes of cooking time. Serve fish and pineapple with Tropical Sauce. *Makes 4 servings*

Grilled Scallops with Avocado Cream & Salsa

4 tablespoons olive oil, divided
1½ teaspoons grated lime peel, divided
3 tablespoons fresh lime juice, divided
1¼ teaspoons salt, divided
½ teaspoon ground cumin
¼ teaspoon black pepper
32 sea scallops
2 firm ripe avocados, halved, pitted and peeled
½ cup finely chopped red onion
¼ cup nonfat plain yogurt
4 (8-inch) flour tortillas, cut into 32 wedges
2 cups shredded iceberg lettuce
¾ cup NEWMAN'S OWN® All Natural Salsa

Whisk together 2 tablespoons oil, ½ teaspoon lime peel, 2 tablespoons lime juice, ¼ teaspoon salt, cumin and pepper in large glass bowl. Add scallops. Cover and marinate in refrigerator 1 hour.

Coarsely mash avocados in medium bowl. Stir in onion, yogurt, remaining 1 tablespoon lime juice, 1 teaspoon lime peel and 1 teaspoon salt until mixture is smooth. Heat remaining 2 tablespoons oil in large nonstick skillet over medium-high heat. Add tortilla wedges in batches and cook 1 to 2 minutes or until golden brown on both sides. Drain on paper towels.

Prepare grill. Place scallops on grid. Grill 3 inches over hot coals 3 to 4 minutes or just until opaque, turning once. To serve, spread 2 teaspoons avocado mixture on tortilla wedge. Layer with 1 tablespoon lettuce, then 1 scallop and top with about 1 teaspoon of Newman's Own® All Natural Salsa. Repeat with remaining ingredients.

Makes 32 appetizers

Summer Vegetable & Fish Bundle

Summer Vegetable & Fish Bundles

4 fish fillets (about 1 pound)
1 pound thinly sliced vegetables*
1 envelope LIPTON® Recipe Secrets® Savory Herb with Garlic or Golden Onion Soup Mix
½ cup water

On two 18 × 18-inch pieces heavy-duty aluminum foil, divide fish equally; top with vegetables. Evenly pour savory herb with garlic soup mix blended with water over fish. Wrap foil loosely around fillets and vegetables, sealing edges airtight with double fold. Grill or broil pouches, seam sides up, 15 minutes or until fish flakes easily with fork. *Makes about 4 servings*

*Use any combination of the following: mushrooms, zucchini, yellow squash or tomatoes.

Serving Suggestion: Serve over hot cooked rice with Lipton® Iced Tea mixed with a splash of cranberry juice cocktail.

Grilled Spiced Halibut, Pineapple and Pepper Skewers

Grilled Spiced Halibut, Pineapple and Pepper Skewers

2 tablespoons lemon juice or lime juice
1 teaspoon minced garlic
1 teaspoon chili powder
½ teaspoon ground cumin
¼ teaspoon ground cinnamon
⅛ teaspoon ground cloves
½ pound boneless skinless halibut steak, about 1 inch thick
½ small pineapple, peeled, halved lengthwise and cut into 24 pieces
1 large green or red bell pepper, cut into 24 squares

Combine juice, garlic, chili powder, cumin, cinnamon and cloves in large resealable food storage bag; knead until blended. Rinse fish and pat dry. Cut into 12 cubes about 1 to 1¼ inch square. Add fish to bag. Seal bag tightly; turn to coat. Marinate in refrigerator 30 minutes to 1 hour. Soak 12 (6- to 8-inch) bamboo skewers in water while fish marinates.

Meanwhile, spray cold grid with nonstick cooking spray. Adjust grid 4 to 6 inches above heat. Prepare grill. Alternately thread 2 pieces pineapple, 2 pieces pepper and 1 piece fish onto each skewer. Place skewers on grid. Cover or tent with foil. Grill 3 to 4 minutes over medium hot coals or until marks are established on bottom. Turn and grill skewers 3 to 4 minutes or until fish is opaque and flakes easily with fork.

Makes 6 appetizer servings

Grilled Lemon-Teriyaki Fish Steaks

⅓ cup KIKKOMAN® Teriyaki Baste & Glaze
¾ teaspoon grated lemon peel
2 tablespoons lemon juice
¾ teaspoon dried basil leaves, crumbled
2 pounds fish steaks (halibut, bass, swordfish or salmon), 1 inch thick

Combine teriyaki baste & glaze, lemon peel, lemon juice and basil. Place fish on oiled grill 4 to 6 inches from hot coals; brush generously with baste & glaze mixture. Cook 4 minutes; turn over. Brush with baste & glaze mixture. Cook 4 minutes longer, or until fish flakes easily with fork, brushing occasionally with remaining baste & glaze mixture. (Or, place fish on rack of broiler pan; brush with baste & glaze mixture. Broil 4 to 5 inches from heat 4 minutes; turn over. Brush with remaining baste & glaze mixture. Broil 4 to 5 minutes longer, or until fish flakes easily with fork.)

Makes 4 servings

Salmon with Chive Sauce

- ½ cup MIRACLE WHIP® Salad Dressing
- ¼ cup finely chopped fresh chives
- 2 tablespoons finely chopped fresh thyme leaves *or* 2 teaspoons dried thyme leaves, crushed
- 2 tablespoons finely chopped fresh dill *or* 2 teaspoons dried dill weed
- ¼ teaspoon salt
- ⅛ teaspoon pepper
- ¼ cup dry white wine or chicken broth
- 2 salmon steaks (about ¾ pound)

• Mix together salad dressing, herbs, salt and pepper until well blended. Reserve ½ cup salad dressing mixture to serve later with cooked salmon. Stir wine into remaining salad dressing mixture; brush on salmon.

• Place salmon on grill over hot coals (coals will be glowing) or rack of broiler pan. Grill, covered, *or* broil 5 to 8 minutes on each side or until fish flakes easily with fork. Serve with reserved salad dressing mixture. *Makes 2 servings*

Prep time: 10 minutes
Grilling time: 16 minutes

Charcoal Grilled Florida Yellowfin Tuna Steaks

- 2 pounds Florida Yellowfin Tuna Steaks, fresh or frozen
- ½ cup vegetable oil
- ¼ cup lemon juice
- 2 teaspoons salt
- ½ teaspoon Worcestershire sauce
- ¼ teaspoon white pepper
- ⅛ teaspoon hot pepper sauce
- Paprika

Thaw tuna if frozen. Prepare grill. Cut tuna into 6 serving-size portions and place in well-greased hinged wire grill basket. Combine all remaining ingredients except paprika in small bowl until well blended; baste tuna with sauce mixture and sprinkle with paprika. Place basket on grid. Grill 4 inches above medium-hot coals 5 to 6 minutes. Turn; baste with sauce mixture and sprinkle with paprika. Grill 4 to 5 minutes more or until tuna has a slightly pink center. *Makes 6 servings*

Favorite recipe from ***Florida Department of Agriculture and Consumer Services***

Salmon with Chive Sauce

Grilled Shrimp Creole

1 can (15 to 16 ounces) red beans
½ cup olive oil, divided
3 tablespoons balsamic or red wine vinegar
3 cloves garlic, minced and divided
1½ pounds raw large shrimp, peeled and deveined
3 tablespoons all-purpose flour
1 green bell pepper, coarsely chopped
1 medium onion, coarsely chopped
2 ribs celery, sliced
1 can (28 ounces) tomatoes, undrained and coarsely chopped
1 bay leaf
1½ teaspoons dried thyme leaves, crushed
¾ teaspoon hot pepper sauce
1 cup uncooked white rice, preferably converted
1 can (about 14 ounces) chicken broth
¼ cup chopped fresh parsley

Place beans in strainer. Rinse under cold running water; drain. Set aside. Combine ¼ cup oil, vinegar and 1 clove garlic in large glass bowl. Add shrimp; toss lightly to coat. Cover and marinate in refrigerator at least 30 minutes or up to 8 hours, turning occasionally.

For tomato sauce, heat remaining ¼ cup oil in large skillet over medium heat. Stir in flour. Cook and stir 10 to 12 minutes or until flour is dark golden brown. Add bell pepper, onion, celery and remaining 2 cloves garlic; cook and stir 5 minutes. Add tomatoes with juice, bay leaf, thyme and hot pepper sauce. Simmer, uncovered, 25 to 30 minutes or until sauce has thickened and vegetables are fork-tender, stirring occasionally. Remove bay leaf. (If desired, tomato sauce may be prepared up to 1 day ahead. Cover and refrigerate. Reheat sauce in medium saucepan over medium heat while shrimp are grilling.)

Prepare grill. Meanwhile, prepare rice according to package directions; substitute broth for 1¾ cups water and omit salt. Stir in beans during last 5 minutes of cooking. Drain shrimp, discarding marinade. Place shrimp in hinged wire grill basket or thread onto metal skewers. Place shrimp on grid. Grill, on uncovered grill, over medium coals 6 to 8 minutes or until shrimp are opaque, turning once.

Arrange rice and beans on 4 serving plates; top with tomato sauce. Remove shrimp from grill basket or skewers. Arrange over tomato sauce. Sprinkle with parsley.
Makes 4 servings

Grilled Key West Fish Steaks

¼ cup KIKKOMAN® Lite Teriyaki Marinade & Sauce
½ teaspoon grated lime peel
1 tablespoon orange juice
2 teaspoons fresh lime juice
4 white fish steaks (halibut, grouper, sea bass or swordfish), *each* ¾ inch thick

Combine lite teriyaki sauce, lime peel, orange juice and lime juice; pour over fish in large plastic food storage bag. Press air out of bag; close top securely. Turn bag over several times to coat all pieces well. Refrigerate 45 to 60 minutes, turning bag over occasionally. Reserving marinade, remove fish; place on grill 4 inches from hot coals. Cook 4 minutes; turn fish over. Brush with reserved marinade. (Discard any remaining marinade.) Cook 3 to 4 minutes longer, or until fish flakes easily with fork. (Or, place fish on rack of broiler pan; broil 4 to 5 inches from heat 4 minutes. Turn fish over; brush with reserved marinade. Broil 3 to 4 minutes longer, or until fish flakes easily with fork.) *Makes 4 servings*

Grilled Shrimp Creole

Grilled Fish with Pineapple Relish

1 DOLE® Fresh Pineapple
⅓ cup finely chopped DOLE® Cucumber
¼ cup finely chopped DOLE® Red Bell Pepper
¼ cup sliced DOLE® Green Onion
2 tablespoons chopped fresh cilantro or parsley
1 tablespoon lime juice
2 teaspoons minced jalapeño pepper
Dash salt
4 halibut steaks or firm white fish fillets

• Twist crown from pineapple. Cut pineapple lengthwise into quarters. Cut fruit from one quarter with knife. Trim off core. Finely chop pineapple to make 1 cup. Slice remaining pineapple crosswise into wedges.

• Prepare grill or preheat broiler. Meanwhile, combine chopped pineapple, cucumber, bell pepper, onion, cilantro, lime juice, jalapeño and salt. Cover; let stand 15 to 30 minutes to blend flavors.

• Grill fish over medium-hot coals or broil on broiler pan, 4 to 6 inches from heat, 10 minutes per inch of thickness, turning once. Transfer to plates. Serve with pineapple wedges. Spoon relish over fish.

Makes 4 servings

Grilled Fish with Pineapple Relish

Swordfish with Honey-Lime Glaze

½ cup lime juice
3½ tablespoons honey
2 cloves garlic, minced
½ to 1 serrano or jalapeño chili pepper, fresh or canned, seeded and minced
1½ teaspoons cornstarch
Salt and black pepper
2 tablespoons finely chopped fresh cilantro (optional)
6 swordfish steaks (*each* at least ¾ inch thick)
2 cups diced seeded tomatoes (about 1½ pounds)
Fresh cilantro sprigs for garnish

To make Honey-Lime Glaze, combine lime juice, honey, garlic, chili pepper, cornstarch and ½ teaspoon salt in a small saucepan. Boil about 1 minute until slightly thickened, stirring constantly. Stir in cilantro, if desired. Reserve half of Honey-Lime Glaze in a small bowl; cool. Rinse steaks; pat dry with paper towels. Season fish with salt and pepper. Brush fish with some of the remaining glaze.

Oil hot grid to help prevent sticking. Grill fish, on a covered grill, over medium KINGSFORD® Briquets, 6 to 10 minutes. Halfway through cooking time, brush top with glaze, then turn and continue grilling until fish turns from transparent to opaque throughout. (Grilling time depends on the thickness of fish; allow 3 to 5 minutes for each ½ inch of thickness.) Stir tomatoes into cooled glaze; serve as a topping. Garnish with cilantro sprigs.

Makes 6 servings

Grilled Antipasto Platter

16 medium scallops
16 medium shrimp, shelled and deveined
12 mushrooms (about 1 inch diameter)
3 ounces thinly sliced prosciutto or deli-style ham
16 slender asparagus spears
1 jar (6½ ounces) marinated artichoke hearts, drained
2 medium zucchini, cut lengthwise into slices
1 large or 2 small red bell peppers, cored, seeded and cut into 1-inch-wide strips
1 head radicchio, cut lengthwise into quarters (optional)
Lemon Baste (recipe follows)
Lemon wedges

Soak 12 long bamboo skewers in water for at least 20 minutes to keep them from burning. Thread 4 scallops on each of 4 skewers and 4 shrimp on each of another 4 skewers. Thread 6 mushrooms on each of 2 more skewers. Cut prosciutto into 2 × 1-inch strips. Wrap 2 asparagus spears together with 2 strips of prosciutto; secure with a toothpick. Repeat with remaining asparagus spears. Wrap each artichoke heart in 1 strip of prosciutto; thread on 2 remaining skewers. Place ingredients except radicchio, Lemon Baste and lemon wedges on a baking sheet. Reserve ¼ cup Lemon Baste. Brush remaining Lemon Baste liberally over ingredients on baking sheet.

Spread medium KINGSFORD® Briquets in a wide single layer over the bed of the grill. Oil hot grid to help prevent sticking. Grill skewers, asparagus bundles, zucchini and red peppers, on an uncovered grill, 7 to 12 minutes until vegetables are tender, seafood firms up and turns opaque and prosciutto around wrapped vegetables is crisp, turning once or twice. Remove each item from grill to a large serving platter as it is done. Pour remaining baste over all. Serve hot or at room temperature. Garnish with radicchio and lemon wedges.

Makes 4 main-dish servings or 8 appetizer servings

Grilled Antipasto Platter

Lemon Baste

½ cup olive oil
¼ cup lemon juice
½ teaspoon salt
¼ teaspoon black pepper

Whisk together all ingredients in small bowl until well blended.

Makes about ¾ cup

Light and Cheesy Grilled Stuffed Fish

Glazed Grilled Trout

6 trout (about 8 ounces *each*), dressed
½ cup KIKKOMAN® Teriyaki Baste & Glaze
4 teaspoons fresh lime juice
1 tablespoon finely chopped fresh dill
Nonstick cooking spray
3 limes, cut into wedges

Score both sides of trout with diagonal slashes ¼ inch deep and 1 inch apart. Combine teriyaki baste & glaze, lime juice and dill; brush trout, including cavities, thoroughly with mixture. Let stand 30 minutes. Meanwhile, prepare coals for grilling. Coat grill rack with cooking spray; place 4 to 5 inches from medium-hot coals. Place trout on rack; cook 5 minutes on each side, or until fish flakes easily with fork, brushing occasionally with baste & glaze mixture. (Or, place trout on rack of broiler pan. Broil 5 minutes on each side, or until fish flakes easily with fork, brushing occasionally with baste & glaze mixture.) Serve with lime wedges.

Makes 6 servings

Light and Cheesy Grilled Stuffed Fish

2 whole fish (such as brook trout, red snapper, baby salmon), cleaned, scaled and boned (1½ to 1¾ pounds *each*)
2 teaspoons Cajun seasoning (optional)
1 cup chicken broth
2 teaspoons dried tarragon leaves, crumbled
2 cups chopped green onions with tops
1½ cups (any style) KAVLI® crispbread crumbs
1 (8-ounce) can water chestnuts, drained and sliced in strips
¼ cup *each* finely chopped red and yellow bell peppers
1 cup (4 ounces) shredded Jarlsberg lite cheese

Prepare grill or preheat oven to 450°F. Open fish, rinse interior and sprinkle with Cajun seasoning, if desired. Bring chicken broth to a boil in medium saucepan over high heat; stir in tarragon and onions. Cover and simmer 2 to 3 minutes or until onions are wilted. Remove from heat. Stir in crispbread crumbs, water chestnuts and peppers. Mix in cheese.

Divide mixture between fish, spreading stuffing evenly in cavities. Fold fish back over filling. Place each fish on large sheet of heavy-duty foil. Fold up foil, leaving space around edges and crimping all ends to make packets. Place packets on grid. Grill fish, on covered grill, over hot coals about 25 minutes or until flesh is white and flakes easily with fork. (For uncovered grill, cook 20 minutes, 8 to 10 inches from hot coals, turning once carefully.)

Makes 4 servings

Favorite recipe from **Norseland, Inc.**

California Shrimp Kabobs

½ DOLE® Fresh Pineapple
Juice from 1 to 2 DOLE® Lemons (½ cup)
¼ cup olive oil
2 teaspoons Dijon mustard
1 teaspoon dried thyme leaves, crumbled
¼ teaspoon crushed red pepper flakes
1 pound (21 to 26) raw jumbo shrimp, shelled and deveined
Salt to taste (optional)
1 *each* DOLE® Red and Green Bell Pepper, chunked
1 teaspoon cornstarch

• Twist crown from pineapple. Cut pineapple lengthwise into quarters. Cut fruit from shell with knife. Slice fruit into chunks; discard shell.

• Prepare grill or preheat broiler. Meanwhile, combine juice, oil, mustard, thyme and pepper flakes in small bowl. Arrange shrimp in shallow casserole dish. Sprinkle with salt, if desired. Pour juice mixture over shrimp. Marinate 15 to 30 minutes. Drain shrimp, reserving marinade.

• Skewer shrimp, pineapple and bell peppers alternately onto 12 (12-inch) bamboo skewers.* Grill over medium-hot coals or broil on broiler pan, 4 to 6 inches from heat, 6 to 8 minutes or until shrimp just turn pink and opaque, turning once. Stir cornstarch into remaining marinade. Microwave on HIGH (100% power) 2 to 3 minutes until sauce boils and thickens. Serve sauce with kabobs.

Makes 4 servings

*Soak bamboo skewers in water 30 minutes to prevent burning.

Grilled Salmon with Cucumber Sauce

¾ cup HELLMANN'S® or BEST FOODS® Real or Light Mayonnaise or Low Fat Cholesterol Free Mayonnaise Dressing
¼ cup snipped fresh dill *or* 1 tablespoon dried dill weed
1 tablespoon lemon juice
6 salmon steaks (4 ounces *each*), ¾ inch thick
1 small cucumber, seeded and chopped
½ cup chopped radishes
Lemon wedges

In medium bowl combine mayonnaise, dill and lemon juice; reserve ½ cup for sauce. Brush fish steaks with remaining mayonnaise mixture. Grill 6 inches from heat, turning and brushing frequently with mayonnaise mixture, 6 to 8 minutes or until fish is firm but moist. Stir cucumber and radishes into reserved mayonnaise mixture. Serve fish with cucumber sauce and lemon wedges.

Makes 6 servings

California Shrimp Kabobs

Shanghai Fish Packets

4 orange roughy or tilefish fillets (4 to 6 ounces *each*)
¼ cup mirin* or Rhine wine
3 tablespoons soy sauce
1 tablespoon Oriental sesame oil
1½ teaspoons grated fresh ginger
¼ teaspoon crushed red pepper
1 tablespoon peanut or vegetable oil
1 clove garlic, minced
1 package (10 ounces) fresh spinach leaves, washed, patted dry and stems removed

Prepare grill. Place orange roughy in single layer in large shallow glass dish. Combine mirin, soy sauce, sesame oil, ginger and crushed red pepper in small bowl; pour over orange roughy. Cover and marinate in refrigerator 30 minutes.

Heat peanut oil in large skillet over medium heat until hot. Add garlic; cook and stir 1 minute. Add spinach; cook and stir about 3 minutes or until wilted, tossing with 2 wooden spoons. Place spinach mixture evenly in centers of four 12 × 12-inch squares of heavy-duty foil. Remove orange roughy from marinade; reserve marinade. Place 1 orange roughy fillet over each mound of spinach. Drizzle reserved marinade evenly over orange roughy. Fold up foil, leaving space around edges and crimping all ends to make packets. Place packets on grid. Grill packets, on covered grill, over medium coals 15 to 18 minutes or until orange roughy flakes easily with fork. *Makes 4 servings*

*Mirin is a Japanese sweet wine available in Japanese markets and the gourmet section of large supermarkets.

Shanghai Fish Packet

Island Surf & Turf Kabobs

1 pound boneless tender beef, 1 inch thick
¼ cup KIKKOMAN® Lite Teriyaki Marinade & Sauce
1 clove garlic, pressed
½ pound medium-size raw shrimp
1 teaspoon sesame seed, toasted (optional)

Trim beef and cut into 1-inch cubes; combine with lite teriyaki sauce and garlic in medium bowl. Marinate 30 minutes. Meanwhile, leaving tails on, shell and devein shrimp. Add shrimp to beef and teriyaki sauce mixture; cover and refrigerate 30 minutes.

Reserving marinade, remove beef and shrimp. Thread each of 8 (10-inch) metal or bamboo* skewers alternately with beef and shrimp. Place on grill 5 inches from hot coals. Cook about 4 minutes; brush with reserved marinade. Cook 4 minutes longer, or until shrimp turn pink. (Or, place skewers on rack of broiler pan. Broil 3 minutes; turn over. Brush with reserved marinade. Broil 3 minutes longer, or until shrimp turn pink.) Sprinkle sesame seed evenly over beef and shrimp before serving, if desired. *Makes 4 to 6 servings*

*Soak bamboo skewers in water 30 minutes to prevent burning.

Glazed Shrimp Skewers

- 1 package (6.5 ounces) RICE-A-RONI® Broccoli Au Gratin
- 3 tablespoons apricot preserves
- 1 tablespoon lemon juice
- 1 teaspoon grated lemon peel
- 1 pound medium raw shrimp, shelled, deveined or large scallops, halved

1. Prepare Rice-A-Roni® Mix as package directs.

2. Combine preserves, juice and ½ teaspoon lemon peel; set aside.

3. On 4 large skewers, thread shrimp. Brush both sides with preserve mixture.

4. Grill over medium coals or broil 5 to 6 inches from heat, 6 to 7 minutes for shrimp or 7 to 9 minutes for scallops, or until seafood is opaque, turning once.

5. Stir remaining ½ teaspoon lemon peel into rice. Serve with cooked seafood.

Makes 4 servings

Barbecued Fish

- 1½ pounds fresh or frozen fish fillets or steaks *or* 4 pan-dressed fish (about 8 ounces *each*)
- ½ cup vegetable oil
- 1 tablespoon Worcestershire sauce
- ½ teaspoon LAWRY'S® Garlic Salt
- ⅛ teaspoon LAWRY'S® Seasoned Pepper

Thaw fish if frozen. Heat grill for medium-hot coals. Cut fish fillets or steaks into 4 portions. For pan-dressed fish, wrap tails in greased aluminum foil. In small bowl, combine oil, Worcestershire sauce, Garlic Salt and Seasoned Pepper; blend well. Place fish in well-greased hinged wire grill basket. Brush fish with oil mixture. Grill, 4 to 5 inches from heat, 5 to 8 minutes. Brush with oil mixture; turn and brush second side. Grill about 5 to 8 minutes longer or until fish flakes easily with fork.

Makes 4 servings

Presentation: Garnish with lemon wedges.

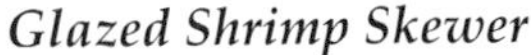

Glazed Shrimp Skewer

Salmon with Cilantro-Lime Sauce

¾ cup HELLMANN'S® or BEST FOODS® Real or Light Mayonnaise or Low Fat Cholesterol Free Mayonnaise Dressing
½ cup chopped fresh cilantro *or* ¼ cup chopped fresh dill
2 tablespoons lime juice
1 medium tomato, seeded and diced
4 salmon or halibut steaks (about 6 ounces *each*), ¾ inch thick
MAZOLA® No Stick cooking spray

In medium bowl combine mayonnaise, cilantro and lime juice. Transfer ½ cup to a small bowl and stir in tomato; set aside. Brush fish steaks with remaining mayonnaise mixture. Spray large skillet with cooking spray. Heat over medium-high heat. Add fish. Cook, turning once, 8 minutes or until fish is firm but moist. Serve with cilantro-lime sauce.

Makes 4 servings

Grilling Directions: Prepare cilantro-lime sauce and fish as directed. Grill fish steaks 6 inches from heat, turning once, about 8 minutes or until firm but moist.

Grilled Trout with Walnut Butter Sauce

Walnut Butter Sauce (recipe follows)
4 whole, cleaned trout or other small whole fish (*each* about 12 ounces)

Prepare Walnut Butter Sauce. Place fish on well-oiled grill rack or in well-oiled fish basket positioned on the grill rack, over medium-hot KINGSFORD® with Mesquite Charcoal Briquets. Grill 13 to 15 minutes, turning after 6 minutes or until fish flakes easily when tested with fork. Serve trout topped with Walnut Butter Sauce.

Makes 4 servings

Salmon with Cilantro-Lime Sauce

Walnut Butter Sauce

½ cup butter or margarine, divided
½ cup chopped walnuts
3 tablespoons Madeira wine

Heat 2 tablespoons butter in large skillet over medium heat until butter is melted. Add walnuts; cook and stir until walnuts are golden and fragrant. Reduce heat to low. Add remaining 6 tablespoons butter; stir until melted. Stir in Madeira. Serve warm.

Grilled Scallop Ceviche

Grilled Scallop Ceviche

- **6 to 7 ounces sea scallops, 1 to 2 inches in diameter**
- **¼ cup lime juice, divided**
- **¼ teaspoon chili powder or paprika**
- **½ large honeydew melon**
- **1 ripe medium papaya or mango *or* ½ large cantaloupe**
- **¼ cup minced onion**
- **1 to 2 fresh jalapeño or serrano peppers, seeded and minced**
- **3 tablespoons minced fresh mint or basil**
- **1 teaspoon honey (optional)**

Rinse scallops and pat dry. Place scallops, 2 tablespoons lime juice and chili powder in large resealable food storage bag. Seal bag tightly; turn to coat. Marinate scallops in refrigerator 30 minutes to 1 hour.

Scoop seeds from melon. Remove fruit from rind with melon baller *or* cut melon into ¾-inch wedges; remove rind and cut fruit into cubes. Halve papaya, scoop out seeds and remove peel with knife; cut fruit into cubes. Place fruit in glass bowl. Stir in remaining 2 tablespoons lime juice, onion and jalapeño. Cover and refrigerate.

Spray cold grid with nonstick cooking spray. Adjust grid 4 to 6 inches above heat. Prepare grill. Drain scallops, discarding marinade. Thread scallops onto 10- to 12-inch metal skewers. Place skewers on grid. Grill over medium-hot coals 3 minutes or until marks are established. Turn skewers over; grill 3 minutes more or until scallops are opaque. Remove scallops from skewers; cut into quarters. Stir into fruit mixture. Cover and refrigerate 30 minutes or up to 24 hours. Stir in mint and honey just before serving, if desired. *Makes 6 servings*

Citrus Marinated Fish Steaks

- **¼ cup frozen orange juice concentrate, thawed**
- **¼ cup REALEMON® Lemon Juice from Concentrate**
- **1 tablespoon vegetable oil**
- **½ teaspoon dill weed**
- **4 (1-inch-thick) salmon, halibut or swordfish steaks, fresh or frozen, thawed (about 1½ pounds)**

In large shallow dish or plastic bag, combine juices, oil and dill; mix well. Add fish. Cover; marinate in refrigerator 2 hours, turning occasionally. Remove fish from marinade; heat marinade thoroughly. Grill or broil until fish flakes with fork, basting frequently with marinade. Garnish as desired. Refrigerate leftovers.

Makes 4 servings

Teriyaki Lemon Fish

⅓ cup HOLLAND HOUSE® White with Lemon Cooking Wine
⅓ cup vegetable oil
2 tablespoons soy sauce
¼ teaspoon ground ginger
4 swordfish, tuna or haddock steaks (4 ounces *each*)

Prepare grill. Combine all ingredients except swordfish in large shallow glass dish. Add swordfish; turn to coat. Cover and marinate in refrigerator 30 minutes. Drain fish, reserving marinade. Place fish on oiled grid. Grill fish over medium-hot coals 10 to 14 minutes, turning once and brushing frequently with marinade. (Do not baste during last 5 minutes of grilling.)

Makes 4 servings

Catfish with Fresh Corn Relish

4 catfish fillets (*each* about 6 ounces and at least ½ inch thick)
2 tablespoons paprika
½ teaspoon ground red pepper
½ teaspoon salt
Fresh Corn Relish (recipe follows)
Lime wedges
Grilled Baking Potatoes (optional) (page 48)
Tarragon sprigs for garnish

Rinse fish; pat dry with paper towels. Combine paprika, red pepper and salt in cup; lightly sprinkle on both sides of fish.

Oil hot grid to help prevent sticking. Grill fish, on a covered grill, over medium KINGSFORD® Briquets, 5 to 9 minutes. Halfway through cooking time, turn fish over and continue grilling until fish turns from translucent to opaque throughout. (Grilling time depends on the thickness of fish; allow 3 to 5 minutes for each ½ inch of thickness.) Serve with Fresh Corn Relish, lime wedges and Grilled Baking Potatoes, if desired. Garnish with tarragon sprigs.

Makes 4 servings

Fresh Corn Relish

¾ cup cooked fresh corn or thawed frozen corn
¼ cup finely chopped green bell pepper
¼ cup finely slivered red onion
1 tablespoon vegetable oil
2 tablespoons seasoned (sweet) rice vinegar
Salt and black pepper
½ cup cherry tomatoes, cut into quarters

Toss together corn, green pepper, onion, oil and vinegar in a medium bowl. Season with salt and pepper. Cover and refrigerate until ready to serve. Just before serving, gently mix in tomatoes.

Makes about 1½ cups

Catfish with Fresh Corn Relish

Szechuan Tuna Steaks

4 tuna steaks (6 ounces *each*), cut 1 inch thick
¼ cup soy sauce
¼ cup dry sherry or sake
1 tablespoon Oriental sesame oil
1 teaspoon hot chili oil *or* ¼ teaspoon crushed red pepper
1 clove garlic, minced
3 tablespoons chopped fresh cilantro

Place tuna in single layer in large shallow glass dish. Combine soy sauce, sherry, sesame oil, hot chili oil and garlic in small bowl. Reserve ¼ cup soy sauce mixture at room temperature. Pour remaining soy sauce mixture over tuna. Cover and marinate in refrigerator 40 minutes, turning once.

Prepare grill. Drain tuna, discarding marinade. Place on grid. Grill tuna, on uncovered grill, over medium-hot coals 6 minutes or until tuna is opaque, but still feels somewhat soft in center,* turning halfway through grilling time. Transfer tuna to carving board. Cut each tuna steak into thin slices; fan out slices onto serving plates. Drizzle tuna slices with reserved soy sauce mixture; sprinkle with cilantro.
Makes 4 servings

*Tuna becomes dry and tough if overcooked. Tuna should be cooked as if it were beef.

Grilled Fish with Chili-Corn Salsa

1 cup cooked whole kernel corn
1 large tomato, seeded and chopped
¼ cup thinly sliced green onions with tops
¼ cup canned diced green chilies
1 tablespoon coarsely chopped fresh cilantro
⅛ teaspoon ground cumin
1 tablespoon lime juice
4 teaspoons olive oil, divided
Salt and black pepper
1½ pounds firm-textured fish steaks or fillets such as salmon, halibut, sea bass or swordfish, *each* 1 inch thick
Fresh cilantro sprigs for garnish

Preheat grill and grease grid. For salsa, combine corn, tomato, green onions, green chilies, cilantro, cumin, juice and 2 teaspoons oil in small bowl; mix well. Add salt and pepper to taste. Let stand at room temperature 30 minutes for flavors to blend.

Brush fish with remaining 2 teaspoons oil; season with salt and pepper. Place fish on grid. Grill 4 to 6 inches over medium-hot coals. Grill, turning once, 4 to 5 minutes on each side or until fish turns opaque and just begins to flake. Serve with salsa. Garnish, if desired. *Makes 4 servings*

Tip: To prevent fish from sticking, cook on a clean well-oiled preheated grill.

Szechuan Tuna Steak

Grilled Vegetable Kabobs

1 large red or green bell pepper
1 large zucchini
1 large yellow squash or additional zucchini
12 ounces large mushrooms
2 tablespoons olive oil
2 tablespoons red wine vinegar
1 package (7.2 ounces) RICE-A-RONI® Herb & Butter
1 large tomato, chopped
¼ cup grated Parmesan cheese

1. Cut red pepper into twelve 1-inch pieces. Cut zucchini and yellow squash crosswise into twelve ½-inch slices. Marinate red pepper, zucchini, yellow squash and mushrooms in combined oil and vinegar 15 minutes.

2. Alternately thread marinated vegetables onto 4 large metal skewers. Brush with any remaining oil mixture; set aside.

3. Prepare Rice-A-Roni® Mix as package directs.

4. While Rice-A-Roni® is simmering, grill kabobs over medium-low coals or broil 4 to 5 inches from heat 12 to 14 minutes or until tender and browned, turning once.

5. Stir tomato into rice. Serve rice topped with kabobs. Sprinkle with cheese.

Makes 4 servings

Grilled Corn in the Husk

6 ears fresh corn, unhusked
½ cup butter or margarine, softened
1 tablespoon LAWRY'S® Seasoned Salt
1 teaspoon LAWRY'S® Seasoned Pepper or freshly ground black pepper
String

Heat grill for medium coals. Peel husks back carefully and remove silk. In small bowl, combine butter, Seasoned Salt and Seasoned Pepper. Spread each ear with seasoned butter. Smooth husks over corn and tie ends together with string. Grill corn, 4 to 5 inches from heat, about 20 minutes or until tender, turning every 5 minutes. *Makes 6 side-dish servings*

Presentation: Extra seasoned butter may be served with corn.

Grilled Vegetable Kabobs

Grilled Vegetable and Ravioli Salad

Fiesta Grilled Polenta

1½ cups corn meal
2 (13¾-ounce) cans chicken broth (3½ cups)
½ cup MIRACLE WHIP® Salad Dressing
½ cup (2 ounces) KRAFT® 100% Grated Parmesan Cheese
⅓ cup *each:* finely chopped red bell pepper, finely chopped green onion
1 (4-ounce) can chopped green chilies, drained
¼ teaspoon ground red pepper

• Stir together corn meal and chicken broth in 2½-quart casserole; cover. Microwave on HIGH 10 to 12 minutes or until thickened, stirring every 4 minutes.

• Stir in remaining ingredients. Spread into lightly greased 13 × 9-inch baking dish; chill until firm.

• Cut mixture into twelve 3-inch squares. Cut each square in half diagonally.

• Place corn meal pieces on greased grill over hot coals (coals will be glowing). Grill, covered, 5 to 6 minutes on each side or until lightly browned.

Makes 8 side-dish servings

Prep time: 15 minutes plus refrigerating
Grilling time: 12 minutes

Grilled Vegetable and Ravioli Salad

1 package (9 ounces) CONTADINA® Refrigerated Fat Free Garden Vegetable Ravioli, cooked and drained
1 pound assorted fresh vegetables, such as zucchini, onion, eggplant, red, yellow or green bell peppers, grilled and diced
1 cup lightly packed, torn assorted salad greens
1⅔ cups (12-ounce container) CONTADINA® Refrigerated Light Garden Vegetable Sauce
2 tablespoons olive oil
2 tablespoons red wine vinegar

In medium bowl, combine ravioli, vegetables and salad greens. In small bowl, combine garden vegetable sauce, oil and vinegar; mix well. Add to pasta; toss well. Serve immediately. *Makes 4 servings*

Creole-Style Corn-on-the-Cob

8 ears fresh corn, unhusked
¾ cup butter or margarine
¼ cup minced green bell pepper
¼ cup minced red bell pepper
¼ cup minced green onions
1 teaspoon minced garlic
2 teaspoons LAWRY'S® Seasoned Salt
1 teaspoon dried thyme leaves, crumbled
1 bay leaf, crumbled
¼ cup dry white wine
1 tablespoon fresh lemon juice

In large bowl, place corn and cover with cold water; let soak overnight. Heat grill for low coals. Grill in husk, 4 to 5 inches from heat, 20 to 25 minutes or until tender. In medium heavy saucepan, melt butter over low heat. Add peppers, onions, garlic, Seasoned Salt, thyme and bay leaf; sauté 1 to 2 minutes. Add wine and lemon juice; cook 2 minutes.

Makes 8 side-dish servings

Presentation: Pull corn husks and silk back to use as "handles." Dip corn in sauce.

Grilled Cajun Potato Wedges

3 large russet potatoes (about 2¼ pounds)
¼ cup olive oil
2 cloves garlic, minced
1 teaspoon salt
1 teaspoon paprika
½ teaspoon dried thyme leaves, crushed
½ teaspoon dried oregano leaves, crushed
¼ teaspoon black pepper
⅛ to ¼ teaspoon ground red pepper
2 cups mesquite chips

Prepare grill. Preheat oven to 425°F. Meanwhile, cut potatoes in half lengthwise, then cut each half lengthwise into 4 wedges. Place potatoes in large bowl. Add oil and garlic; toss to coat well. Combine salt, paprika, thyme, oregano, black pepper and ground red pepper in small bowl. Sprinkle over potatoes; toss to coat well. Place potato wedges in single layer in shallow roasting pan. (Reserve remaining oil mixture left in large bowl.) Bake 20 minutes. Meanwhile, cover mesquite chips with cold water; soak 20 minutes.

Drain mesquite chips; sprinkle over coals. Place potato wedges on their sides on grid. Grill, on covered grill, over medium coals 15 to 20 minutes or until potatoes are browned and fork-tender, brushing with reserved oil mixture halfway through grilling time and turning once.

Makes 4 to 6 side-dish servings

Grilled Cajun Potato Wedges

Skewered Vegetables

2 medium zucchini, cut lengthwise into halves, then cut into 1-inch slices
8 pearl onions, cut into halves
½ red bell pepper, cut into 1-inch pieces
8 medium fresh mushrooms (optional)
16 lemon slices
2 tablespoons butter or margarine, melted
Salt and black pepper

Place zucchini, onions and red pepper in medium saucepan with enough water to cover. Bring to a boil. Cover; boil for 1 minute. Remove with slotted spoon and drain well. Alternately thread zucchini, onions, red pepper, mushrooms and lemon slices onto 8 metal or bamboo skewers. (Soak bamboo skewers in water at least 20 minutes to keep them from burning.)

Grilled Tri-Colored Pepper Salad

Oil hot grid to help prevent sticking. Grill vegetables, on a covered grill, over medium-hot KINGSFORD® Briquets, 6 minutes or until tender, carefully turning skewers once and basting with butter. Season with salt and pepper to taste. Serve immediately. *Makes 8 side-dish servings*

Grilled Tri-Colored Pepper Salad

Fresh basil leaves
1 *each* large red, yellow and green bell pepper, cut into halves or quarters
⅓ cup extra-virgin olive oil
3 tablespoons balsamic vinegar
2 cloves garlic, minced
¼ teaspoon salt
¼ teaspoon black pepper
⅓ cup crumbled goat cheese (about 1½ ounces)

Prepare grill. Meanwhile, layer basil leaves with largest leaf on bottom, then roll up jelly-roll style. Slice basil roll into very thin slices; separate into strips. Slice enough leaves to measure ¼ cup. Set aside. Place bell peppers, skin sides down, on grid. Grill, on covered grill, over hot coals 10 to 12 minutes or until skin is charred. To steam bell peppers and loosen skin, place charred bell peppers in paper bag. Close bag; set aside to cool 10 to 15 minutes. Remove skin with paring knife; discard skin.

Place bell peppers in shallow glass serving dish. Combine oil, vinegar, garlic, salt and black pepper in small bowl; whisk until well combined. Pour over bell peppers. Let stand 30 minutes at room temperature. (Or, cover and refrigerate up to 24 hours. Bring bell peppers to room temperature before serving.) Sprinkle bell peppers with cheese and basil just before serving.

Makes 4 to 6 side-dish servings

Grilled Corn-on-the-Cob

¼ pound butter or margarine, softened
1 tablespoon KIKKOMAN® Soy Sauce
½ teaspoon dried tarragon leaves, crumbled
6 ears fresh corn

Thoroughly blend butter, soy sauce and tarragon leaves. Husk corn. Lay each ear on piece of foil large enough to wrap around it; spread ears generously with seasoned butter. Wrap foil around corn; seal edges. Place on grill 3 inches from hot coals; cook 20 to 30 minutes, or until corn is tender, turning over frequently. (Or, place wrapped corn on baking sheet. Bake in 325°F oven 30 minutes.) Serve immediately.

Makes 6 side-dish servings

Note: Butter-soy mixture may also be spread on hot boiled corn.

Grilled Corn-on-the-Cob

Grilled Sweet Potato Packets with Pecan Butter

¼ cup chopped pecans
4 sweet potatoes (about 8 ounces *each*)
1 large sweet or Spanish onion, thinly sliced and separated into rings
3 tablespoons vegetable oil
⅓ cup butter or margarine, softened
2 tablespoons packed light brown sugar
¼ teaspoon salt
¼ teaspoon ground cinnamon

Prepare grill. Meanwhile, to toast pecans, spread in single layer on baking sheet. Bake in preheated 350°F oven 8 to 10 minutes or until golden brown, stirring frequently. Remove pecans from baking sheet; cool to room temperature. Set aside.

To prepare sweet potatoes, peel with vegetable peeler. Slice potatoes crosswise into ¼-inch-thick slices. Alternately place potato slices and onion rings on four 14 × 12-inch sheets of heavy-duty foil. Brush tops and sides with oil to prevent drying. Fold up foil, leaving space around edges and crimping all ends to make packets. Place packets on grid. Grill, on covered grill, over medium coals 25 to 30 minutes or until potatoes are fork-tender.

Meanwhile, to prepare Pecan Butter, combine butter, sugar, salt and cinnamon in small bowl; mix well. Stir in pecans. Open packets carefully; top each with dollop of Pecan Butter. *Makes 4 side-dish servings*

Grilled Vegetable Pizzas

1 package active dry quick-rise yeast
1 teaspoon sugar
⅔ cup warm water (105° to 115°F)
2 cups all-purpose flour
¾ teaspoon salt
3 tablespoons olive oil, divided
1 clove garlic, minced
1 red bell pepper, cut into quarters
4 slices red onion, cut ¼ inch thick
1 medium zucchini, halved lengthwise
1 medium yellow squash, halved lengthwise
1 cup prepared pizza sauce
¼ teaspoon crushed red pepper
2 cups (8 ounces) shredded fontinella or mozzarella cheese
¼ cup sliced fresh basil leaves

Sprinkle yeast and sugar over warm water in small bowl; stir until yeast is dissolved. Let stand 5 minutes or until mixture is bubbly.* Combine flour, yeast mixture and salt in large bowl. Beat with electric mixer at medium speed until dough forms a ball. Add 1 tablespoon oil; beat until well mixed.

Place dough on lightly-floured surface; flatten slightly. Knead dough 8 to 9 minutes or until dough is smooth and elastic. Shape dough into a ball; place in large greased bowl. Turn to grease entire surface. Cover with clean kitchen towel and let dough rise in warm place (80° to 85°F) 30 minutes or until doubled in bulk.

Meanwhile, prepare grill. Combine remaining 2 tablespoons oil and garlic in small bowl; brush over bell pepper, onion, zucchini and squash. Place vegetables on grid. Grill, on covered grill, over medium coals 10 minutes or until crisp-tender, turning halfway through grilling time. Remove vegetables from grill. Slice bell pepper lengthwise into ¼-inch strips. Cut zucchini and squash crosswise into ¼-inch slices. Separate onion slices into rings.

Punch dough down; divide into 4 equal balls. Flatten each ball into circle on lightly floured surface. Using lightly floured rolling pin, roll out each ball into 8-inch circle, starting at center and rolling to edges. Place 2 dough circles on grid. Grill, on covered grill, over medium coals 4 minutes or until bottoms are lightly browned. Transfer to large plates, grilled sides up. Repeat with remaining 2 dough circles.

Combine pizza sauce and crushed red pepper in small bowl; spread evenly over grilled sides of crusts. Sprinkle with cheese; top with grilled vegetables.

Place 2 pizzas on grid. Grill, on covered grill, over medium coals 5 minutes or until cheese is melted and crusts are cooked through. Repeat with remaining 2 pizzas. Sprinkle pizzas with basil; cut into wedges. Serve warm or at room temperature.

Makes 4 main-dish or 8 appetizer servings

*If yeast does not bubble, it is no longer active. Discard mixture and start over with new yeast. Always check expiration date on yeast package. Also, water that is too hot will kill yeast; it is best to use a thermometer.

Grilled Potatoes

4 medium baking potatoes, diced
½ cup Lipton® Onion Butter (page 208)
Chopped parsley

On four 18 × 10-inch pieces heavy-duty aluminum foil, divide potatoes equally; top each with 2 tablespoons Lipton® Onion Butter and sprinkle with parsley. Wrap foil loosely around potatoes, sealing edges airtight with double fold. Grill 30 minutes or until tender. *Makes 4 servings*

Serving Suggestion: Serve with Marinated Flank Steak (page 18) and Lipton® Iced Tea.

Grilled Vegetable Pizza

Grilled Vegetables

Grilled Vegetables

¼ cup minced fresh herbs, such as parsley, thyme, rosemary, oregano or basil
1 small eggplant (about ¾ pound), cut into ¼-inch-thick slices
½ teaspoon salt
1 *each* red, green and yellow bell pepper, quartered and seeded
2 zucchini, cut lengthwise into ¼-inch-thick slices
1 fennel bulb, cut lengthwise into ¼-inch-thick slices
Nonstick cooking spray

Combine herbs of your choice in small bowl; set aside.

Place eggplant in large colander over bowl; sprinkle with salt. Drain 1 hour. Prepare grill. Spray vegetables with cooking spray and sprinkle with herb mixture. Grill over medium-hot coals 10 to 15 minutes or until fork-tender and lightly browned on both sides. (Cooking times vary depending on type of vegetable; remove vegetables as they are done to avoid overcooking.)

Makes 6 side-dish servings

Variation: Cut vegetables into 1-inch cubes and thread onto skewers. Spray with cooking spray and sprinkle with herb mixture. Grill as directed.

Serving Suggestion: Serve over pasta or rice for a delicious vegetarian entrée.

Italian Bread with Tomato Appetizers

3 medium tomatoes, seeded and finely chopped
2 tablespoons finely chopped red onion
1 tablespoon chopped fresh basil leaves
¼ teaspoon ground black pepper (optional)
8 tablespoons WISH-BONE® Italian Dressing,* divided
1 loaf Italian or French bread (about 18 inches long)

In small bowl, combine tomatoes, onion, basil, pepper and 2 tablespoons Italian dressing; set aside.

Slice bread diagonally into 18 slices. Brush 1 side of each slice with remaining 6 tablespoons dressing. Grill or broil bread until golden, turning once. Evenly top grilled slices with tomato mixture.

Makes 18 appetizer servings

*Also terrific with Wish-Bone® Robusto Italian or Lite Italian Dressing.

Note: Tomato mixture can be prepared ahead.

Grilled Ratatouille

- 3 tablespoons red wine vinegar
- 1 tablespoon olive oil
- 2 teaspoons fresh thyme leaves
- ½ teaspoon ground black pepper
- 4 small Japanese eggplants, cut lengthwise into ½-inch-thick slices
- 2 small zucchini, cut in half lengthwise
- 1 medium red onion, quartered
- 1 red bell pepper, halved and seeded
- 1 yellow bell pepper, halved and seeded
- 6 ounces uncooked ziti or penne pasta
- ½ cup ⅓-less-salt chicken broth
- 1 tablespoon honey
- 1 tablespoon Dijon mustard
- ½ teaspoon Italian seasoning
- ¼ teaspoon salt
- 1 cup cherry tomato halves

Combine vinegar, oil, thyme and black pepper in large shallow glass bowl. Add eggplants, zucchini, onion and bell peppers; toss to coat evenly. Let stand at room temperature 1 hour or cover and refrigerate overnight.

Prepare grill. Meanwhile, cook pasta according to package directions, omitting salt. Drain and rinse well under cold water; set aside. Remove vegetables, reserving marinade. Grill vegetables over medium-hot coals about 3 to 4 minutes per side or until tender. Cool vegetables; cut into 1-inch pieces.

Combine vegetables and pasta in large bowl. Add broth, honey, mustard, Italian seasoning and salt to reserved marinade; whisk to combine. Pour over vegetable-pasta mixture. Gently stir in tomato halves. Serve chilled or at room temperature.

Makes 9 (1-cup) servings

Savory Grilled Potatoes in Foil

- ½ cup MIRACLE WHIP® Salad Dressing
- 3 cloves garlic, minced
- ½ teaspoon paprika
- ¼ teaspoon *each:* salt, pepper
- 3 baking potatoes, cut into ¼-inch slices
- 1 large onion, sliced

• Mix salad dressing and seasonings in large bowl until well blended. Stir in potatoes and onions to coat.

• Divide potato mixture evenly among six 12-inch square pieces of heavy-duty foil. Seal each to form packet.

• Place foil packets on grill over medium-hot coals (coals will have slight glow). Grill, covered, 25 to 30 minutes or until potatoes are tender. *Makes 6 side-dish servings*

Prep time: 15 minutes
Grilling time: 30 minutes

Savory Grilled Potatoes in Foil

South-of-the-Border Vegetable Kabobs

5 cloves garlic, peeled
½ cup A.1.® BOLD Steak Sauce
¼ cup margarine, melted
1 tablespoon finely chopped cilantro
¾ teaspoon ground cumin
¼ teaspoon coarsely ground black pepper
⅛ teaspoon ground red pepper
3 ears corn, cut crosswise into 1½-inch-thick slices and blanched
3 medium plum tomatoes, cut into ½-inch slices
1 small zucchini, cut lengthwise into thin slices
1 cup baby carrots, blanched

South-of-the-Border Vegetable Kabobs

Mince 1 garlic clove; halve remaining garlic cloves and set aside. In small bowl, combine steak sauce, margarine, cilantro, minced garlic, cumin and peppers; set aside.

Alternately thread vegetables and halved garlic cloves onto 6 (10-inch) metal skewers. Grill kabobs over medium heat for 7 to 9 minutes or until vegetables are tender, turning and basting often with steak sauce mixture. Remove from skewers; serve immediately. *Makes 6 servings*

Grilled Corn Soup

4 ears Grilled Corn-on-the-Cob (recipe follows)
5 green onions
4 cups chicken broth, divided
Salt and black pepper

Cut kernels from cobs to make 2 to 2½ cups. Slice green onions, separating the white part from the green. Place corn, the white part of onions and 2 cups chicken broth in a blender or food processor; process until mixture is slightly lumpy. Place corn mixture in large saucepan; add remaining chicken broth. Simmer gently 15 minutes. Stir in sliced green onion tops; season with salt and pepper to taste.
Makes 4 to 6 servings

Grilled Corn-on-the-Cob: Turn back corn husks; do not remove. Remove silks with stiff brush; rinse corn under cold running water. Smooth husks back into position. Grill ears, on a covered grill, over medium-hot KINGSFORD® Briquets, about 25 minutes or until tender, turning corn often. Remove husks and serve.

Tip: Grilled corn-on-the-cob is an all-time favorite, so grill extra, and turn it into a fabulous quick soup the next day.

Herbed Mushroom Vegetable Medley

- **4 ounces button or crimini mushrooms, thinly sliced**
- **1 medium red or yellow bell pepper, cut into ¼-inch-wide strips**
- **1 medium zucchini, cut crosswise into ¼-inch-thick slices**
- **1 medium yellow squash, cut crosswise into ¼-inch-thick slices**
- **3 tablespoons butter or margarine, melted**
- **1 tablespoon chopped fresh thyme leaves *or* 1 teaspoon dried thyme leaves, crushed**
- **1 tablespoon chopped fresh basil leaves *or* 1 teaspoon dried basil leaves, crushed**
- **1 tablespoon chopped fresh chives *or* green onion tops**
- **1 clove garlic, minced**
- **¼ teaspoon salt**
- **¼ teaspoon black pepper**

Prepare grill. Combine mushrooms, bell pepper, zucchini and squash in large bowl. Combine butter, thyme, basil, chives, garlic, salt and black pepper in small bowl. Pour over vegetable mixture; toss to coat well.

Transfer mixture to 20 × 14-inch sheet of heavy-duty foil. Fold up foil, leaving space around edges and crimping all ends to make packet. Place packet on grid. Grill packet, on covered grill, over medium coals 20 to 25 minutes or until vegetables are fork-tender. Open packet carefully to serve.

Makes 4 to 6 side-dish servings

Herbed Mushroom Vegetable Medley

Grilled Vegetables

- **2 medium yams or sweet potatoes**
- **2 medium Japanese eggplants**
- **2 medium crookneck squash, zucchini or patty pan squash**
- **2 small turnips with tops**
- **¼ cup virgin olive oil**
- **1 teaspoon LAWRY'S® Red Pepper Seasoned Salt**

Heat grill for medium-hot coals. Scrub skins of vegetables but do not peel; trim ends. Slice yams lengthwise into ¾-inch-thick slices. Cut remaining vegetables in half lengthwise. In small bowl, combine olive oil and Red Pepper Seasoned Salt; brush generously on vegetables. Grill vegetables, cut sides down, 4 to 5 inches from heat, 10 to 15 minutes or until tender when pierced with a skewer, turning once.

Makes 6 to 8 side-dish servings

Presentation: Serve with other favorite barbecued foods.

Hint: You may substitute any vegetable combination.

Grilled Coriander Corn

4 ears fresh corn, unhusked
3 tablespoons butter or margarine, softened
1 teaspoon ground coriander
¼ teaspoon salt (optional)
⅛ teaspoon ground red pepper

Pull outer husks from top to base of each corn; leave husks attached to ear. (If desired, remove 1 strip of husk from inner portion of each ear; reserve for later use.) Strip away silk from corn. Place corn in large bowl. Cover with cold water; soak 20 to 30 minutes.

Meanwhile, prepare grill. Remove corn from water; pat kernels dry with paper towels. Combine butter, coriander, salt and ground red pepper in small bowl. Spread evenly over kernels. Bring husks back up over each ear of corn; secure at top with paper-covered metal twist-ties. (Or, use reserved strips of corn husk to tie knots at the top of each ear, if desired.) Place corn on grid. Grill, on covered grill, over medium-hot coals 20 to 25 minutes or until corn is hot and tender, turning halfway through grilling time.

Makes 4 side-dish servings

Note: For ember cooking, prepare corn as directed, but omit soaking in cold water. Wrap each ear securely in heavy-duty foil. Place directly on coals. Grill, in covered grill, on medium-hot coals 25 to 30 minutes or until corn is hot and tender, turning every 10 minutes.

Grilled Garlic and Vegetables

8 whole heads fresh garlic*
2 artichokes, trimmed and quartered
4 ears corn, cut crosswise in half
2 carrots, cut into 1-inch chunks
2 zucchini, cut into 1-inch chunks
1 cup butter or margarine
8 sprigs fresh rosemary *or* 4 teaspoons dried rosemary, crushed
½ cup sliced almonds
Salt and black pepper

Prepare grill. Peel outer skin from garlic, keeping cloves intact. Cut 16 (12-inch) squares of heavy-duty foil. On double thickness of foil, place 1 whole head garlic, 1 artichoke quarter, 1 corn half and ⅛ *each* of carrot and zucchini chunks. Repeat to obtain 7 more packets. Dot *each* packet with 2 tablespoons butter; top with sprig of rosemary *or* ½ teaspoon dried rosemary, 1 tablespoon almonds and sprinkle with salt and pepper to taste. Fold up foil, leaving space around edges and crimping all ends to make packets. Place packets on grid. Grill over hot coals 40 to 45 minutes or until vegetables are tender, turning occasionally. *Makes 8 side-dish servings*

*The whole garlic bulb is called a head.

Favorite recipe from **Christopher Ranch Garlic**

Grilled Coriander Corn

Grilled Pasta Salad

Grilled Pasta Salad

- **4 medium zucchini and/or yellow squash, sliced**
- **1 medium Spanish onion, halved and cut into large chunks**
- **1 envelope LIPTON® Recipe Secrets® Savory Herb with Garlic Soup Mix***
- **¼ cup olive or vegetable oil**
- **8 ounces penne, rotini or ziti pasta, cooked and drained**
- **¾ cup diced roasted red peppers**
- **¼ cup red wine vinegar, apple cider vinegar or white vinegar**

*Also terrific with Lipton® Recipe Secrets® Italian Herb with Tomato or Golden Onion Soup Mix.

On heavy-duty aluminum foil or on broiler pan, arrange zucchini and onion. Brush with savory herb with garlic soup mix blended with oil. Grill or broil 5 minutes or until golden brown and crisp-tender. In large bowl, toss cooked pasta, vegetables, roasted peppers and vinegar. Serve warm or at room temperature.

Makes about 4 main-dish or 8 side-dish servings

Serving Suggestion: Serve with hot crusty bread and a spinach salad.

Grilled Vegetables al Fresco

- **2 large red bell peppers**
- **2 medium zucchini**
- **1 large eggplant**

Spicy Marinade

- **⅔ cup white wine vinegar**
- **½ cup soy sauce**
- **2 tablespoons minced fresh ginger**
- **2 tablespoons olive oil**
- **2 tablespoons Oriental sesame oil**
- **2 large cloves garlic, minced**
- **2 teaspoons TABASCO® pepper sauce**

Core and seed red peppers; cut each pepper into quarters. Cut each zucchini lengthwise into ¼-inch-thick strips. Slice eggplant into ¼-inch-thick rounds. In 13 × 9-inch baking dish, combine Spicy Marinade ingredients. Place vegetable pieces in mixture; toss to mix well. Cover and refrigerate vegetables at least 2 hours or up to 24 hours, turning occasionally.

About 30 minutes before serving, prepare grill. Place red peppers, zucchini and eggplant slices on grill rack. Grill, 5 to 6 inches over medium coals, 4 minutes or until vegetables are tender, turning once and brushing with marinade occasionally.

Makes 4 side-dish servings

Hot Blue Cheese Dip with Grilled Vegetables

2 tablespoons margarine
2 tablespoons all-purpose flour
1½ cups milk
¾ cup A.1.® Steak Sauce, divided
⅓ cup crumbled blue cheese (about 1½ ounces)
1 medium eggplant, quartered lengthwise and cut into ½-inch-thick slices
2 small zucchini, cut into ½-inch rounds
12 medium mushrooms (about 4 ounces)
8 green onions, cut into 2-inch pieces
2 small red bell peppers, cut into 1-inch strips
2 tablespoons olive oil

Soak 12 (10-inch) wooden skewers in water for at least 30 minutes. In medium saucepan, over medium heat, melt margarine. Stir in flour; cook for 1 minute. Gradually stir in milk; cook and stir until mixture thickens and begins to boil. Stir in ½ cup steak sauce and cheese; heat until cheese melts. Keep cheese dip warm.

Alternately thread vegetables onto skewers. Combine remaining steak sauce and oil. Grill vegetables over medium heat for 8 to 10 minutes or until vegetables are tender, turning and brushing with steak sauce/oil mixture. Serve with cheese dip.

Makes 12 appetizer servings

Skewered Grilled Potatoes

2 pounds red potatoes, quartered
⅓ cup cold water
½ cup MIRACLE WHIP® Salad Dressing
¼ cup dry white wine or chicken broth
2 teaspoons dried rosemary leaves, crushed
1 teaspoon garlic powder

• Place potatoes and water in 2-quart microwave-safe casserole; cover.

• Microwave on HIGH 12 to 15 minutes or until tender, stirring after 8 minutes. Drain.

• Mix remaining ingredients until well blended. Stir in potatoes. Refrigerate 1 hour. Drain, reserving marinade.

• Arrange potatoes on skewers. Place on grill over hot coals (coals will be glowing). Grill, covered, 6 to 8 minutes or until potatoes are tender and golden brown, brushing occasionally with reserved marinade and turning after 4 minutes.

Makes 8 side-dish servings

Prep time: 20 minutes plus refrigerating
Grilling time: 8 minutes
Microwave cooking time: 15 minutes

Skewered Grilled Potatoes

BURGERS & SANDWICHES

Ranch Burgers

1¼ pounds lean ground beef
¾ cup prepared HIDDEN VALLEY RANCH® Original Ranch® Salad Dressing
¾ cup dry bread crumbs
¼ cup minced onions
1 teaspoon salt
¼ teaspoon black pepper
Sesame seed buns
Lettuce, tomato slices and red onion slices (optional)
Additional Original Ranch® Salad Dressing

In large bowl, combine beef, salad dressing, bread crumbs, onions, salt and pepper. Shape into 6 patties. Grill over medium-hot coals 4 to 5 minutes for medium doneness. Place on sesame seed buns with lettuce, tomato and red onion slices, if desired. Serve with a generous amount of additional salad dressing.

Makes 6 servings

Mushroom-Stuffed Pork Burgers

1½ pounds lean ground pork
2 teaspoons butter or margarine
¾ cup thinly sliced fresh mushrooms
¼ cup thinly sliced green onion
1 clove garlic, minced
1 teaspoon Dijon mustard
1 teaspoon Worcestershire sauce
¼ teaspoon salt
⅛ teaspoon black pepper
Hamburger buns (optional)

Prepare grill. Melt butter in small skillet; add mushrooms, onion and garlic. Cook and stir over medium-high heat about 2 minutes or until tender; set aside.

Combine ground pork, mustard, Worcestershire, salt and pepper; mix well. Shape into 12 patties, about 4 inches in diameter. Spoon mushroom mixture onto center of 6 patties. Spread to within ½ inch of edge. Top with remaining 6 patties; seal edges to enclose filling. Place patties on grid. Grill about 6 inches over medium coals 10 to 15 minutes, turning once. Serve on buns, if desired. *Makes 6 servings*

Prep time: 15 minutes
Cooking time: 15 minutes

Favorite recipe from ***National Pork Producers Council***

Ranch Burger

Open-Faced Mesquite Steak Sandwiches

Tomato-Cheese Burgers

2 pounds ground beef
¼ cup KIKKOMAN® Soy Sauce
3 tablespoons instant minced onion
½ teaspoon garlic salt
1 large tomato, cut into 6 slices
6 cheese slices

Thoroughly combine beef, soy sauce, onion and garlic salt; shape into 12 patties. On each of 6 patties, place 1 slice of tomato. Top with remaining patties; pinch edges together to seal. Place on grill 4 to 5 inches from hot coals; cook 3 minutes on each side (for rare), or to desired doneness. (Or, broil patties 3 minutes on each side [for rare], or to desired doneness.) Top burgers immediately with cheese.

Makes 6 servings

Open-Faced Mesquite Steak Sandwiches

1 pound flank steak
½ cup LAWRY'S® Mesquite Marinade with Lime Juice
8 slices sourdough bread or thin French bread
4 ounces refried beans
1 small red onion, thinly sliced
1 medium-sized green bell pepper, thinly sliced
½ cup chunky-style salsa
4 ounces Cheddar cheese, sliced

Heat grill for medium coals or heat broiler. Pierce steak several times with fork. In large resealable plastic bag or shallow glass baking dish, place steak. Pour Mesquite Marinade with Lime Juice over steak. Seal bag or cover dish. Marinate in refrigerator at least 30 minutes. Remove steak, discarding marinade. Grill or broil, 4 to 5 inches from heat source, 4 to 5 minutes on each side or to desired doneness. Thinly slice steak across the grain of meat; set aside. Spread bread slices with refried beans; cover with meat, onion and bell pepper. Top with salsa and cheese. Grill or broil 1 minute or just until cheese is melted.

Makes 4 servings

Presentation: Serve warm with a crisp green salad or mixed vegetables.

Mediterranean Burgers

½ cup feta cheese (2 ounces)
¼ cup A.1.® Steak Sauce, divided
2 tablespoons sliced ripe olives
2 tablespoons mayonnaise
1 pound ground beef
4 regular pita breads
4 lettuce leaves
4 tomato slices

In small bowl, combine feta cheese, 2 tablespoons steak sauce, olives and mayonnaise. Cover; chill until ready to serve.

Shape beef into 4 patties; grill over medium heat for 5 minutes on each side or to desired doneness, brushing with remaining 2 tablespoons steak sauce. Split open top edge of each pita bread. Place 1 lettuce leaf in each pita pocket; top each with burger, tomato slice and 2 tablespoons prepared sauce. Serve hot. *Makes 4 servings*

Vegetarian Burgers

½ cup A.1.® Steak Sauce, divided
¼ cup plain yogurt
⅔ cup slivered almonds
⅔ cup salted peanuts
⅔ cup sunflower kernels
½ cup chopped green bell pepper
¼ cup chopped onion
1 clove garlic, minced
1 tablespoon red wine vinegar
4 (5-inch) pita breads, halved
4 lettuce leaves
4 tomato slices

In small bowl, combine ¼ cup steak sauce and yogurt; set aside.

In food processor or blender, process almonds, peanuts, sunflower kernels, green pepper, onion and garlic until coarsely chopped. With motor running, slowly add remaining steak sauce and vinegar until blended; shape mixture into 4 patties.

Grill burgers over medium heat for 1½ minutes on each side or until heated through, turning once. Split open top edge of each pita bread. Layer lettuce, burger, tomato slice and 2 tablespoons prepared sauce in each pita bread half. Serve immediately. *Makes 4 servings*

Note: Sauce may also be served with beef burgers.

Giant Cheeseburgers

1½ cups shredded Monterey Jack cheese (about 6 ounces)
1 can (2¼ ounces) chopped ripe olives, drained
⅛ teaspoon hot pepper sauce
1¾ pounds ground beef
¼ cup finely chopped onion
1 teaspoon salt
½ teaspoon black pepper
6 whole wheat hamburger buns
Butter or margarine, melted

Combine cheese, olives and pepper sauce; mix well. Divide mixture evenly and shape into 6 balls. Mix ground beef with onion, salt and pepper; shape into 12 thin patties. Place a cheese ball in center of 6 patties and top each with a second patty. Seal edges of each patty to enclose cheese ball. Lightly oil grid. Grill patties, on a covered grill, over medium-hot KINGSFORD® Briquets 5 to 6 minutes on each side or to desired doneness. Split buns, brush with butter and place, buttered sides down, on grill to heat through. Serve cheeseburgers on buns.
Makes 6 servings

Vegetarian Burger

Savory Stuffed Turkey Burgers

- **1 pound ground turkey**
- **¼ cup A.1.® BOLD Steak Sauce, divided**
- **¼ cup chopped onion**
- **½ teaspoon dried thyme leaves**
- **¼ teaspoon ground black pepper**
- **½ cup prepared herb bread stuffing**
- **½ cup whole berry cranberry sauce**
- **4 slices whole wheat bread, toasted**
- **4 lettuce leaves**

In medium bowl, combine turkey, 2 tablespoons steak sauce, onion, thyme and pepper; shape into 8 thin patties. Place 2 tablespoons prepared stuffing in center of each of 4 patties. Top with remaining patties. Seal edges to form 4 patties; set aside.

In small bowl, combine remaining 2 tablespoons steak sauce and cranberry sauce; set aside.

Savory Stuffed Turkey Burger

Grill burgers over medium heat for 10 minutes on each side or until no longer pink. Top each bread slice with lettuce leaf and burger. Serve immediately topped with prepared cranberry sauce mixture.

Makes 4 servings

Charcoal Broiled Burgers Cha Cha Cha

- **2 pounds lean ground beef**
- **½ cup *each* prepared salsa and finely crushed tortilla chips**
- **2 teaspoons chili powder**
- **½ teaspoon salt**
- **8 hamburger buns, split**
- **2 cups (8 ounces) SARGENTO® Classic Supreme Shredded Cheese For Tacos**
- **¾ cup chopped fresh tomatoes**
- **¾ cup shredded leaf lettuce *or* chopped pepperoncini (optional)**

Prepare grill. Combine ground beef, salsa, tortilla chips, chili powder and salt in large bowl; mix lightly but thoroughly. Shape into 8 (½-inch-thick) patties, about 4 inches in diameter. Place bun tops, cut sides up, in foil pan large enough to hold in one layer. Divide Taco cheese evenly over bun tops. Cover with foil. Place on one edge of grid and place patties in center of grid. Grill patties over medium-hot coals about 5 minutes on each side for medium or to desired doneness. Serve patties on bun bottoms; top with tomatoes and lettuce or pepperoncini, if desired. Cover with bun tops, cheese sides down.

Makes 8 servings

Cowboy Burgers

1 pound ground beef
½ teaspoon LAWRY'S® Seasoned Salt
½ teaspoon LAWRY'S® Seasoned Pepper
2 tablespoons *plus* 2 teaspoons butter or margarine
1 large onion, thinly sliced and separated into rings
1 package (1.25 ounces) LAWRY'S® Taco Spices & Seasonings
4 slices Cheddar cheese
4 kaiser rolls
Lettuce leaves
Tomato slices

Heat grill for medium-hot coals or heat broiler. In medium bowl, combine ground beef, Seasoned Salt and Seasoned Pepper; shape into 4 patties. Grill or broil, 4 to 5 inches from heat source, 4 minutes on each side for rare or to desired doneness. Meanwhile, in medium skillet, melt butter. Add onion and Taco Spices & Seasonings; blend well. Sauté until onion is tender and translucent. Top each patty with cheese. Return to grill or broiler until cheese is melted. On bottom half of each roll, place lettuce, tomato and patty; cover with onion and top half of roll. *Makes 4 servings*

Presentation: Serve with hot baked beans.

Cowboy Burger

Grilled Eggplant Sandwiches

1 eggplant (about 1¼ pounds)
Salt and black pepper
6 thin slices Provolone cheese
6 thin slices deli-style ham or mortadella
Fresh basil leaves (optional)
Olive oil

Cut eggplant into 12 (⅜-inch-thick) rounds; sprinkle both sides with salt and pepper. Top each of 6 eggplant slices with a slice of cheese, a slice of meat (fold or tear to fit) and a few basil leaves, if desired. Cover with a slice of eggplant. Brush one side with olive oil. Secure each sandwich with 2 or 3 toothpicks.

Oil hot grid to help prevent sticking. Grill eggplant, oil side down, on a covered grill, over medium KINGSFORD® Briquets, 15 to 20 minutes. Halfway through cooking time, brush top with oil, then turn and continue grilling until eggplant is tender when pierced. (When turning, position sandwiches so toothpicks extend down between spaces in grid.) If eggplant starts to char, move to a cooler part of the grill. Let sandwiches cool about 5 minutes, then cut into halves or quarters, if desired. Serve warm or at room temperature.

Makes 6 sandwiches

Serving Suggestion: Cut into halves or quarters, these sandwiches make terrific hors d'oeuvres.

Greek Burgers

Yogurt Sauce (recipe follows)
1 pound ground beef
2 teaspoons ground cumin
1 tablespoon chopped fresh oregano *or* 1 teaspoon dried oregano leaves
½ teaspoon salt
Dash ground red pepper
Dash black pepper
2 tablespoons red wine
4 pita breads, cut in half
Lettuce
Chopped tomatoes

Prepare Yogurt Sauce. Soak 4 bamboo skewers in water 30 minutes to prevent burning. Meanwhile, combine ground beef, seasonings and wine in medium bowl; mix lightly. Divide mixture into 8 equal portions; form each portion into an oval, each about 4 inches long. Cover; chill 30 minutes.

Preheat grill. Insert skewers lengthwise through centers of ovals, placing 2 on each skewer. Place skewers on grid. Grill over medium-hot coals about 8 minutes or to desired doneness, turning once. Fill each pita bread half with lettuce, burger and chopped tomatoes. Serve with Yogurt Sauce. *Makes 4 servings (2 halves each)*

Yogurt Sauce

2 cups plain yogurt
1 cup chopped red onion
1 cup chopped cucumber
¼ cup chopped fresh mint *or* 4½ teaspoons dried mint leaves
1 tablespoon chopped fresh marjoram *or* 1 teaspoon dried marjoram leaves

Combine ingredients in small bowl. Cover; refrigerate up to 4 hours before serving.

Grilled Chicken Croissant Monterey

½ cup A.1.® Steak Sauce, divided
1 tablespoon olive oil
1 tablespoon finely chopped parsley
1 teaspoon dried minced onion
¼ cup mayonnaise
4 boneless chicken breast halves, gently pounded (about 12 ounces)
4 slices Muenster cheese (about 3 ounces)
4 croissants (6 × 3 inches *each*), split
4 lettuce leaves
1 small avocado, peeled, pitted and sliced
4 tomato slices

In small bowl, combine ¼ cup steak sauce, oil, parsley and onion; set aside for basting.

In separate bowl, combine remaining ¼ cup steak sauce and mayonnaise; set aside. (Discard any remaining basting sauce.)

Grill chicken over medium heat for 6 minutes or until no longer pink in center, turning and brushing often with basting sauce. Top each chicken breast with cheese slice; grill until cheese melts.

To serve, spread 1 tablespoon reserved steak sauce/mayonnaise mixture on bottom of each croissant; top with lettuce leaf, avocado slices, tomato slice and chicken breast. Spread 1 tablespoon steak sauce/mayonnaise mixture on each chicken breast; top with croissant top. Serve immediately. *Makes 4 servings*

Greek Burgers

Lahaina Burgers

Lahaina Burgers

1¼ pounds lean ground beef
¼ cup *plus* 1 tablespoon KIKKOMAN® Lite Teriyaki Marinade & Sauce, divided
4 green onions and tops, chopped
1 teaspoon minced fresh ginger root
1 large clove garlic, minced
1 egg, slightly beaten
1 slice bread, torn into small pieces
1 can (8 ounces) sliced pineapple, drained

Thoroughly combine beef, ¼ cup lite teriyaki sauce, green onions, ginger, garlic, egg and bread; shape into 4 patties. Place on grill 4 to 5 inches from hot coals. Cook 3 minutes; turn over. Cook 3 minutes longer (for rare), or to desired doneness. During last 2 minutes of cooking time, place pineapple slices on grill. Cook 1 minute. Turn over and brush with remaining 1 tablespoon lite teriyaki sauce. Cook 1 minute longer. (Or, place patties on rack of broiler pan. Broil 4 minutes; turn over. Broil 3 minutes longer [for rare], or to desired doneness. During last 2 minutes of cooking time, place pineapple slices on broiler pan. Broil 1 minute. Turn over and brush with remaining 1 tablespoon lite teriyaki sauce. Broil 1 minute longer.) Top patties with pineapple just before serving.

Makes 4 servings

BelGioioso Gorgonzola Burgers

4 ounces BelGioioso Gorgonzola cheese (soft and creamy)
1½ pounds ground chuck
Salt and black pepper to taste
Olive oil
4 hamburger buns, split
8 thin slices red onion
4 thick slices tomato
Spicy Dijon mustard

Prepare grill. Cut Gorgonzola into 4 pieces and shape each piece into a flat round. Divide ground chuck into 8 patties. Place 1 Gorgonzola piece in center of 4 patties. Top with remaining patties; seal edges to form 4 patties. Season with salt and pepper.

Place burgers on grid. Grill over medium coals 4 minutes on each side or to desired doneness. Meanwhile, brush olive oil on buns. Grill, oil sides down, or toast buns. Serve burgers on buns with onion, tomato and mustard. *Makes 4 servings*

Favorite recipe from ***Auricchio Cheese, Inc.***

Swiss Burgers

1½ pounds ground beef
¾ cup shredded Swiss cheese (about 3 ounces)
1 can (8 ounces) sauerkraut, drained and heated
½ cup WISH-BONE® Thousand Island or Lite Thousand Island Dressing

Shape ground beef into 6 patties. Grill or broil to desired doneness. Top evenly with cheese, sauerkraut and Thousand Island dressing. Serve with rye or pita bread, if desired. *Makes about 6 servings*

Burgers Canadian

½ cup mayonnaise
⅓ cup A.1.® Steak Sauce
2 tablespoons prepared horseradish
1 pound ground beef
2 ounces Cheddar cheese, sliced
4 slices Canadian bacon (4 ounces)
4 sesame sandwich rolls, split and lightly toasted
4 curly lettuce leaves

In small bowl, combine mayonnaise, steak sauce and horseradish. Cover; chill until serving time.

Shape ground beef into 4 patties. Grill burgers over medium heat for 4 minutes on each side or to desired doneness. When almost done, top with cheese; grill until cheese melts. Grill Canadian bacon over medium heat for 1 minute on each side or until heated through. Spread 2 tablespoons sauce on each roll bottom; top with burger, warm Canadian bacon slice, lettuce leaf and roll top. Serve immediately with remaining sauce for dipping.
Makes 4 servings

Gourmet Olé Burgers

1½ pounds ground beef
1 package (1.25 ounces) LAWRY'S® Taco Spices & Seasonings
¼ cup ketchup
Monterey Jack cheese slices
Salsa

Heat grill for medium-hot coals or heat broiler. In medium bowl, combine ground beef, Taco Spices & Seasonings and ketchup; blend well. Shape into patties. Grill or broil, 4 inches from heat source, 5 to 7 minutes on each side or to desired doneness. Top each burger with a slice of cheese. Return to grill or broiler until cheese melts. Top with a dollop of salsa.
Makes 6 to 8 servings

Presentation: Serve on lettuce-lined hamburger buns. Garnish with avocado slices, if desired.

Hint: Cut cheese with cookie cutters for interesting shapes.

Gourmet Olé Burger

Seasoned Burgers

1½ pounds lean ground beef
1½ teaspoons WYLER'S® or STEERO® Beef-Flavor Instant Bouillon

Combine ingredients; shape into patties. Grill or broil 5 to 7 minutes on each side or to desired doneness. Garnish as desired. Refrigerate leftovers. *Makes 4 servings*

Italian Burgers: Combine beef mixture with 2 tablespoons grated Parmesan cheese and 1 teaspoon Italian seasoning. Cook as directed. Serve with pizza sauce. Garnish as desired.

Oriental Burgers: Combine beef mixture with 1 (8-ounce) can water chestnuts, drained and chopped, and ¼ cup sliced green onions. Cook as directed. Top with pineapple slice; serve with BENNETT'S® Sweet & Sour Sauce. Garnish as desired.

Mexican Burgers: Combine beef mixture with 1 (4-ounce) can chopped green chilies, drained, and ¼ cup chopped onion. Cook as directed. Serve with BORDEN® or MEADOW GOLD® Sour Cream and salsa.

German Burgers: Combine beef mixture with 2 tablespoons chopped dill pickle and 1 teaspoon caraway seed. Cook as directed. Serve with sauerkraut.

Clockwise from top right: Mexican Burger, Italian Burger, Garden Burger and Oriental Burger

Garden Burgers: Combine beef mixture with 1 tablespoon chopped green bell pepper and 2 tablespoons Thousand Island dressing. Cook as directed. Serve with cole slaw and chopped tomato.

Grilled Pork Chop Sandwich with Goat Cheese Crostini

4 boneless pork chops, ¾ inch thick
1 (12-inch) loaf French bread, cut crosswise in half
2 teaspoons olive oil
4 ounces garlic-and-herb flavored goat cheese
2 tablespoons chopped fresh oregano *or* 2 teaspoons dried oregano leaves
1 cup shredded iceberg lettuce
¼ cup Italian salad dressing

Prepare grill. Place chops on grid. Grill over medium-hot coals 3 to 4 minutes on each side or until chops are juicy and barely pink in center. Remove chops to a serving platter; keep warm. Preheat broiler. Meanwhile, cut French bread pieces lengthwise in half. Brush cut sides of bread with olive oil, then spread with goat cheese. Sprinkle with oregano. Place bread pieces on foil-lined baking sheet and place under broiler 4 to 5 inches from heat; broil 1 to 2 minutes or until cheese is heated through. Sprinkle with lettuce. Thinly slice pork chops across grain. Arrange pork slices on top of lettuce. Drizzle with Italian dressing. *Makes 4 servings*

Prep time: 10 minutes
Cooking time: 10 minutes

Favorite recipe from **National Pork Producers Council**

Parmesan Burgers

1 pound ground beef
⅓ cup A.1.® Steak Sauce, divided
2 tablespoons grated Parmesan cheese
½ cup prepared spaghetti sauce
4 mozzarella cheese slices (about 2 ounces)
4 English muffins, split and grilled or toasted

In medium bowl, combine ground beef, 3 tablespoons steak sauce and Parmesan cheese; shape mixture into 4 patties. Set aside.

In small bowl, combine remaining steak sauce and spaghetti sauce; set aside.

Grill burgers over medium heat for 4 minutes on each side or to desired doneness. When almost done, top each with mozzarella cheese; grill until cheese melts. Spread 1 tablespoon steak sauce mixture on each muffin bottom; top each with burger, some of remaining sauce and muffin top. Serve immediately.
Makes 4 servings

Grilled Kikko-Burgers

1 pound ground beef
2 tablespoons instant minced onion
¼ teaspoon pepper
¼ teaspoon ground ginger
2 tablespoons KIKKOMAN® Soy Sauce

Thoroughly combine beef, onion, pepper, ginger and soy sauce; shape into 4 patties. Place 4 to 5 inches from hot coals; cook 6 minutes (for rare), or to desired doneness, turning over after 3 minutes. (Or, place patties on rack of broiler pan; broil 3 minutes on each side [for rare], or to desired doneness.) *Makes 4 servings*

Zesty Burgers

2 pounds ground beef
½ cup WISH-BONE® Italian Dressing*
2 tablespoons horseradish (optional)
1 carrot, grated
1 medium onion, finely chopped
2 eggs
1 cup plain dry bread crumbs

In large bowl, combine all ingredients; shape into 6 patties. Grill or broil to desired doneness. Serve on hamburger rolls, if desired. *Makes 6 servings*

*Also terrific with Wish-Bone® Robusto Italian.

Barbecued Pork Tenderloin Sandwiches

1 large red onion
½ cup ketchup
⅓ cup packed brown sugar
2 tablespoons bourbon or whiskey (optional)
1 tablespoon Worcestershire sauce
½ teaspoon dry mustard
¼ teaspoon ground red pepper
1 clove garlic, minced
2 whole pork tenderloins (about ¾ pound *each*), well trimmed
6 hoagie rolls or kaiser rolls, split

Prepare grill. Meanwhile, cut onion crosswise into six ¼-inch-thick slices. Set aside. Combine ketchup, sugar, bourbon, Worcestershire, mustard, red pepper and garlic in small heavy saucepan with ovenproof handle; mix well. (If not ovenproof, wrap heavy-duty foil around handle.)

Set saucepan on one side of grid.* Place tenderloins on center of grid. Grill tenderloins, on uncovered grill, over medium-hot coals 8 minutes. Simmer sauce 5 minutes or until thickened, stirring occasionally. Turn tenderloins; grill, uncovered, 5 minutes more. Add onion slices to grid. Set aside half the sauce; reserve for serving. Brush tenderloins and onions with some of remaining sauce. Grill, uncovered, 7 to 10 minutes or until pork is juicy and barely pink in center, brushing with remaining basting sauce and turning onions and tenderloins halfway through grilling time. (If desired, insert instant-read thermometer** into center of thickest part of tenderloins. Thermometer should register 160°F.)

Carve tenderloins crosswise into thin slices; separate onion slices into rings. Divide pork and onion rings among rolls; drizzle with reserved sauce. *Makes 6 servings*

*If desired, sauce may be prepared on range top. Combine ketchup, sugar, bourbon, Worcestershire, mustard, red pepper and garlic in small saucepan. Bring to a boil over medium-high heat. Reduce heat to low and simmer, uncovered, 5 minutes or until thickened, stirring occasionally.

**Do not leave instant-read thermometer in tenderloins during grilling since the thermometer is not heatproof.

Barbecued Pork Tenderloin Sandwich

Zesty Turkey Burger

Zesty Turkey Burgers

1 pound ground turkey
¼ cup BENNETT'S® Chili Sauce
1 teaspoon WYLER'S® or STEERO® Chicken-Flavor Instant Bouillon

Combine ingredients; shape into patties. Grill, broil or pan-fry until turkey is no longer pink. Serve with additional chili sauce if desired. Refrigerate leftovers.

Makes 4 servings

Inside-Out Brie Burgers

1 pound ground beef
5 tablespoons A.1.® Steak Sauce, divided
3 ounces Brie, cut into 4 slices
¼ cup dairy sour cream
2 tablespoons chopped green onion
1 medium red bell pepper, cut into ¼-inch rings
4 (2½-inch) slices Italian or French bread, halved
4 radicchio or lettuce leaves

In medium bowl, combine ground beef and 3 tablespoons steak sauce; shape into 8 thin patties. Place 1 slice of Brie in center of each of 4 patties. Top with remaining patties. Seal edges to form 4 patties; set aside.

In small bowl, combine remaining steak sauce, sour cream and onion; set aside.

Grill burgers over medium heat for 7 minutes on each side or to desired doneness. Place pepper rings on grill; grill with hamburgers until tender, about 4 to 5 minutes. Top each of 4 bread slice halves with radicchio, burger, pepper ring, 2 tablespoons prepared sauce and another bread slice half; serve immediately.

Makes 4 servings

Nutty Burgers

1½ pounds ground beef
1 medium onion, finely chopped
1 cup dry bread crumbs
⅔ cup pine nuts
⅓ cup grated Parmesan cheese
⅓ cup chopped fresh parsley
2 eggs
1 clove garlic, minced
1½ teaspoons salt
1 teaspoon black pepper
12 slices French bread (*each* ¼ inch thick) *or* 6 hamburger buns
Chopped green onions for garnish

Combine beef, onion, bread crumbs, pine nuts, cheese, parsley, eggs, garlic, salt and pepper in medium bowl. Shape meat mixture into 6 thick patties.

Oil hot grid to help prevent sticking. Grill patties, on a covered grill, over medium-hot KINGSFORD® Briquets, 10 minutes for medium doneness, turning once. Serve on French bread. Garnish with green onions, if desired.

Makes 6 servings

America's Favorite Cheddar Beef Burgers

1 pound ground beef
⅓ cup A.1.® Steak Sauce, divided
1 medium onion, cut into strips
1 medium green or red bell pepper, cut into strips
1 tablespoon margarine
4 ounces Cheddar cheese, sliced
4 hamburger rolls
4 tomato slices

In medium bowl, combine ground beef and 3 tablespoons steak sauce; shape mixture into 4 patties. Set aside.

In medium skillet, over medium heat, cook onion and pepper in margarine until tender, stirring occasionally. Stir in remaining steak sauce; keep warm.

Grill burgers over medium heat for 4 minutes on each side or to desired doneness. When almost done, top with cheese; grill until cheese melts. Spoon 2 tablespoons onion mixture onto each roll bottom; top each with burger, tomato slice, some of remaining onion mixture and roll top. Serve immediately.

Makes 4 servings

The Other Burger

1 pound ground pork (80% lean)
1 teaspoon black pepper
¼ teaspoon salt
Hamburger buns (optional)

Prepare grill. Gently mix together ground pork, pepper and salt; shape into 4 burgers about ¾ inch thick. Place burgers on grid. Grill, on covered grill, over medium-hot coals 5 minutes on each side or until barely pink in center. Serve on hamburger buns, if desired.

Makes 4 servings

Eastern Burger: Add 2 teaspoons soy sauce, 2 tablespoons dry sherry and 1 tablespoon grated ginger root to pork mixture; grill as directed.

Veggie Burger: Add 3 drops hot pepper sauce, 1 grated carrot and 3 tablespoons chopped parsley to pork mixture; grill as directed.

South-of-the-Border Burger: Add ¼ teaspoon *each* ground cumin, dried oregano leaves, seasoned salt and crushed red pepper to pork mixture; grill as directed.

Italian Burger: Add 1 pressed garlic clove, 1 teaspoon crushed fennel seeds and 2 teaspoons *each* red wine and olive oil to pork mixture; grill as directed.

Prep time: 10 minutes
Cooking time: 10 minutes

Favorite recipe from **National Pork Producers Council**

America's Favorite Cheddar Beef Burger

Sizzling Chicken Sandwiches

4 boneless, skinless chicken breast halves
1 package (1.27 ounces) LAWRY'S® Spices & Seasonings for Fajitas
1 cup chunky salsa
¼ cup water
Lettuce
4 large sandwich buns
4 slices Monterey Jack cheese
Red onion slices
Avocado slices
Additional chunky salsa

In large resealable plastic bag, place chicken. In small bowl, combine Spices & Seasonings for Fajitas, 1 cup salsa and water; pour over chicken. Marinate in refrigerator 2 hours. Heat grill for medium coals or heat broiler. Remove chicken, reserving marinade. Grill or broil, 4 to 5 inches from heat source, 5 to 7 minutes on each side or until chicken is no longer pink in center, basting frequently with marinade. Place on lettuce-lined sandwich buns. Top with cheese, onion, avocado and salsa.

Makes 4 servings

Hint: Do not baste chicken with marinade during last 5 minutes of cooking.

Sizzling Chicken Sandwich

Honey-Mustard Burgers

3 tablespoons Dijon mustard
2 tablespoons honey
3 teaspoons minced fresh oregano leaves,* divided
1 pound ground beef (80% lean)
¼ cup finely chopped onion
¼ teaspoon black pepper
4 leaf lettuce leaves
4 crusty rolls, split
4 slices onion, separated into rings (optional)

Prepare grill. Combine mustard, honey and 1 teaspoon oregano in small bowl; set aside. Combine ground beef, 2 tablespoons mustard sauce, remaining 2 teaspoons oregano, chopped onion and pepper in large bowl; mix lightly but thoroughly. Divide beef mixture into 4 equal portions; shape into patties 4 inches in diameter.

Place patties on grid. Grill over medium-hot coals 4 to 6 minutes on each side or to desired doneness. Place 1 lettuce leaf on each bottom roll half; top with a burger. Spoon remaining mustard sauce over burgers; garnish with onion rings, if desired. Add top halves of rolls.

Makes 4 servings

*Substitute ¾ teaspoon dried oregano leaves, crushed, for fresh oregano. Combine ¼ teaspoon with mustard and honey; add remaining ½ teaspoon to ground beef mixture.

Favorite recipe from **National Live Stock & Meat Board**

Blue Cheese Burgers with Red Onions

2 pounds ground chuck
2 cloves garlic, minced
1 teaspoon salt
½ teaspoon black pepper
4 ounces blue cheese
⅓ cup coarsely chopped walnuts, toasted
1 torpedo (long) red onion *or* 2 small red onions, sliced into ⅜-inch-thick rounds
2 baguettes (*each* 12 inches long)
Olive or vegetable oil

Combine beef, garlic, salt and pepper in a medium bowl. Shape meat mixture into 12 thin oval patties. Mash cheese and blend with walnuts in a small bowl. Divide cheese mixture equally onto centers of 6 meat patties. Top with remaining meat patties; tightly pinch edges together to seal in filling.

Oil hot grid to help prevent sticking. Grill patties and onions, if desired, on a covered grill, over medium KINGSFORD® Briquets, 7 to 12 minutes for medium doneness, turning once. Cut baguettes into 4-inch lengths; split each piece and brush cut sides with olive oil. Move cooked burgers to edge of grill to keep warm. Grill bread, oil side down, until lightly toasted. Serve burgers with onions on toasted baguettes.

Makes 6 servings

Serving Suggestion: These are terrific plain, but they're even better served with a spread of one part mayonnaise to one part Dijon mustard. Offer accompaniments such as sliced tomatoes and soft-leaf lettuce (Boston, Bibb, butter or red leaf).

Blue Cheese Burger with Red Onions

Pizza Burgers

1 pound lean ground beef
1 cup (4 ounces) shredded mozzarella cheese
1 tablespoon minced onion
1½ teaspoons chopped fresh oregano *or* ½ teaspoon dried oregano leaves
1 tablespoon chopped fresh basil *or* 1 teaspoon dried basil leaves
½ teaspoon salt
Dash black pepper
Prepared pizza sauce, warmed
2 English muffins, split and toasted

Prepare grill. Meanwhile, combine ground beef, cheese, onion and seasonings in medium bowl; mix lightly. Shape into 4 patties.

Place burgers on grid. Grill over medium-hot coals 8 minutes or to desired doneness, turning once. Top with pizza sauce. Serve on English muffins. *Makes 4 servings*

Mexicali Burgers

Guacamole (recipe follows)
1 pound ground chuck
⅓ cup prepared salsa or picante sauce
⅓ cup crushed tortilla chips
3 tablespoons finely chopped fresh cilantro
2 tablespoons grated onion
1 teaspoon ground cumin
4 slices Monterey Jack or Cheddar cheese
4 kaiser rolls or hamburger buns, split
Lettuce leaves (optional)
Sliced tomatoes (optional)

Prepare grill with rectangular metal or foil drip pan. Bank briquets on either side of drip pan for indirect cooking. Meanwhile, prepare Guacamole. Combine ground chuck, salsa, chips, cilantro, onion and cumin in medium bowl. Mix lightly but thoroughly. Shape mixture into 4 (½-inch-thick) burgers, 4 inches in diameter.

Place burgers on grid. Grill, on covered grill, over medium coals 8 to 10 minutes for medium or to desired doneness, turning halfway through grilling time. Place 1 slice cheese on each burger to melt during last 1 to 2 minutes of grilling. If desired, place rolls, cut sides down, on grid to toast lightly during last 1 to 2 minutes of grilling. Place burgers between rolls; top burgers with Guacamole. Serve with lettuce and tomatoes. *Makes 4 servings*

Guacamole

1 ripe avocado, seeded
1 tablespoon prepared salsa or picante sauce
1 teaspoon fresh lime or lemon juice
¼ teaspoon garlic salt

Scoop avocado flesh out of shells; place in medium bowl. Mash roughly with fork, leaving avocado slightly chunky. Stir in salsa, juice and garlic salt. Let stand at room temperature while grilling burgers. (Can be prepared up to 3 hours in advance. Cover; refrigerate. Bring to room temperature before serving.)

Makes about ½ cup

Turkey Burgers

½ cup lightly packed (2 ounces) shredded Cheddar or Monterey Jack cheese
2 tablespoons mayonnaise
1 green onion with tops, thinly sliced
1 teaspoon prepared horseradish (optional)
1 pound ground turkey
Salt and black pepper
8 slices French bread (*each* ¼ inch thick) *or* 4 hamburger buns
Olive oil or melted butter

Combine cheese, mayonnaise, onion and horseradish, if desired, in a small bowl; set aside. Shape turkey into 4 patties about ½ inch thick. Season with salt and pepper.

Oil hot grid to help prevent sticking. Grill turkey, on a covered grill, over medium KINGSFORD® Briquets, 12 to 16 minutes until burgers are no longer pink in center, turning once. Spoon cheese topping on burgers 3 to 4 minutes before removing from grill. Cheese should melt slightly. Move cooked burgers to edge of grill to keep warm. Brush bread lightly with oil. Grill bread, oil side down, until lightly toasted. Serve burgers on bread.

Makes 4 servings

Mexicali Burger

English Burger

Two-Way Burgers

Grilled Burgers

1 pound ground beef
¼ cup minced onion
¼ teaspoon black pepper

Prepare grill. Combine ground beef, onion and pepper, mixing lightly but thoroughly. Divide beef mixture into 4 equal portions and form into patties 4 inches in diameter. Place patties on grid. Grill over medium coals 10 to 12 minutes or to desired doneness, turning once. Prepare desired recipe and assemble as directed.

Makes 4 beef patties

Tip: Prepare Grilled Burgers and choose one of two different burger recipes—California Burgers or English Burgers.

California Burgers

1 recipe Grilled Burgers
¼ cup plain yogurt
1 teaspoon Dijon mustard
4 whole wheat hamburger buns, split
12 large spinach leaves, stems removed
4 thin slices red onion
4 large mushrooms, sliced
1 small avocado, peeled, seeded and cut into 12 wedges

Combine yogurt and mustard. On bottom half of each bun, layer an equal amount of spinach leaves, onions and mushrooms; top each with a Grilled Burger. Arrange 3 avocado wedges on each patty; top with an equal amount of yogurt mixture. Close each sandwich with bun top.

Makes 4 servings

English Burgers

1 recipe Grilled Burgers
¼ cup *each* horseradish sauce and chopped tomato
2 tablespoons crumbled crisply cooked bacon*
4 English muffins, split and lightly toasted

Combine horseradish sauce, tomato and bacon. Place a Grilled Burger on each muffin half. Spoon an equal amount of horseradish sauce mixture over each patty. Cover with remaining muffin half.

Makes 4 servings

*One tablespoon bottled real bacon bits may be substituted for cooked bacon.

Favorite recipe from **National Live Stock & Meat Board**

Grilled Chicken & Vegetable Sandwich with Salsa Mayonnaise

6 tablespoons NEWMAN'S OWN® All Natural Salsa, divided
4 tablespoons nonfat or low fat mayonnaise, divided
1 tablespoon chopped fresh cilantro
1 tablespoon fresh lime juice
½ teaspoon grated lime peel
½ teaspoon ground cumin
1 clove garlic, pressed
1 whole chicken breast (8 ounces), skinned, boned and halved
2 tablespoons vegetable oil
½ teaspoon ground chili powder
4 ounces yellow squash, cut into ½-inch slices
1 red bell pepper, quartered and seeded
4 slices red onion, ½ inch thick
1 crusty Italian bread (12 inch loaf), halved lengthwise
1 cup shredded iceberg lettuce

Combine 2 tablespoons Newman's Own® All Natural Salsa, 2 tablespoons mayonnaise, cilantro, juice, lime peel, cumin and garlic in medium glass bowl. Add chicken; toss to coat. Cover and marinate in refrigerator 30 to 60 minutes.

Prepare grill or preheat broiler. Combine oil and chili powder in small bowl. Brush vegetables with oil mixture. Grill or broil chicken and vegetables 8 to 10 minutes or until chicken is no longer pink in center, turning once. Transfer to plate. Combine 4 tablespoons Newman's Own® All Natural Salsa and 2 tablespoons mayonnaise.

To serve, spread salsa mayonnaise on each bread half. Place lettuce on bottom half of bread, then layer with chicken and vegetables. Place top half of bread over chicken and vegetables. Cut sandwich in half. *Makes 2 (6-inch) sandwiches*

Big D Ranch Burgers

1 cup sliced onions
⅓ cup sliced green bell pepper strips
⅓ cup sliced red bell pepper strips
1 tablespoon margarine
3 tablespoons A.1.® Steak Sauce
2 teaspoons prepared horseradish
1 pound ground beef
4 onion rolls, split

In medium skillet, over medium heat, cook onions, green pepper and red pepper in margarine until tender-crisp. Stir in steak sauce and horseradish; keep warm.

Shape ground beef into 4 patties. Grill burgers over medium heat for 5 minutes on each side or to desired doneness. Place burgers on roll bottoms; top each with ¼ cup pepper mixture and roll top. Serve immediately. *Makes 4 servings*

Big D Ranch Burger

Scandinavian Burgers

1 pound lean ground beef
¾ cup shredded zucchini
⅓ cup shredded carrot
2 tablespoons finely minced onion
1 tablespoon chopped fresh dill *or* 1 teaspoon dried dill weed
½ teaspoon salt
Dash black pepper
1 egg, beaten
¼ cup beer or nonalcoholic beer
4 whole wheat buns or rye rolls (optional)

Prepare grill. Combine beef, zucchini, carrot, onion and seasonings in medium bowl; mix lightly. Stir in egg and beer. Shape into 4 patties; place on grid. Grill over medium-hot coals 8 minutes or to desired doneness, turning once. Serve on buns, if desired. *Makes 4 serving*

Top to bottom: Scandinavian Burgers and Grilled Smoked Sausage (page 71)

Lipton® Onion Burgers

1 envelope LIPTON® Recipe Secrets® Onion Soup Mix*
2 pounds ground beef
½ cup water

In large bowl, combine all ingredients; shape into 8 patties. Grill or broil to desired doneness. *Makes about 8 servings*

*Also terrific with Lipton® Recipe Secrets® Beefy Onion, Onion-Mushroom or Italian Herb with Tomato Soup Mix.

Serving Suggestion: Serve with lettuce, tomato, pickles and potato salad.

Teriyaki Burgers

1 pound lean ground beef
¼ cup LAWRY'S® Teriyaki Marinade with Pineapple Juice
¼ cup finely chopped onion
¼ cup finely chopped green bell pepper
½ teaspoon LAWRY'S® Garlic Powder with Parsley
4 whole wheat or onion rolls
1 can (5¼ ounces) pineapple slices, drained
Tomato slices
Lettuce

Heat grill for medium-hot coals or heat broiler. In medium bowl, blend together beef, Teriyaki Marinade with Pineapple Juice, onion, bell pepper and Garlic Powder with Parsley. Let stand 5 minutes. Form into 4 patties. (Mixture will be moist.) Grill or broil, 5 inches from heat source, 3 to 5 minutes on each side or to desired doneness. On bottom half of each roll, place patty; cover with pineapple slice, tomato slice, lettuce and top half of roll.

Makes 4 servings

Hint: Lightly grill pineapple slices to warm; brush with extra Teriyaki Marinade with Pineapple Juice.

Grilled Chicken Breast and Peperonata Sandwiches

- **1 tablespoon olive or vegetable oil**
- **1 medium red bell pepper, sliced into strips**
- **1 medium green bell pepper, sliced into strips**
- **¾ cup onion slices (about 1 medium)**
- **2 cloves garlic, minced**
- **¼ teaspoon salt**
- **¼ teaspoon black pepper**
- **4 boneless skinless chicken breast halves (about 1 pound)**
- **4 small French rolls, split and toasted**

Prepare grill. Heat oil in large nonstick skillet over medium heat until hot. Add bell peppers, onion and garlic; cook and stir 5 minutes. Reduce heat to low; cook and stir about 20 minutes or until vegetables are very soft. Stir in salt and black pepper.

Place chicken on grid. Grill, on covered grill, over medium-hot coals 10 minutes on each side or until chicken is no longer pink in center. (Or, broil chicken, 6 inches from heat source, 7 to 8 minutes on each side or until chicken is no longer pink in center.) Place chicken in rolls. Spoon pepper mixture evenly over chicken.

Makes 4 servings

Grilled Chicken Breast and Peperonata Sandwich

Blackened Burgers

- **1 pound ground beef**
- **5 tablespoons A.1.® Steak Sauce, divided**
- **4 teaspoons coarsely cracked black pepper, divided**
- **4 kaiser rolls, split**
- **4 tomato slices**

In medium bowl, combine ground beef, 3 tablespoons steak sauce and 1 teaspoon pepper; shape mixture into 4 patties. Brush patties with remaining steak sauce; coat with remaining pepper.

Grill burgers over medium heat for 5 minutes on each side or to desired doneness. Top each roll bottom with burger, tomato slice and roll top. Serve immediately.

Makes 4 servings

Hawaiian-Style Burgers

1½ pounds ground beef
⅓ cup chopped green onions
2 tablespoons Worcestershire sauce
⅛ teaspoon black pepper
⅓ cup pineapple preserves
⅓ cup barbecue sauce
6 pineapple slices
6 hamburger buns, split and toasted

Prepare grill. Combine beef, onions, Worcestershire and pepper in large bowl. Shape into 6 (1-inch-thick) patties. Combine preserves and barbecue sauce in small saucepan. Bring to a boil over medium heat, stirring often.

Place patties on grid. Grill, uncovered, over medium coals 4 minutes on each side or to desired doneness, brushing often with sauce. Place pineapple on grid. Grill 1 minute or until browned, turning once. To serve, place patties on buns with pineapple.
Makes 6 servings

Broiling Directions: Arrange prepared patties on rack in broiler pan. Broil 4 inches from heat 4 minutes on each side or to desired doneness, brushing often with sauce. Broil pineapple 1 minute, turning once. Serve as directed.

Cheesy Lamburger

1 pound lean ground American lamb
¼ cup shredded Cheddar cheese (1 ounce)
2 tablespoons sweet pickle relish
2 tablespoons finely chopped onion
1 tablespoon finely chopped green bell pepper
1 teaspoon Dijon mustard
4 multi-grain hamburger buns, toasted
4 lettuce leaves
4 slices tomato

Prepare grill. Combine cheese, relish, onion, pepper and mustard in small bowl. Shape lamb into 8 thin patties about 4 inches in diameter. Spoon cheese mixture onto centers of 4 patties. Top each with another patty, pressing edges to seal filling inside. Place burgers on grid. Grill 4 inches over medium coals 5 minutes on each side or to desired doneness. Serve on buns with lettuce and tomato. *Makes 4 servings*

Variation: Substitute dill pickle relish and Monterey Jack or Swiss cheese for the sweet relish and Cheddar.

Prep time: 15 minutes
Cooking time: 10 to 15 minutes

Favorite recipe from **American Lamb Council**

Grilled Reuben Burgers

1 envelope LIPTON® Recipe Secrets® Onion-Mushroom Soup Mix*
1½ pounds ground beef
½ cup water
½ cup shredded Swiss cheese (about 2 ounces)
1 tablespoon crisp-cooked crumbled bacon or bacon bits
½ teaspoon caraway seeds (optional)

In large bowl, combine all ingredients; shape into 6 patties. Grill or broil to desired doneness. Top, if desired, with heated sauerkraut and additional bacon.
Makes 6 servings

*Also terrific with Lipton® Recipe Secrets® Onion or Beefy Onion Soup Mix.

Serving Suggestion: Serve with coleslaw, pickles and Lipton® Iced Tea.

Hawaiian-Style Burger

SAUCES & MARINADES

Mushroom Bacon Sauce

5 slices bacon, cut into ¼-inch pieces (about 4 ounces)
1 (10-ounce) package mushrooms, sliced (about 4 cups)
¼ cup A.1.® Steak Sauce
2 tablespoons sherry cooking wine

In large skillet, over medium-high heat, cook bacon until crisp. Remove bacon with slotted spoon. Reserve 2 tablespoons drippings.

In same skillet, sauté mushrooms in reserved drippings for 5 minutes or until tender. Stir in steak sauce, sherry and bacon; bring to a boil. Reduce heat; simmer 5 minutes. Serve hot with cooked beef, burgers or poultry. *Makes 1½ cups*

K.C. Masterpiece® Spread

¼ cup K.C. MASTERPIECE® Barbecue Sauce
¼ cup reduced-calorie or regular mayonnaise

Combine barbecue sauce and mayonnaise in a small bowl until smooth. Serve with grilled beef, turkey, chicken or pork.
Makes 1 cup

Lemon-Garlic Grilling Sauce

½ cup butter or margarine, melted
¼ cup fresh lemon juice
1 tablespoon Worcestershire sauce
½ teaspoon TABASCO® pepper sauce
1 to 3 cloves garlic, minced
¼ teaspoon black pepper

Combine ingredients in small bowl until well blended. Brush on fish, seafood, poultry or vegetables during grilling or broiling. Heat any remaining sauce to a boil and serve with grilled foods.
Makes ¾ cup

Steak Marinade Italiano

¼ cup A.1.® Steak Sauce
¼ cup prepared Italian salad dressing
1 teaspoon garlic powder

In small nonmetal bowl, combine steak sauce, salad dressing and garlic powder. Use to marinate beef, poultry or pork for about 1 hour in the refrigerator.
Makes ½ cup

Mushroom Bacon Sauce

Red Onion Jam

Tomato-Chile Marinade

1 can (8 ounces) tomato sauce
1 can (4 ounces) diced green chilies
¼ cup chopped onion
1 tablespoon *each* wine vinegar and olive oil
¼ teaspoon salt
2 tablespoons chopped fresh cilantro or parsley

Combine ingredients in medium bowl. Use as marinade *or* sauce for grilled beef, chicken or fish. *Makes 1⅔ cups*

Favorite recipe from ***Canned Food Information Council***

Bold Pepper Sauce

1 cup thinly sliced red bell pepper
1 cup thinly sliced green bell pepper
2 tablespoons margarine
¾ cup A.1.® BOLD Steak Sauce
1 tablespoon dry sherry

In medium skillet, over medium-high heat, sauté peppers in margarine until tender-crisp, about 5 minutes. Stir in steak sauce and sherry; heat to a boil. Reduce heat; simmer 5 minutes. Serve warm with cooked beef or poultry. *Makes 1¾ cups*

Red Onion Jam

3 cups peeled red onions (about 1 pound)
1½ cups apple juice
½ cup red wine vinegar
1½ teaspoons rubbed sage
½ teaspoon pepper
4 cups granulated sugar
¾ cup firmly packed light brown sugar
1 box SURE•JELL® Fruit Pectin
½ teaspoon margarine or butter

Boil jars on rack in large pot filled with water 10 minutes. Place flat lids in saucepan with water. Bring to a boil. Remove from heat. Let jars and lids stand in hot water until ready to fill. Drain well before filling.

Peel, quarter and thinly slice red onions. Measure 3 cups into 6- or 8-quart saucepot. Stir in apple juice, vinegar, sage and pepper.

Combine sugars in separate bowl. Stir fruit pectin into onion mixture in saucepot. Add margarine. Bring mixture to full rolling boil on high heat, stirring constantly. Quickly stir in sugars. Return to full rolling boil and boil exactly 5 minutes, stirring constantly. Remove from heat. Skim off any foam with metal spoon.

Ladle quickly into prepared jars, filling to within ⅛ inch of tops. Wipe jar rims and threads. Cover with two-piece lids. Screw bands tightly. Invert jars 5 minutes, then turn upright. After jars are cool, check seals. *Makes 6 (1-cup) jars*

Mediterranean Marinade

⅓ cup olive or vegetable oil
¼ cup REALEMON® Lemon Juice from Concentrate
3 tablespoons dry sherry or water
2 teaspoons rosemary leaves, crushed
2 cloves garlic, finely chopped
1½ teaspoons WYLER'S® or STEERO® Chicken- or Beef-Flavor Instant Bouillon

In large shallow glass dish or resealable plastic bag, combine ingredients; add chicken, beef or pork. Cover or seal bag; marinate in refrigerator 4 hours or overnight, turning occasionally. Remove meat from marinade; grill or broil as desired, basting frequently with marinade. (Do not baste during last 5 minutes of grilling.) Refrigerate leftover meat.

Makes about 1 cup

Curried Barbecue Sauce

¼ cup chopped green onions
1 clove garlic, crushed
1 tablespoon vegetable oil
1 teaspoon curry powder
⅓ cup Dijon mustard
⅓ cup A.1.® Steak Sauce
½ cup plain lowfat yogurt

In small saucepan, over low heat, cook onions and garlic in oil until tender, stirring frequently. Stir in curry powder; cook 1 minute. Stir in mustard and steak sauce. Remove saucepan from heat; cool slightly. Stir in yogurt. Use as a baste while grilling poultry, lamb or pork.

Makes about 1⅓ cups

Mediterranean Marinated Chicken

Thai Marinade

½ cup A.1.® Steak Sauce
⅓ cup peanut butter
2 tablespoons soy sauce

In small nonmetal bowl, combine steak sauce, peanut butter and soy sauce. Use to marinate beef, poultry or pork for about 1 hour in the refrigerator. *Makes 1 cup*

Jamaican BBQ Sauce

⅓ cup molasses
⅓ cup prepared mustard
⅓ cup red wine vinegar
3 tablespoons Worcestershire sauce
¾ teaspoon TABASCO® pepper sauce

Combine ingredients in small bowl until well blended. Use as a baste while grilling beef, chicken, pork or game.

Makes 1 cup

Thai Marinade

Fresh Nectarine Sauce

½ pound ripe nectarines
2 tablespoons sugar
2 tablespoons KIKKOMAN® Lite Teriyaki Marinade & Sauce
1 teaspoon cornstarch
2 tablespoons water

Peel, pit and coarsely chop nectarines; place in blender or food processor container. Add sugar and lite teriyaki sauce; cover. Process on low speed until smooth. Blend cornstarch and water in small saucepan; stir in nectarine mixture. Cook, stirring constantly, until sauce boils and thickens. Transfer to serving bowl; refrigerate until well chilled. Serve over cooked pork or chicken. *Makes 1 cup*

Lipton® Onion Butter

1 envelope LIPTON® Recipe Secrets® Onion Soup Mix
1 container (8 ounces) whipped butter or soft margarine *or* ½ pound butter or margarine, softened

In small bowl, thoroughly blend onion soup mix with butter. Store covered in refrigerator. *Makes about 1¼ cups*

Serving Suggestions: Brush Lipton® Onion Butter on sliced red onion, eggplant, tomatoes or corn-on-the-cob; grill or broil until vegetables are tender. Spread Lipton® Onion Butter between slices of French or Italian bread; wrap in aluminum foil and grill until butter is melted.

Bacon & Onion Relish

½ pound sliced bacon, cut into small pieces
2 large yellow onions, thinly sliced
2 tablespoons red wine vinegar
Salt and black pepper

Cook bacon in medium skillet over low heat until almost crisp. Drain off drippings. Add onions; cook and stir over medium heat until golden brown. Stir in vinegar; season with salt and pepper to taste. Serve hot. Refrigerate leftovers. *Makes 1 cup*

Serving Suggestion: Serve as a topping for grilled BOB EVANS FARMS® Sandwich Patties on a bun.

Gazpacho Relish

4 teaspoons tomato paste
2 teaspoons red wine vinegar
2 teaspoons lime juice
1½ teaspoons olive oil
½ pound tomatoes, peeled, seeded and chopped
¼ cup minced green bell pepper
¼ cup peeled and chopped cucumber
4 canned artichoke hearts, chopped
2 teaspoons minced shallots
2 teaspoons chopped fresh dill
¼ teaspoon black pepper
3 to 6 drops hot pepper sauce

Place tomato paste, vinegar, juice and oil in blender or food processor; process until smooth. Transfer mixture to medium bowl and stir in remaining ingredients. Cover and refrigerate several hours before serving. Serve cold. Refrigerate leftovers. *Makes 1 cup*

Serving Suggestion: Serve as an accompaniment to grilled BOB EVANS FARMS® Sandwich Patties or chicken.

Top to bottom: Bacon & Onion Relish, Sweet & Sour Relish and Gazpacho Relish

Sweet & Sour Relish

1 medium onion, chopped
1 stalk celery, chopped
½ cup prepared chili sauce
2 tablespoons dark brown sugar
2 tablespoons cider vinegar
Dash dried tarragon leaves

Combine ingredients in medium saucepan. Bring to a boil over medium-high heat. Reduce heat to low; simmer 5 minutes, stirring occasionally. Serve hot or cold. Refrigerate leftovers and reheat if necessary. *Makes 1 cup*

Serving Suggestion: Serve with grilled BOB EVANS FARMS® Bratwurst, Smoked Sausage or Kielbasa.

Mexican Hamburger Topping

½ cup HELLMANN'S® or BEST FOODS® Real or Light Mayonnaise or Low Fat Cholesterol Free Mayonnaise Dressing
½ cup prepared chunky salsa, drained
½ cup (2 ounces) shredded Cheddar cheese
½ cup refried beans

In small bowl combine mayonnaise, salsa, cheese and beans. Serve with hamburgers.
Makes about 1⅔ cups

Bacon Hamburger Topping: Combine 1 cup mayonnaise and ¼ cup crumbled cooked bacon or real bacon bits. Makes about 1 cup.

Green Onion Hamburger Topping: Combine 1 cup mayonnaise and ¼ cup sliced green onions. Makes about 1 cup.

Midwest Bar-B-Q Sauce

1 tablespoon olive oil
1 medium onion, finely chopped
1 bottle (20 ounces) ketchup
¾ cup packed brown sugar
½ cup beer (optional)
2 tablespoons Worcestershire sauce
1 tablespoon minced garlic
1 teaspoon liquid smoke seasoning
½ teaspoon AC'CENT® Flavor Enhancer

In medium saucepan, heat oil over medium-high heat until hot. Add onion; cook and stir until tender. Add remaining ingredients. Bring to a boil over high heat; reduce heat to low and simmer 10 minutes. Store covered in refrigerator. Use as a baste while grilling beef, ribs or chicken.
Makes 2½ cups

Top to bottom: Bacon, Mexican and Green Onion Hamburger Toppings

Barbecued Garlic

8 whole heads fresh garlic*
¼ cup butter or margarine
4 sprigs fresh rosemary or oregano *or* 2 teaspoons dried rosemary or oregano leaves, crushed

Preheat grill. Peel outer skin layers of garlic, leaving cloves and head intact. Place heads on double thickness of foil; drizzle with butter and sprinkle with herbs. Fold up foil, leaving space around edges and crimping all ends to make packet. Place packet on grid. Grill over hot coals 40 to 45 minutes, turning occasionally. Serve 1 whole head per person. Squeeze cooked cloves from skin onto cooked meat and vegetables or spread on French or rye bread.
Makes 8 servings

*The whole garlic bulb is called a head.

Favorite recipe from **Christopher Ranch Garlic**

Tomato-Corn Relish

¾ pound (2 medium) fresh California tomatoes, seeded and finely chopped
1 cup fresh corn kernels
½ cup finely chopped green bell pepper
½ cup finely chopped celery
½ red onion, chopped
2½ tablespoons white wine vinegar
1 clove garlic, minced
½ teaspoon sugar
1 tablespoon Dijon mustard
¼ teaspoon crushed red pepper

Combine ingredients in medium bowl. Serve with hot dogs and hamburgers.
Makes 2½ cups

Favorite recipe from **California Tomato Board**

Left to right: New Mexico Marinade and Wyoming Wild Barbecued Sauce

Wyoming Wild Barbecue Sauce

1 cup chili sauce
1 cup ketchup
¼ cup steak sauce
1 tablespoon Worcestershire sauce
1 tablespoon garlic, finely chopped
2 tablespoons horseradish
3 tablespoons dry mustard
2 tablespoons TABASCO® pepper sauce
1 tablespoon dark molasses
1 tablespoon red wine vinegar

Combine ingredients in medium bowl. Whisk until sauce is well blended. Store in 1-quart covered jar in refrigerator up to 7 days. Use as a baste while grilling beef, chicken, pork or game. *Makes 3 cups*

New Mexico Marinade

1½ cups beer
½ cup chopped fresh cilantro
3 cloves garlic
½ cup lime juice
2 teaspoons chili powder
1 teaspoon TABASCO® pepper sauce
1½ teaspoons ground cumin

Place ingredients in food processor or blender; process until well combined. Store in 1-pint covered jar in the refrigerator up to 3 days. Use to marinate beef, pork or chicken in refrigerator. *Makes 2 cups*

Tangy Lemon Glaze

½ cup apple juice
¼ cup firmly packed brown sugar
½ cup A.1.® Steak Sauce
2 tablespoons lemon juice
1 tablespoon cornstarch
1 teaspoon grated lemon peel

In small saucepan, blend apple juice and brown sugar. Stir in steak sauce, lemon juice, cornstarch and lemon peel. Over medium heat, heat to a boil, stirring constantly. Boil 1 minute; remove from heat and cool slightly. Use as a baste while grilling poultry, pork or ham.
Makes about 1¼ cups

Chili Marinade

¼ cup A.1.® Steak Sauce
¼ cup chili sauce

In small nonmetal bowl, combine steak sauce and chili sauce. Use to marinate beef or pork for about 1 hour in the refrigerator.
Makes ½ cup

West Coast Bar-B-Q Sauce

2 tablespoons cornstarch
¼ cup fresh lemon juice
1 can (15½ ounces) crushed pineapple, undrained
1¼ cups honey
¼ cup Dijon mustard
3 tablespoons soy sauce
1 tablespoon minced garlic
1 teaspoon ground ginger
½ teaspoon AC'CENT® Flavor Enhancer

In medium saucepan, stir together cornstarch and lemon juice until cornstarch is dissolved. Add remaining ingredients. Bring to a boil over high heat; reduce heat to low and simmer 10 minutes. Store covered in refrigerator. Use as a baste while grilling beef, ribs or chicken.

Makes 3 cups

Soy Marinade

½ cup REALEMON® Lemon Juice from Concentrate
½ cup soy sauce
½ cup vegetable oil
3 tablespoons ketchup
3 to 4 cloves garlic, finely chopped
¼ teaspoon pepper

In large shallow glass dish or resealable plastic bag, combine ingredients; add beef, chicken or pork. Cover or seal bag; marinate in refrigerator 4 hours or overnight, turning occasionally. Remove meat from marinade; heat marinade thoroughly. Grill or broil meat as desired, basting frequently with marinade. (Do not baste during last 5 minutes of grilling.) Refrigerate leftovers.

Makes about 1½ cups

Soy Marinated London Broil

Pineapple Salsa

1 can (20 ounces) DOLE® Crushed Pineapple, drained
½ cup finely chopped DOLE® Red Bell Pepper
¼ cup finely chopped DOLE® Green Bell Pepper
1 tablespoon chopped DOLE® Green Onion
2 teaspoons chopped fresh cilantro or parsley
2 teaspoons finely chopped jalapeño peppers
1 teaspoon grated lime peel

• Combine ingredients in small bowl.

• Serve salsa at room temperature or slightly chilled over grilled chicken or fish.

Makes 8 servings

Prep time: 20 minutes

Pineapple Salsa

Italian Marinade

1 envelope GOOD SEASONS® Italian, Zesty Italian or Garlic & Herb Salad Dressing Mix
⅓ cup oil
⅓ cup dry white wine or water
2 tablespoons lemon juice

Mix salad dressing mix, oil, wine and lemon juice in cruet or medium bowl until well blended. Reserve ¼ cup marinade for basting; refrigerate. Pour remaining marinade over 1½ to 2 pounds meat, poultry or seafood. Toss to coat well; cover. Refrigerate to marinate. Drain before grilling.

Makes ⅔ cup

Aioli

1 cup reduced-calorie mayonnaise
4 cloves garlic, pressed
1 tablespoon Dijon mustard
1 tablespoon lemon juice or to taste

Combine ingredients in small bowl until well blended. Cover; refrigerate 1 to 2 hours to allow flavors to blend. Serve with grilled beef, poultry, pork or fish.

Makes 1 cup

Favorite recipe from ***The Kingsford Products Company***

Orange Barbecue Sauce

¾ cup orange marmalade
½ cup A.1.® BOLD Steak Sauce
½ cup Dijon mustard
¼ cup finely chopped onion

In small bowl, combine marmalade, steak sauce, mustard and onion. Use as a baste while grilling poultry, ribs or pork.

Makes about 2 cups

Onion Wine Sauce

4 cups onion wedges
2 cloves garlic, minced
2 tablespoons margarine
½ cup A.1.® Steak Sauce
2 tablespoons red cooking wine

In large skillet, over medium-high heat, cook and stir onions and garlic in margarine until tender, about 10 minutes. Stir in steak sauce and wine; heat to a boil. Reduce heat; simmer 5 minutes. Serve hot with cooked beef or poultry.

Makes 2½ cups

Red Relish

1 red bell pepper, quartered and seeded
1 large tomato, cut into halves, seeded and squeezed to drain some juice
2 tablespoons balsamic vinegar*
2 tablespoons chopped fresh basil
Salt and black pepper to taste

Grill red pepper, skin side down, on an uncovered grill, over medium KINGSFORD® Briquets, until skin starts to blister and pepper turns limp. Add tomato to grill 2 minutes after the pepper. Grill until tomato begins to turn limp. Remove from grill and let cool. Chop pepper and tomato; combine with remaining ingredients. Serve with grilled beef, turkey, chicken, pork or fish.

Makes about 1⅓ cups

*Substitute 1 tablespoon red wine vinegar plus ½ teaspoon sugar for the balsamic vinegar.

Onion Wine Sauce

Lone Star Barbecue Sauce

½ cup melted butter
¼ cup sugar
¼ teaspoon TABASCO® pepper sauce
½ teaspoon dry mustard
1 cup vegetable oil
1 bottle (12 ounces) ketchup
¼ cup Worcestershire sauce
2 cloves garlic, minced
1 large onion, chopped
Juice from 1 lemon

Combine ingredients in medium bowl until well blended. Brush both sides of beef or chicken before grilling and frequently during grilling. (Do not baste during last 5 minutes of grilling.)

Makes about 3½ cups

Honey Barbecue Sauce

1 can ($10\frac{3}{4}$ ounces) condensed tomato soup
½ cup honey
2 tablespoons Worcestershire sauce
2 to 3 tablespoons vegetable oil
1 tablespoon lemon juice
1 teaspoon prepared mustard
Dash ground red pepper or bottled hot pepper sauce (optional)

Combine ingredients in medium saucepan. Bring to a boil over medium heat. Reduce heat to low and simmer, uncovered, 5 minutes. Use as a baste while grilling beef, ribs or poultry. *Makes about 2 cups*

Favorite recipe from **National Honey Board**

Honey Strawberry Salsa

1½ cups diced sweet red pepper
1 cup sliced fresh strawberries
1 cup diced green bell pepper
1 cup diced fresh tomato
¼ cup chopped Anaheim pepper
2 tablespoons finely chopped fresh cilantro
⅓ cup honey
¼ cup lemon juice
1 tablespoon tequila (optional)
½ teaspoon crushed dried red chili pepper
½ teaspoon salt
¼ teaspoon pepper

Combine ingredients in glass container; mix well. Cover tightly and refrigerate overnight to allow flavors to blend. Serve on grilled fish or chicken.

Makes 3 to 4 cups

Favorite recipe from **National Honey Board**

Creamy Horseradish Sauce

1 (8-ounce) package cream cheese, softened
⅓ cup A.1.® Steak Sauce
3 tablespoons prepared horseradish, drained
2 tablespoons chopped green onion

In medium bowl, blend cream cheese, steak sauce and horseradish; stir in onion. Cover; chill at least 1 hour or up to 2 days. Serve cold or at room temperature with cooked beef, sausage, fish or baked potatoes.

Makes 1½ cups

Herbed Honey Lime Sauce

½ cup minced onion
1 tablespoon olive oil
1 cup dry white wine or chicken broth
¼ cup honey
¼ cup lime juice
2 teaspoons dry mustard
1 teaspoon minced fresh rosemary
½ teaspoon salt
Dash pepper
1 teaspoon cornstarch
1 teaspoon water

Cook and stir onion in olive oil in medium saucepan over medium heat until onion is softened. Stir in wine, honey, lime juice, mustard, rosemary, salt and pepper; mix well and bring to a boil. Combine cornstarch and water in small bowl or cup, mixing well; add to sauce. Cook over low heat, stirring until sauce comes to a boil and thickens. Serve over cooked turkey, chicken, fish or pork. *Makes 2 cups*

Favorite recipe from **National Honey Board**

Top to bottom: Honey Barbecued Sauce, Honey Strawberry Salsa and Herbed Honey Lime Sauce

Acknowledgments

The publisher would like to thank the companies and organizations listed below for the use of their recipes and photographs in this publication.

American Lamb Council
Auricchio Cheese, Inc.
Best Foods, a Division of CPC International Inc.
Bob Evans Farms®
Borden Kitchens, Borden, Inc.
California Table Grape Commission
California Tomato Board
California Tree Fruit Agreement
Canned Food Information Council
Christopher Ranch Garlic
The Dannon Company, Inc.
Delmarva Poultry Industry, Inc.
Del Monte Corporation
Dole Food Company, Inc.
Florida Department of Agriculture and Consumer Services
Golden Grain/Mission Pasta
Heinz U.S.A.
The HVR Company
Kikkoman International Inc.
The Kingsford Products Company
Kraft Foods, Inc.
Lawry's® Foods, Inc.
Thomas J. Lipton Co.
McIlhenny Company
MOTT'S® U.S.A., a division of Cadbury Beverages Inc.
Nabisco Foods Group
National Honey Board
National Live Stock & Meat Board
National Pork Producers Council
National Turkey Federation
Nestlé Food Company
Newman's Own, Inc.
Norseland, Inc.
Pace Foods, Ltd.
Perdue® Farms
Pet Incorporated
The Procter & Gamble Company
Sargento Foods Inc.®
USA Rice Council

INDEX

D

E

F

G

H

I

J

K

T

V

W

Z

METRIC CONVERSION CHART

VOLUME MEASUREMENTS (dry)

1/8 teaspoon = 0.5 mL
1/4 teaspoon = 1 mL
1/2 teaspoon = 2 mL
3/4 teaspoon = 4 mL
1 teaspoon = 5 mL
1 tablespoon = 15 mL
2 tablespoons = 30 mL
1/4 cup = 60 mL
1/3 cup = 75 mL
1/2 cup = 125 mL
2/3 cup = 150 mL
3/4 cup = 175 mL
1 cup = 250 mL
2 cups = 1 pint = 500 mL
3 cups = 750 mL
4 cups = 1 quart = 1 L

VOLUME MEASUREMENTS (fluid)

1 fluid ounce (2 tablespoons) = 30 mL
4 fluid ounces (1/2 cup) = 125 mL
8 fluid ounces (1 cup) = 250 mL
12 fluid ounces (1 1/2 cups) = 375 mL
16 fluid ounces (2 cups) = 500 mL

WEIGHTS (mass)

1/2 ounce = 15 g
1 ounce = 30 g
3 ounces = 90 g
4 ounces = 120 g
8 ounces = 225 g
10 ounces = 285 g
12 ounces = 360 g
16 ounces = 1 pound = 450 g

DIMENSIONS

1/16 inch = 2 mm
1/8 inch = 3 mm
1/4 inch = 6 mm
1/2 inch = 1.5 cm
3/4 inch = 2 cm
1 inch = 2.5 cm

OVEN TEMPERATURES

250°F = 120°C
275°F = 140°C
300°F = 150°C
325°F = 160°C
350°F = 180°C
375°F = 190°C
400°F = 200°C
425°F = 220°C
450°F = 230°C

BAKING PAN SIZES

Utensil	Size in Inches/Quarts	Metric Volume	Size in Centimeters
Baking or Cake Pan (square or rectangular)	8×8×2	2 L	20×20×5
	9×9×2	2.5 L	22×22×5
	12×8×2	3 L	30×20×5
	13×9×2	3.5 L	33×23×5
Loaf Pan	8×4×3	1.5 L	20×10×7
	9×5×3	2 L	23×13×7
Round Layer Cake Pan	8×1½	1.2 L	20×4
	9×1½	1.5 L	23×4
Pie Plate	8×1¼	750 mL	20×3
	9×1¼	1 L	23×3
Baking Dish or Casserole	1 quart	1 L	—
	1½ quart	1.5 L	—
	2 quart	2 L	—